THE CRISIS
OF LIBERALISM

_____

NEW ISSUES OF DEMOCRACY

By

J. A. HOBSON

First published in 1909

This edition published by Read Books Ltd.
Copyright © 2019 Read Books Ltd.
This book is copyright and may not be
reproduced or copied in any way without
the express permission of the publisher in writing

British Library Cataloguing-in-Publication Data
A catalogue record for this book is available
from the British Library

The tendency of all strong Governments has always been to suppress liberty, partly in order to ease the processes of rule, partly from sheer disbelief in innovation.

J. A. HOBSON

CONTENTS

PREFACE

THE constitutional *fracas* caused by the invasion of the ancient privileges of the House of Commons by the House of Lords well serves to indicate, though by no means to comprehend, the crisis with which English Liberalism is confronted. No English Liberal of the 'seventies would have deemed it possible that so evidently obsolescent an organ of Government as the House of Lords should, within a single generation, have come to show so vigorous a spirit of encroachment. Nor could it, had not Liberalism itself shown defects of vision and of purpose which sowed doubt and distraction among its followers.

Before the great new tasks of political reconstruction and social reform, which lay along the plain path of progress, the party quailed. The first test issue, Home Rule, was the signal, not merely for open schism and wholesale desertion, but for reluctance and despondency among large sections of those who formally accepted the policy. For then for the first time Liberalism was urged to apply the principles of self-government in such a manner as involved reformation in the ownership of property. The failure to carry through this policy in the mid-'eighties was a humiliation which bred self-distrust. Though this period synchronised with fresh and full disclosures of poverty and sweating in our towns, of the decay of rural industry and population, of conflicts of capital and labour assuming graver and more dangerous aspects, Liberalism made no serious endeavour to formulate an organic policy of social reform. The old *laissez faire* individualism was still too dominant a doctrine among her intellectual leaders.

For over a quarter of a century Liberalism has wandered in this valley of indecision, halting, weak, vacillating, divided, and concessive. Not gaining ground, it yielded it. For the great arch-enemy of the age, Imperialism, found a too facile entrance among the ranks of her dejected followers, bringing as its natural ally Militarism. No one, clearly analysing the play of modern forces, can doubt that the course of British Imperialism which, swelling up in the late 'eighties and dominating our Asiatic and African policy, found its climax and its direct expression in the Boer War, was exploited by Conservatism to break and dissipate the new forces of social reform which were beginning to assert themselves in Liberalism. The diversion was only too successful. By the close of the century this Imperialism, composed of force, finance, and false philanthropy, now masquerading as defence, now as mission, now as commercial policy, had secretly eaten its way into the vitals of the Liberal Party. The connivance, condonance, nay the active participation, of Liberals in the wreckage of South Africa was a revelation of the measure of this betrayal of Liberal principles. What wonder if the champions of reaction should have thought it an easy task to recapture one by one the constitutional and economic positions wrested from them in the struggles of the nineteenth century! Why should not a nation which had yielded so far to Imperialism and Militarism be forced to accept their natural ally Protection, dressed out with Imperial trappings as its policy of national finance?

Shaken by the Free Trade victory of 1906, the confidence of Conservatism is not broken. Its energetic leaders do not believe that Liberalism contains within itself that sincerity of purpose, that clearness of vision, and that solidarity of movement, which will enable it to carry out a vigorous, comprehensive, and popular policy. Recognising among its chief counsellors men who ten years ago betrayed the older Liberalism, they do not accredit it with audacity or energy enough to travel far, or willingly, along the road of a newer and more hazardous Liberalism. These men, they hold, have been partly forced by circumstances, partly manœuvred by more advanced companions, into a Social-Radicalism which does not command their intellectual assent or their genuine sympathy, and which they will be prepared to abandon when a favourable opportunity presents itself. Every really dangerous onrush of progressive forces has always been checked by a free desertion of moderate Liberals to the enemy. As the new social-economic policy opens out into an " attack on property " there will be a further shedding of " the Whigs." Although the emergency of a Free Trade Party, committed by its own cowardice to heavy expenditure on armaments, and by opportunist pledges to large measures of social reform, has compelled resort to a " revolutionary " Budget, this advanced economic and financial policy does not, in the judgment of Conservatives, represent the accepted Liberalism of the future. Nor, in their judgment, will Liberalism be able to arouse and sustain that firm popular faith in its future without which it is not possible to do great works.

It is this disbelief in the spiritual strength of Liberalism, thus derived, that explains why Conservatism, defeated in its assault upon the fortress of Free Trade, rallies again to a more formidable attack upon the principle of popular representative government.

To many Liberals this movement of the Lords seems wanton folly. But it is not. It is a half-conscious recognition of the intrinsic or essential nature of the new Liberalism, which during the last few years has moved forward quickly from the shadowy background of the political stage towards actuality in statecraft. The reason, a quite sufficient one, why Conservatives have decided to stake the very constitution in the hazard of the present fight, is that they recognise in the New Liberalism, to which they think the Government has been reluctantly committed by Mr. George and Mr. Churchill, the beginnings of an unceasing and an enlarging attack upon the system of private property and private industrial enterprise. Actuated rather by a true instinct of self-defence than by a fully reasoned policy, they have decided to fight this New Liberalism before it has captured the firm adhesion of the party and the imagination of the people. In the valuation clauses of the Budget, the higher graduation of estate duties and income tax, and in the explicit assertion of a scrutiny into 'origin' of wealth as a test of taxable capacity, they read the handwriting on the wall. When the essential distinction between earned and unearned income and property is once clearly accepted, not merely as a theory but as a first principle of public policy, to be applied, progressively, as an instrument for financing 'social reform,' resistance may be too late. From the standpoint of the 'vested interests,' as from that of Liberalism, the situation is indeed 'critical,' and the crisis is even more momentous than is indicated by the struggle for the 'veto.' The forces of Conservatism must use every weapon in their armoury, constitutional, legal, electoral, educational; every art of menace, cajolery, misrepresentation, and corruption, which their control of a party machinery, landlordism, 'the trade,' finance, the Press, the Church, 'Society,' 'sport,' the 'services,' place at their disposal, will be plied with unexampled ardour. The House of Lords only forms the first line of trenches. Behind it lies a whole row of defences, represented by the laws and the judiciary, the bureaucracy, the Court, the electoral machinery (favouring at every turn the power of the purse), the secret unrepresentative character and working of Cabinet Government, the manipulation of electoral opinion through the public house, the Press, the pulpit, and those other instruments of popular instruction which depend for their financial support upon the charity of the propertied classes.

All these forces will be brought into action to meet the New Liberalism, which, in the name of ' social reform,' proceeds to the attack upon ' monopolies ' and unearned property.

Will Liberalism, reformed and dedicated to this new, enlarged, and positive task of realising liberty, carry its adherents with unbroken ranks with persistent vigour along this march of social progress?

The real crisis of Liberalism lies here, not in the immediate capacity to resist the insolent encroachment of the unrepresentative House, but in the intellectual and moral ability to accept and execute a positive progressive policy which involves a new conception of the functions of the State.

It is true that no sudden reversal of policy is required : the old individualism has long since been replaced by various enlargements of public activity. But hitherto these interferences and novel functions of the State have been mostly unconnected actions of an opportunist character : no avowed principle or system has underlain them. This opportunism, this studied disavowal of ulterior meaning, disarmed much opposition in the ranks of Liberalism : so long as " Socialistic " measures were shown as single moves in a party game, played by both sides, little offence was caused.

Our crisis consists in the substitution of an organic for an opportunist policy, the adoption of a vigorous, definite, positive policy of social reconstruction, involving important modifications in the legal and economic institutions of private property and private industry. For any faithful analysis of our existing economic system will show that nothing less can fulfil the demand, which Mr. Churchill has expressed, that " property—be associated in the minds of the mass of the people with ideas of reason and justice."

No one who follows the new crystallisation of Liberal policy, as displayed in the anti-destitution and insurance proposals of the Government, to which substance is already given in Old Age Pensions, Wages Boards, and Labour Exchanges, in the public provision for the development of our natural resources, in the Small Holdings and Town Planning policy, and in the financial claims of the State to participation in "unearned increments," can fail to recognise a coherency of purpose, an organic plan of social progress, which implies a new consciousness of Liberal statecraft.

The full implications of this movement may not be clearly grasped, but Liberalism is now formally committed to a task which certainly involves a new conception of the State in its relation to the individual life and to private enterprise. That conception is not Socialism, in any accredited meaning of that term, though implying a considerable amount of increased public ownership and control of industry. From the standpoint which best presents its continuity with earlier Liberalism, it appears as a fuller appreciation and realisation of individual liberty contained in the provision of equal opportunities for self-development. But to this individual standpoint must be joined a just apprehension of the social, viz., the insistence that these claims or rights of self-development be adjusted to the sovereignty of social welfare.

How far the historical Liberal Party in the country is capable of the intellectual and moral re-orientation demanded for the successful undertaking of this new career, is the fundamental issue at stake. In most European countries Liberalism has failed, because it has tied itself too rigorously to a set of narrow intellectual principles. Political parties in this country have never been dominated to the same extent by ideas: this logical weakness, we often boast, perhaps with reason, has been a source of practical strength. It implies at any rate an adaptability, a plasticity, perhaps an instinctive virtue of adjustment, that may enable British Liberalism to avoid the shipwreck which Continental Liberalism has suffered when it was driven on the submerged reefs of the economic problem in politics.

This volume, though consisting of articles contributed to various publications during recent years, has been composed with the definite object of relating the present constitutional struggle to the larger and more important issue of the future of Liberalism in this country. In the First Part, I seek to indicate the place which the fight around the Lords' veto occupies in the larger struggle for democratic government. The destruction of the veto must be accompanied or followed by other important reforms in our electoral institutions, and by a measure which shall associate the people more directly with the art of government, by assigning to it that power of mandate which the Lords falsely pretend that it possesses. The case for a Referendum is set forth with some detail of argument, and the experience of Switzerland is cited in support of it as a serviceable complement of representative government. Recognising that behind the issues of Constitutional Reform lies the policy of Social Reform, whose financial implications have precipitated the present struggle between the Houses, I have devoted the Second Part of the volume to the relations between New Liberalism and Socialism, indicating the chief developments of the modern State required to protect citizens against the abuses of property and of private industrial enterprise, and to furnish substantial equality of economic and intellectual opportunity.

The last section is devoted to a discussion of certain broader questions, in part political, in part intellectual and ethical, which are bound up with the substance of democracy, such as the function of private charity, organised or free, in its relation to problems of Poverty and Education, and the new issues of Imperialism and national morality, with their bearings upon the control of lower or of backward peoples.

The future of Liberalism depends upon the willing-
ness and the ability of its professed adherents to confront
courageously and hopefully these large demands for the
restatement of the Liberal creed, and its realisation in
the new economic and moral world opening out before us.

To the Editor of the *Manchester Guardian*, *The
Nation*, the *Contemporary Review*, and the *English
Review* I am indebted for kind permission to republish
articles contributed to these publications.

J. A. Hobson.

Limpsfield,

    December 1st, 1909.

Part I
DEMOCRACY

CHAPTER I

THE CRISIS OF LIBERALISM

Readers of Lord Morley's " Life of Gladstone " will understand that it was possible for a great Liberal statesman of the Victorian age to conduct a long political career of large and fruitful effort without confronting in its full shape any of those great social-economic issues which now in this, as in every other civilised country, occupy the front places on the stage of politics. The tenure of land in Ireland did indeed engage his serious attention, but the hardly less urgent problems of rural and urban ownership in Great Britain never really occupied his field of vision, while constructive legislation coping with pauperism, sweating, unemployment, old-age destitution, or engaging the State in constructive work for the development of the productive resources of our land and labour, lay outside his conception of practical or even legitimate politics. Nay, the whole conception of the State disclosed by these new issues, as an instrument for the active adaptation of the economic and moral environment to the new needs of individual and social life, by securing full opportunities of self-development and social service for all citizens, was foreign to the Liberalism of the last generation. Now, in England, as elsewhere, these positive, constructive and primarily economic proposals are clamouring for consideration. The old *laissez-faire* Liberalism is dead. Its early demise might indeed have been predicted from the time when Cobden recognised the necessity of " freeing "

3

the land of England as he had helped to " free " her trade. For the effective liberation of the land, as we now perceive, involves large permanent measures of public control, and brings in its wake a long series of further enlargements of State activity in transport, credit, housing, and other matters. The slow education which the land question has conducted upon the nature of monopoly and socially-created values, was bound in time to bear fruit in a growing recognition of similar elements of monopoly and social values inherent not only in liquor licences and other legalised monopolies but everywhere throughout the industrial system where competition is impeded or estopped. So, quite apart from any theoretic Socialism, there has been formed in the public mind a firm conviction that, wherever these obstructions to economic liberty are found, the State must exert its powers, either to restore free competition, or, where that is impracticable or unwise, to substitute a public monopoly in which all share for a private monopoly the profits of which pass to a favoured few.

The New Liberalism has absorbed this teaching and is preparing to put it into practice. These legal or economic privileges, which impede or cancel competition, are also recognised to be responsible for the degrading toil and poverty of the lower strata of our population and the equally degrading idleness and luxury of the upper strata, the two counterparts of the same economic facts. These truths are constantly becoming clearer to a larger number of our citizens and are generating increased energy for political reform.

But when the people, possessed by this new energy, seek to realise their objects by political endeavour, they continually find themselves thwarted by certain seen and other unseen obstacles. The demands even for redress of crying grievances are denied, delayed, or side-tracked, or else conceded in some trivial, unsatisfying form. Hence a huge waste of reform energy, bitter disappointment, and a sense of impotency which more than all else paralyses the popular spirit of reform.

What are these obstacles? For the most part they consist of economic interests firmly entrenched at certain coigns of vantage along the march of political achievement. Every one of the social-economic reforms to which I have alluded has to fight its way through a series of electoral, legislative, administrative and judicial processes in any one of which it is liable to meet the open or the secret opposition of a powerful party, class or clique which believes the proposal to be injurious to its interests. Sometimes this opposition of an economic interest is complicated and screened by some other feeling or judgment, of a social, patriotic or even a religious character, which serves to hide even from those who are the strongest opponents the naked force of the self-interest which directs their opposition.

Now the main importance of the present crisis in English politics consists in the fact that a strong search-light has thrown out in the most vivid colours one persistent barrier to reform. The House of Lords has come out into the open. Under the thin and quite ridiculous pretence of thought-reading the national will, they have substituted the economic and social interests of their order for the national welfare which they profess to serve. Every measure sent to them by the Commons which directly affected property or the control of property, especially in land, houses, and licences, those forms of property most strongly represented in their House, they have either destroyed or mutilated, and encouraged by success they have even dared, in the defence of their property, to invade the region of financial legislation reserved by long constitutional usage for the sole control of the House of Commons.

The first effect of this action has been to convince social and economic reformers of the folly of endeavouring to pluck the fruits of democracy before the tree which should bear them has been shaped and grown. The false pretence that democracy exists, has proved the subtlest defence of privilege. The belief that the popular will is realisable effectively through the representative system in England, France or the United States, has caused a greater waste of reform energy than any other single cause. For so long as this belief prevails, reformers will refuse to undertake the laborious work of perfecting the constitutional machinery of democracy. In England, as elsewhere where a fervid passion of social reform has arisen, reformers have been indignant at the suggestion that it may be more economical to postpone the immediate realisation of their proposals until they have removed obstructions in electoral and legislative institutions. They are tired, they say, of tinkering with political machinery; a popular franchise already exists, the people can now get their will if they stand together and shout loud enough. Now all who have made a close study of the actual operation of the so-called democratic machinery, in Europe or in America, perceive that this view is false. Ostrogorski's study of the mechanics of the party system in the United States and in Great Britain shows to what perilous abuses the forms of representative government are exposed, and how feebly and irregularly the real spirit of democracy pulses through them. The defects of representation are not the same in the two countries. In America it is the " spoils," corrupting the party system from the national convention down to the ward " primary," and the rigours of a written constitution which preclude amendment. In England it is the refusal to give completeness to the representative forms and to provide democratic safeguards against abuses of them.

The experience of our Liberal Government during the last four years has forced upon us an era of constitutional reform. But there is even yet little realisation of the magnitude and the variety of the constitutional changes that must ensue if democratic government is to be achieved in Great Britain. So deeply ingrained has been the very principle of Opportunism in our politics, that it is safe to say that the great majority of our reformers at present ask nothing more than the destruction of the veto of the House of Lords, while many even would be well contented with such structural reforms of the Second Chamber as would subordinate the hereditary to a new representative element drawn from the official and professional classes. Though feeling for the moment may run high against the insolence of a body of landowners and rich men presuming to encroach upon the prerogatives of the representative House, there will be serious risk, after the preliminary battle has been won by the Commons, of a compromise which shall still leave an effective veto upon ordinary legislation to a sham representative Second Chamber. When the first line of trenches has been carried by the democratic attack, a stout rally will be made for a reformed Second Chamber, retaining the same constitutional powers as the present House of Lords, only abandoning all claim to interference with finance. A whole crop of specious proposals will be raised for a Senate of great, wise, and eminent persons, not elected by the direct vote of the people, but appointed by methods which will ensure a permanent majority of members who, by instinct, training, economic interests and social connections, can be relied upon to defend vested interests and to check the " extravagances " of a popularly elected chamber. But suppose more drastic counsels should prevail, and that no reformed Second Chamber should be left with an effective veto. Shall we then have got real democracy? Will the great measures of social reform which are pressing move forward surely and swiftly towards achievement? Not at all. There can be no more foolish error than to represent the veto of the House of Lords as the only, or even the chief barrier to the free realisation of the will of the people in this country. The true importance of this present crisis is that it must furnish an introduction to the far larger task of restating the principles of democracy and recasting the forms which shall express them. To this task the destruction of the Lords' veto is but the prelude. Suppose this destruction is accomplished, in what case does democracy stand? In name we have a single-chamber Government, an all-powerful elected House of Commons, the chosen representatives of the people. These men are supposed to initiate and determine legislation, to control the executive government, and to decide what revenue shall be raised and how it shall be spent. Do they really and effectively exercise these powers? Not at all. Though much has been said of the very real encroachments made by the House of Lords upon the power of the Commons during Liberal Administrations of the last quarter of a century, little attention has been drawn to the continuous encroachments made upon the privileges of the House of Commons during the same period by the Cabinet. " The English system," writes Professor Lowell,* " seems to be approximating more and more to a condition where the Cabinet initiates everything, frames its own policy, submits that policy to a searching criticism in the House, and adopts such suggestions as it deems best; but where the House, after all this has been done, must accept the acts and proposals of the Government as they stand, or pass a vote of censure, and take the chances of a change of Ministry or a dissolution." Nor does this express the full measure of Cabinet control. For the party whip, often enforced by pressure through the local caucus and the use of party funds, commonly confines all " searching criticism," except in rare instances of independence, to the Opposition, relieving the ordinary " follower " of the Government

---

* "The Government of England," vol. i. p. 327.

from any real part in shaping the measures to which he gives his formal assent. The ordinary Parliamentarian, it matters not upon which side of the House he sits, has virtually no opportunity of introducing any Bill with a chance of carrying it into law; the time placed at the disposal of private Members has been continually reduced; the liberty of taking part effectively in debate has been curtailed at the discretion of the Government; while large restrictions have been placed upon the ventilation of grievances by questions. Almost the whole time and energy of legislation in the Commons are placed at the well-nigh absolute disposal of the Cabinet which decides what measures shall be introduced, what time shall be allotted to them, what portions of them shall be discussed adequately or at all, and which shall be dropped or presented to the House of Lords. On foreign affairs the House of Commons has become virtually impotent. The Foreign Secretary needs rarely appear in the House of Commons, needs seldom answer questions, and can take the most revolutionary steps in foreign relations without seeking even the formal assent of the representatives of the people and without troubling himself to give them full information afterwards. Since foreign policy determines in the main our naval and military expenditure and policy, this autocracy in foreign affairs virtually restricts the power of the Commons over finance and, through finance, over the whole range of domestic policy.

I am well aware of the explanations that are given for this enlargement of Cabinet control. The complexity of the modern work of central government is such, we are told, that the most rigorous economy of the time of Parliament is needed to execute it: the new Cabinet control is not a planned invasion of old parliamentary liberties but an expedient necessary for the conduct of public business. This may well be true, but none the less the process marks a diminution of

|representative government and a failure of democracy. For the shifting of control from the House of Commons to the Cabinet must at best be taken to mean the functioning of the popular will at two removes instead of one. But it means more than this. The Cabinet is seldom a just reflection or representation of the majority of the Commons in which the Government is nominally vested. Though it must be sufficiently representative to command the faithful allegiance of the party, that consideration, interpreted in the light of the facts adduced above, admits considerable licence. No one would, for example, contend that the Liberal majority returned at the polls four years ago would have chosen a Cabinet composed, as was the actual Cabinet, if a party vote by secret ballot had been taken.

Thus the great practical increase of Cabinet power in legislative and executive work, however expedient for other reasons, must be regarded as a reduction of popular self-government. In point of fact the substance of this grievance is even heavier than the form. For rank, social position, and tradition still weigh so heavily, even in Liberal Administrations, that a comparatively small number of ruling families are always largely, often dominantly, represented upon the front bench, without real reference to personal ability. Though such a statement is necessarily insusceptible of proof, no one acquainted with the *personnel* of recent Governments is likely to dispute it. It implies a very real distortion of representative government.

It will doubtless be said, and private Members often comfort themselves by repeating it, that though the Cabinet does make all important decisions, it considers and consults the party, listens to deputations of Members and moulds its policy accordingly. Here, of course, we are again in the region of immeasurable influences. But while a Government with a small majority must evidently be careful not to alienate votes, a situation which gives importance to cave-men or

" kickers," a strong Government is able to defy any ordinary recalcitrance and usually browbeats grumblers into submission. And the whole tendency of our party system, working upon the present exaggerated swing of the electoral pendulum, favours strong Governments.

But it is not alone the encroachments of Cabinet rule that have curtailed the authority and liberty of the House of Commons. The caucus system and the growth of organisations for the promotion of particular reforms, or for the furtherance of special trading or other interests, have, by exacting pledges, gone far towards changing a Member of Parliament from a representative into a delegate. Now, while genuine delegacy is a defensible mode by which the popular will may obtain expression, the sort of delegacy now imposed is definitely undemocratic. Under it small well-organised local minorities are frequently enabled to obtain a body of pledged support in Parliament far in excess of that to which their numbers entitle them. The illusory character of many of these pledges, though averting the worst consequences of this abuse of our representative system, does not prevent them from exercising a most demoralising influence upon the course of politics. Moreover, this practice excludes from Parliamentary life many men whose independent character forbids them to give the pledges necessary to secure election.

Were the proposed destruction of the Lords' veto to leave the House of Commons vested with supreme authority of government, a large stride towards effective democracy might seem to have been taken. By securing an extended franchise, shorter parliaments and adequate reforms of electoral machinery, the representative assembly might at least become a genuine expression of the popular will. There would no doubt be many even among Liberals, distrustful of uni-cameral government, where the absence of a written constitution would confer upon a single chamber, possibly elected on some heated party issue, an unlimited power to change the very foundations and fabric of government. But this danger is under the present system greatly enhanced by the fact that the mere abolition of the veto would establish not the supremacy of the House of Commons, but a Cabinet autocracy qualified in certain electoral conditions by the power of some enclave or " cave " in a party. There are circumstances under which this state of affairs might easily lead to Cæsarism, where a magnetic party leader either succeeded in capturing the imagination of the populace or in engineering a supremacy among competing politicians.

The consideration of the wider issues of democracy cannot be postponed. Though in pursuance of our customary method of dealing with " one thing at a time " we may first proceed to abolish the Lords' veto, we cannot halt there. That change, as we perceive, will not leave other things as they were, but will demand a thorough-going many-sided reconstruction of our representative system, unless we wish to abandon the cause of political self-government.

Several reforms are needed, besides the destruction of the Lords' veto, in order to convert the present representative system into an effective instrument of democracy. The House of Commons must be made more accurately representative, and representative government must be supplemented by a measure of direct democratic control. In order to make the House of Commons representative of the will of the people, it must be in direct and frequent contact with the needs, aspirations, and experience of the whole people. Though capacity to serve the State is the true basis of the suffrage, and this capacity must be greater in some citizens than in others, no safe method of enforcing this theoretically justifiable discrimination is discoverable. Adult suffrage is the only practicable expedient for securing the required contact between representatives and people. In every country where democracy has taken root the basis of representation has broadened towards this shape. The admission of women to an equal voice with men thus needs no separate argument. It inheres in the very nature of democracy. For a democracy maimed by the exclusion of the direct representation of the needs, aspirations, and experience of half the people would be a mere androcracy.

With the same object of rendering the House of Commons a truer expression of the popular will, some form of proportional representation must be incorporated in our electoral system. Three definite evils are traceable to the defective working of the present system. First, there is the party majority in the House of Commons exaggerated beyond all proper proportion to the aggregate electoral majority in the country, and lending itself, as we have seen, to Cabinet autocracy. Secondly, there is the abuse of pledges imposed upon candidates by minorities which, under proportional representation with fairly large areas, would spend their electoral strength upon electing a few zealous supporters of their special causes. Thirdly, there is the loss to the State of many of her ablest and most honourable legislators who cannot hope or desire to obtain election under the existing system of polling. The single transferable vote, applied in areas of sufficient size to enable every considerable minority to be represented, is so simple and so manifestly just a reform that it could not fail to win popular acceptance, if a fair opportunity were secured for the recasting of our electoral machinery.

If to these major reforms we added the destruction of the present plural vote and the payment of members and electoral expenses out of public funds, we should have secured the forms of sound representation. But two democratic requirements would still remain unfulfilled. Though proportional representation would mitigate the tyranny of majority rule, and would curb to some extent the autocracy of Governments, astute party management or personal ambition might generate new abuses such as attend the play of the group system in some continental legislatures. Moreover, it is unlikely that the reforms of electoral institutions, here proposed, would of themselves so strengthen the House of Commons as to reverse the tendency towards increased Cabinet control. A real and firm check upon abuse of power on the part of a Cabinet and a House of Commons called upon to deal with new and urgent issues upon which the electorate had not been consulted, is an essential of democracy. Nor are such the only occasions which require a check. Elected legislators, mostly amateurs, will of necessity be influenced strongly, sometimes predominantly, by those able permanent officials who, in the intricate processes of modern government, must necessarily come to play a growing part in the construction and administration of laws. Now this official mind, eminently serviceable, has its inevitable defects; authoritative, excessively conservative, mechanical, and usually contemptuous of the lay civic mind, it is apt to use every opportunity to impose itself upon new legislative proposals, and to substitute, as far as possible, the official will for the representative will. Now, though in nine cases out of ten this co-operation of the skilled official may be highly beneficial, there will be certain cases where his determinant influence will definitely conflict with the wisdom of the will of the people. This is no matter of mere theory. The fact cannot be blinked that, for some time to come, high officials in this country will, by their economic interests, their upbringing, and their social habits, be in most imperfect sympathy with the aspirations of democracy. Consciously, or more often unconsciously, these class sentiments or interests will obtrude themselves into the advisory and formative work of legislation and administration which falls to them. How should it be otherwise? Until a far fuller measure of equality of economic and intellectual opportunity exists than now, a powerful support must continue to be rendered by the higher bureaucracy to the defence of vested interests upon the political field.

The only effective check upon these defects or abuses of representative government is a direct appeal to the people. This Referendum is based upon a recognition that no form of representation is perfect, and that certain particular defects in representative government can best be met by a special and direct appeal to the fount of government. The will or consent of the people is in fact always claimed on behalf of every important measure of our legislature. But there exists no means of testing this claim. Electoral pledges, or post-electoral resolutions of caucuses or of other gatherings of electors, are, as we have seen, ineffective and often injurious methods of conveying a mandate or a consent. But the growing part they play in politics must be interpreted as an instinctive endeavour of the popular will to express particular judgments and to supplement the purely representative principle by some closer and more intimate control.

In every " democratic " country there is evinced this growing desire of the people to register its will through certain determinant acts of judgment upon concrete issues. The desire is commonly fed by a distrust of the efficacy of a representative system which so often lends itself to the manipulation of business or class interests or falls under the too complete control of professional politicians. But the roots of the desire lie far deeper down in the nature of democracy. There is in every people a half-conscious recognition of the fact that the will of the people is not really operative unless it is able to perform concrete acts of government. The instinctive craving for self-realisation through responsible conduct is a collective as well as an individual feeling. This feeling is not satisfied by the act of choosing a representative once in five or six years. The instinct of self-government is starved on such a fare. As an individual needs the responsibility for concrete acts of conduct in order to maintain and educate his personality, so it is with the collective personality of a nation. This is no revolutionary demand, but one enforced by the sober study of national psychology. An electorate will remain little better than a " mob " so long as it is treated like a mob, deprived of all opportunity of sober reflection and judgment upon 'intelligible issues, and goaded at intervals to orgies of electoral excitement in which passion, prejudice, business and sporting instincts are set to determine the representation of the people.

It is not, however, my purpose here to argue the case for Adult Suffrage, Proportionate Representation, and the Referendum, nor to consider the important effects which such measures would involve in the working of our party system. I merely desire to insist that a surgical operation upon the veto of the Lords must entail important after-treatment in the shape of constructive constitutional reforms, and that such proposals as are here set forth must at an early date be brought into the forefront of practical politics. The evolution of democracy would have proceeded far more slowly had the veto of the Lords, following the Royal Prerogative, slowly narrowed down from precedent to precedent until it had passed into the limbo of rudimentary survivals. The reversal of this process during the last two generations, for the political defence of vested interests, has brought fuller consciousness and purpose into the struggle for popular government. The application of constitutional force against the unconstitutional conduct of the Lords will compel the people to heal the breach they will have made by large considered measures of reform. It is of profound importance that the necessity of this constructive work should be clearly recognised, and that thoughtful politicians should set themselves without delay to the educative work that it entails.

CHAPTER II

THE LORDS OR THE REFERENDUM?

I

The grave constitutional struggle now opening between the Commons and the Lords has long been recognised as an inevitable incident in the history of British democracy. No theoretical objection to an hereditary house of legislature as inconsistent with the principles or practice of popular self-government has provoked the struggle. The temper of our people is such that it will acquiesce in the retention of the strangest anomalies, the most glaring inconsistencies, until they are recognised to be the immediate causes of present urgent grievances. So it has been with the House of Lords. The incompatibility of the principle of an hereditary control, to which it belonged, with the modern doctrine of the paramountcy of the will of the people has been quite apparent ever since the Reform Bill of 1832. From that time, too, has dated a steadily growing opposition between the Houses upon all issues of reform. " Although," said Mr. Gladstone in 1893, " there was contrariety between the House of Lords and the House of Commons before the Reform Bill of 1832, there never was conflict. When the Reform Bill became law, and for the first time the great principle was established that no man must sit in the House of Commons except by the voice of the constituency— then it was plain that this contrariety of the two Houses must develop, must sharpen into more pronounced differences and conflicts between the two Houses."

The real essence of this conflict consists, however, in the attitude assumed by the Lords towards the two great political parties and their policies. Since 1832 the House of Lords has definitely and continuously maintained the status of an appanage of the Conservative Party. When the electorate has returned a majority of Conservative members to the Lower House, and a Conservative Government has taken office, the conduct of the House of Lords has been little else than a formal registration of the Ministerial will; when the same electorate has placed in office a Liberal Government the Lords have become a recognised and permanent instrument of opposition. The alternatives of acquiescence and antagonism have been a constant shock and hindrance to the free play of our system of party government; under Conservative Ministers the consultatory and revising functions of a Second Chamber have been suspended, and unicameral government has virtually prevailed; under Liberal Ministers the House of Lords has been used as a party engine of obstruction. The " cup " has been " filling " for three-quarters of a century; the legicidal record of the Lords is long and various, extending over the entire area of political, social, and economic progress. Take a list of the most representative acts of legislative reform relating to religious liberty, freedom of the press, purity of elections, improvements in municipal government; turn to the long array of reforms of our criminal and civil codes, the building up of our public system of education, the structure of Factory and Workshop Acts and of other laws relating to the protection of workers, sanitary legislation, Irish legislation, and in particular laws attempting to repeal or modify the power of landlordism, and to secure to the people of Great Britain or Ireland a freer access to and fuller use of their native land—there will be found hardly a single important measure belonging to any of these orders which in its endeavour to express the popular will that gave it birth has not

suffered death or mutilation at the hands of the House
of Lords.

There may be those who would make the duration
of this grievance a reason for delaying any present
drastic remedy, holding that what has been endured
so long can be endured still longer.   It is therefore
needful to recognise that two changes have taken place
in recent years which render the earlier arts of
accommodation practised by Liberal Governments to
secure some modicum of progressive legislation no
longer feasible.

Since 1885 the Conservative majority in the Lords
has been overwhelming in magnitude. The rejection of
the first Reform Bill, in 1831, was carried in the Lords
by 199 to 158, a majority of only 41.   Even a generation later, in 1860, the rejection of the Paper Duty
Repeal Bill was carried by a majority of only 89.   But
in 1885 the Lords threw out the Home Rule Bill by no
less than 419 votes to 41.   From that time to this the
number of avowed and active Liberals, in a House of
Lords containing about 600 members, has remained
about 45.   Such an access of brute force is, of course,
in itself a danger, making it easier for any little group
of wreckers, out of party bias, class feeling, or economic
interest, to kill even those humbler measures of public
utility which in former times often got through alive.

The other novel factor in the situation is the demand
for stronger measures of social-economic reform which
stands in the forefront of the battle of Liberalism. Land
ownership, the Church, " the trade," and other powerful
" vested interests" are subjected to direct attacks, and
are organising co-operative methods of defence towards
which it is natural that the House of Lords should
be expected to contribute.   The more " Socialistic "
character of modern Radicalism forces the Lords to the
defence of their economic entrenchments.   The fear of
the early success of some " confiscatory" policy is for the
first time really felt by the abler Conservative leaders,

and if the legicidal power of the Lords is left intact they will be impelled to a use of it even more ruthless than in past times, because they will be more conscious of fighting for their " rights " and " privileges."

Unless Liberalism is to be sterilised for effective action, it is therefore manifest that Liberals must now " face the music." We have to destroy the power of the Lords to kill, mutilate, or unduly delay Liberal measures. What is that power? What is it that the Lords claim to have a right to do? Upon this point there is some popular misapprehension that requires removal. It has not for a long time been claimed by the Lords that they possess the same full power of accepting and rejecting Bills as the House of Commons. It is, of course, notorious that they may not amend money bills. This power they lost as the result of a resolution of the House of Commons in 1678. Though formally they still retain the power of rejecting money bills, the practice and probably the power to do so was lost in 1860 in the famous struggle over the Paper Duties Repeal Act, to which we shall make further reference.

But it is most important to realise that in ordinary legislation the powers of the Lords are limited by precedent and authority. Even at the period of the Reform struggle, in 1832, an unlimited arbitrary power of rejection without reference to the popular will was not claimed. The Duke of Wellington's contention then was almost identical with the doctrine affirmed recently by *The Times* in these words :—" It claims the right of asking the country to judge between the two Houses." The passing of the Reform Bill indisputably curtailed the power of the Lords, though Mr. Bagehot's statement that " since the Reform Act the House of Lords has become a revising and suspending House " is a somewhat extreme description of the actual change. The following more precise statement by the same authority may be considered a sound account of the

real constitutional position in the mid-Victorian days :
" It can alter bills, it can reject bills on which the House
of Commons is not yet thoroughly determined. Their
veto is a sort of hypothetical veto." Advancing a
generation, we may append the brief commentary of
Professor Dicey (1886), who holds that the Lords
must give way " whenever it is clearly proved that the
will of the House of Commons represents the deliberate
will of the nation."

It may well appear that the recent conduct of the
Lords and their defence of it during the present
Parliament is substantially opposed to this constitutional
definition, and marks a new encroachment or endeavour
to recover powers of arbitrary rejection which had
already passed away. This is in substance true. The
Lords are encroaching, and the Commons in resenting
this encroachment pursue a conservative policy. But
it must be noted that the encroachment is covered by a
defence which though false in substance is correct in
form. The Lords, we are told, fully admit that the
" will of the people " should operate in legislation, but
they claim to use an equal right with the Commons
to determine whether a particular bill does or does not
express the popular will. Both Mr. Balfour and Lord
Lansdowne have recently restated this position in language which is memorable for its frankness. The former,
addressing the Junior Carlton Club on November 28th,
1906, said : " I do not for one moment believe that the
Lords, in the exercise of the high functions entrusted
to them by the Constitution, will waver in their duty.
Their duty is not to thwart the will of the nation, but to
see that its will is really and truly carried out." The
Plural Voting Bill and some of the chief provisions of the
Education Bill did not, in the judgment of the Lords,
express " the will of the nation ; " hence they were
entitled and required to reject them. The same doctrine
was consistently applied in still more instructive fashion
in the acceptance of the Trades Disputes Bill. This

measure, though denounced by Lord Lansdowne and Lord Halsbury as " disastrous," " calamitous," " unjust," and " tyrannical," was accepted on the express ground that " the constituencies " demanded such a measure. " If your lordships," said Lord Lansdowne, "were to refer this bill back to the country, what would be the result? Can we have any doubt as to the answer the constituencies would give? I believe we should find a demand for a similar bill renewed with greater intensity, and in a form embittered by the suggestion that the House of Lords was in conflict with the general desire of the working men of this country." One other passage in this remarkable speech deserves to be put on record as a statement of this doctrine of the mandate: " I believe it is the duty of your lordships' House to arrest the progress of such measures when we believe they have not been properly considered, and are not in accord with the judgment of the country."

It is this claim of the Lords to veto measures or parts of measures which have not been properly considered and which have not behind them a popular mandate that is the point at issue. The Government denies *in toto* the validity of this claim, on the grounds, first, that no such mandate as is here pretended is in fact requisite for legislation; secondly, that there exists no method whereby the House of Lords can ascertain whether a particular bill possesses a mandate; and, lastly, that the application of this principle by the Lords to bills passed respectively by a Liberal or a Conservative House of Commons is such as to give the lie to any claim that their policy is genuinely determined by any such consideration. How can a House of Lords claim to be guided exclusively by its reading of popular mandates when it accepts every important controversial measure proposed by a Conservative Government and rejects almost every measure of similar character proposed by a Liberal Government?

II

To represent the Constitutional issue that has arisen as confined to the adjustment of the relations between the two Houses of Parliament is to underestimate its scope and difficulties. The governmental function of the people is directly involved, for the radical complaint is that the popular will, seeking expression through legislation, is impeded or perverted through the defects of Parliamentary machinery. In considering remedies for these defects we must not confine ourselves to some measure for the easing of the immediate situation, but must seek some basis of more enduring settlement. That any remedy involves some alteration of the structure of the Constitution is tolerably apparent. Such an experiment cannot be lightly undertaken, and its delicacy and its unknown risks demand that the immediate measure of reform shall be such as to involve the smallest amount of organic change consistent with the attainment of the desired end, viz., the rendering of the popular will effective through the use of Parliamentary government. Since the immediate grievance is the abuse of the power of veto contained in the legislative function of the House of Lords, the first and simplest remedy has appeared to some to be that the Commons should, by resolution and by legislative action, aim to destroy this power of veto in the Lords or to reduce it to a harmless weapon of delay. In a few quarters there is talk of " ending " the Lords or of destroying outright their " veto " by passing through a House packed for this purpose a measure enacting that a law passed by the House of Commons shall forthwith be presented to the King for the Royal Assent, the assent of the Lords being no longer necessary. But the advocates of such direct proposals of legislation by a single Chamber are comparatively few. A far wider vogue belongs to the proposal to crush the legicidal efficacy of the Lords' veto by placing a short time-limit on its operation.

Those who favour this form of remedy usually suggest the duration of the existing session or of the existing Parliament for the operative power of the veto. If this change were effected the Commons would over-ride the rejection of a measure by the Lords by a formal re-introduction of the rejected Bill at the beginning of the following session, or at such other short interval as might be prescribed.

Now, upon these proposals of a short time suspensory veto we have one plain judgment to express. The veto they leave is not a substantial power to deny or to delay. To reduce the power of rejection in the Lords to a sessional or parliamentary veto is virtually to destroy our two-Chamber system of legislation and to substitute a single-Chamber system. In measures of first-class legislative import—and it is the treatment of such measures by the Lords that is in question—delay of a few months, or even years, cannot be regarded as of material consequence. The real aim and result of such a reform would be to make the House of Commons the sole effective instrument of legislation. It is right that the suspensory veto proposal, when regarded as the sole and sufficient method of " dealing with the Lords," should be seen in its true light, that of a proposal to give omnipotence to the House of Commons in law-making. We are thus enabled to confront the important question whether a single-Chamber legislature in this country is safe, desirable, and in accordance with the wishes of the people. Single-Chamber governments are not unknown. Greece and a few South American States are governed by single Chambers at the present time. But no representative House has ever possessed an extent of power comparable to that which the British House of Commons would possess if the check of the Lords were removed and no new check introduced. In most representative Houses some legislative powers are reserved by a written or an unwritten constitution, and wherever a written constitution exists in a modern democratic State the power of the representative assembly to effect constitutional changes is limited. Our House of Commons, thus rid of the veto of the Lords, would stand in the unique position of having sucked into itself by a gradual process of absorption all those legislative powers which once belonged to the Crown and to the Peers, besides those powers which in most democratically-ordered States are still reserved to the veto of the people.

Do we seriously desire to endow the House of Commons with an absolutism which is only checked by an intrusion of the popular will at intervals of five or six years, the time and distinctive circumstances of which are determined by the same supreme body? It may be said that British democracy is irrevocably committed to the principle of representation, that the House of Commons embodies this principle, and that therefore no extension of the powers of the Commons can be regarded as a dangerous excess. But the representative principle is susceptible of various applications and modifications in practice. In most forms of popular government two focuses of representation are applied, so as to yield two elected assemblies serving as a check or balance to one another, or frequent periodical retirements of large sections of one or both assemblies enable the popular will constantly to renew its impress upon the Legislature. In this country the effect of the virtual cancelment of the Lords' veto as the sufficient remedy for present grievances would simply mean that every government would be endowed with that same power of defying public opinion and disregarding public interests exhibited by the Parliament which sat during the years 1902-5. It is idle in face of recent experience to pretend, by means of general references to the representative principle, that the application of that principle to the election of a House of Commons affords security against the gravest abuses of governmental power.

Moreover, we cannot ignore the notorious fact that

the growth of the power of the Cabinet in recent years, involving as it does the diminution of the control of the body of the Commons over the course of legislation, implies a weakening of the representative system. Taken at the best, the Cabinet is representative at two removes; at its worst it may, and does, imply that the actual course of legislation in the House of Commons is determined by a small committee which is not even an approximately accurate reflex of the feelings and interests of the party majority in the House, and whose relation to the electorate is so slight and distant as to be almost negligible. The exigencies of modern Parliamentary government have combined to diminish the legislative power directly wielded by the House of Commons and to increase that wielded by the Cabinet. To destroy the Lords' veto would be, then, to establish that same qualified Cabinet autocracy in a Liberal Government which, with a quiescent House of Lords, has long prevailed under Conservative Governments. It may well be held that a Liberal Government, with its fuller trust in the people, will be disposed to maintain a more genuinely representative spirit in its legislative action. But in considering an enduring basis of reform we must take under our survey all sorts of Governments—a Government raised to a long spell of power in a moment of artfully stimulated passion as well as one elected to carry out a series of carefully discussed and widely demanded reforms. In other words, are the conditions under which the popular will expresses itself in legislation through the House of Commons so satisfactory as to justify the conviction that we may safely bestow a plenary power of law-making upon a single Chamber so elected and so controlled for periods of seven years?

It is doubtless true that a House of Commons after its election maintains some sympathetic contact with the electorate, and is bound to pay some sort of regard to public opinion. So likewise the Cabinet and the

Ministry, though not elected by the House and containing often a large element of the peerage, cannot disregard the feelings and views of the party in the Commons, whose Members habitually employ their opportunities of informing, urging, warning, and even menacing Ministers. But when we put the plain question, " Does this method of representation afford such reasonably full security for the interpretation of the will of the people through acts of legislation that we are prepared to stake the working of our democratic Government upon its success?" an affirmative answer is seen to be impossible.

Nor is it merely that the House of Commons, as the single instrument of representative government, is defective. It is also felt to be unsafe. There exists a very widespread feeling that the conditions under which a general election takes place are liable to be those of a rush of feeling and a falsification of political issues. The people require and desire some protection against the grave dangers of misrepresentation involved therein, lest they should have committed themselves too rashly to a long line of policy which was in no true sense their will. The nation will not support any proposal formally or virtually to establish in this country a single-Chamber Legislature. The possibilities of an abuse of power are too great and the consequences of such abuse too grave. The following words of J. S. Mill are as true to-day as when he wrote them : " The consideration which tells most in my judgment in favour of two Chambers is the evil effect produced upon the mind of any holder of power, whether an individual or an assembly, by the consciousness of having only themselves to consult."

III

Many of those who favour the proposal to establish single-Chamber legislation by reducing the Lords' veto to a power of delay for one or more sessions are ready to concede that the House of Commons, as at present constituted, is not so faithful a reflection of popular opinion and aspirations as it might be. They recognise that the absorption of the control of public business by the Cabinet, with its corresponding diminution of the liberty of ordinary Members to initiate and carry laws, to take part in discussions, and even to raise grievances, implies some decline of the effective representative character of the people's House. It is not desirable, such men admit, to remedy the Liberal grievance against the Lords by imparting to every Government that power to disregard the plainest intimations of the popular will which was subject to such grave abuse by the 1900 Government during its last years of office. " But," it is contended, " once crush the Lords' veto upon Liberal legislation, and it will be possible to effect great reforms, electoral and constitutional. Shorter Parliaments can curb excesses of independence; the second ballot, or the adoption of proportionate representation, will check that exaggerated swing of the pendulum which tends to make every House a caricature of the state of feeling in the country; large devolution of legislative and administrative business from the Imperial Parliament upon provinces and smaller areas of local government, relieving the present congestion of business in the House of Commons, will restore some of the liberties of legislation and debate which have been curtailed." But granted that such reforms of the House are in themselves desirable and can be compassed, the question still remains, Is the nation prepared to assign unlimited powers of legislative change to a single elected Chamber for a term of years? Shall we consent to put all our legislative eggs in one basket? is the accepted form in which the question will present itself to the ordinary citizen, and the answer will be a clear, decisive negative. To entrust to a single elected Assembly greater unchecked powers than have ever before been entrusted will be realised as too hazardous an undertaking.

The conservative instincts of the nation will, unless we are mistaken, express themselves in two demands— first, that a Second Chamber shall continue to exist, possessing some measure of real legislative influence, though not the present absolute power of veto; secondly, that the people shall be endowed with some more effective control over the course of legislation than is provided by the machinery of a general election. The maintenance of a second advisory Chamber, with power to influence the course of legislation, will generally be approved, and innumerable schemes for the construction of such a second House have been propounded, the more conservative based upon the idea of converting the existing House of Lords into a more effective instrument by various processes of selection, rejection, and appointment, the more radical aiming at the substitution of an entirely new sort of elected House. Any attempt here to distinguish and discuss the comparative merits of these diverse structures would bewilder and impede us in our main object —that of discovering the safest and most profitable distribution of legislative powers. But we may take it for granted that public opinion will favour the erection of a Second Chamber capable of exercising, by initiative, consultation, and authoritative weight, a genuine and valuable influence upon the legislative work of the Government. To do this implies a combination of two conditions. Such a Second Chamber must gather within itself men of superior and acknowledged intellect and character, many of them possessed of experience in the making and administration of laws. At the same time it should possess a fuller public confidence and a closer and more sympathetic relation to the body of the people than consorts with the idea of a Chamber of hereditary or of merely nominated members. In other words, the prime essential of an effective Senate is that, in the main at any rate, it should be composed of elected persons, but that the mode and qualifications for election and for the holding of office should be such as to secure high qualities of political experience, intellect, and public spirit. This might be compassed by a process of direct popular election, with larger electoral areas, and on a proportional plan which would secure a great variety of political opinions and less party attachment than is found in the House of Commons. Or the electorate for the Second Chamber might, as Mr. A. R. Wallace suggested in the *Fortnightly Review*, be confined to the members of the various parish, district, borough, and county councils throughout the country. There would be some advantage in securing for Members of this House a longer and a safer tenure of office than is requisite or desirable for the House of Commons. It would not be proposed to transfer to this new Second Chamber the full power over legislation enjoyed by the present House of Lords. To set up a new Second Chamber, with whatever safeguards of election, possessed of the absolute veto of the present House of Lords, would not, indeed, meet the necessities of the case for reform. For such senate of statesmen, consisting, as it is desirable it should, largely of men of official experience, will of necessity lean unduly towards Conservatism, and will almost certainly be weighted with class feelings and view-points. Such will be the inevitable defects of its qualities, whatever the methods of election or appointment. To leave to such a Chamber an absolute veto would be to misconceive the public service it is capable of rendering and endow it with a harmful power of hindering popular legislation. The same objection, though in a milder degree, is applicable to the proposal that, where a difference of judgment upon a Bill has arisen between the two Chambers, they should, following the precedent of France, and of some of our own colonies, sit together and determine the issue by a joint vote. The advantage of some provision for

conference between the Chambers in such cases is great
and evident; but if we are right in our conviction that
the sort of Second Chamber most serviceable for advice
and criticism will of necessity remain predominantly
conservative in judgment and in action, any provision
securing equal efficacy for a vote of the Member of the
Second Chamber with that of a Member of the House
of Commons, will prove a drag upon progressive
legislation.

The true functions of the reformed Second Chamber
should be purely advisory and deliberative, and its influence should reside not in the " brute force " of a veto,
but in the dignity and authority, intellectual and moral,
which the character of its composition and deliberations
will command. The rough-and-tumble of party play in
the House of Commons leaves ample scope for work of
incomparable worth in detailed criticism of Bills. Moreover, there is no reason why the initiation of measures
in the Second Chamber should be curtailed. Such an
Assembly as is here contemplated would find, perhaps,
its most useful work in that skilled draughtsmanship
which is so lacking in many measures that originate in
the haste and turmoil of the House of Commons.

But is this Chamber of statesmen to be allowed to
exercise no determinant influence whatever upon the
course of legislation? Is it not to support its intellectual
and moral authority by any formal power? We have
already indicated the nature of the reply to this vital
question. Some check upon the legislative freedom of
the Commons must remain with the Second Chamber,
but that check must not be an absolute veto.

This proposal of a suspensory veto over a general
election, though less likely to become a weapon of Conservative obstruction under a reformed and elected
Second Chamber, will appear to most men an excessive
check upon progressive legislation. In substance, indeed,
it differs little, if at all, from the power nominally
claimed for the existing House of Lords under the

theory of the " mandate " as recently expounded. The House of Lords, we are told, only claims the right to compel the Commons to obtain a " mandate " for its measure by submitting it as a definite issue at a general election. The larger power of " suspensory veto " suggested for a reformed Upper House recalls too forcibly the possibility of similar abuse to make it likely that such a veto will be accorded to any Second Chamber, however constituted. The real grievance of the possession of an unpopular obstructive instrument in the shape of a permanently Conservative Second Chamber will not have been redressed until a means is devised for referring directly to the people the determination of an important difference of judgment between the two Chambers.' The formal legislative power left to the new Second Chamber should be the power of causing a Bill of the Commons which they disapprove to be submitted to a separate vote of the electorate, in order to test the question whether or not the people desires that the disputed Bill should become law.

IV

The proposal that a reformed Second Chamber, wholly or mainly elected under conditions likely to secure Members of high intellectual calibre, independent judgment, and political experience, should be entrusted with a power of submitting to a Referendum any Bill passed by the House of Commons which, in their judgment, has not received the sanction of the popular will, has several claims to our favourable consideration as an instrument of government. Its possession would secure for the Second Chamber a real power of checking hasty, ill-advised, or unauthorised legislation by the House of Commons or the Ministry, without leaving it any final right of causing rejection or considerable delay. It might even be permissible for the Second Chamber to reject a measure once, or to amend it, so that the House of Commons might have the opportunity of reconsidering the Bill in the light of the criticism of the Second Chamber. But the Bill as presented a second time must either receive the formal assent of the Second Chamber, or, in case this assent is refused, must be submitted in due form, and after a short but sufficient interval to a vote of the entire electorate of the country, whose acceptance or refusal shall determine whether the measure is presented for the Royal assent, and so passes into law, or is dropped.

The first and principal advantage of this proposal is that it provides an effective curb upon any legicidal or obstructive tendencies which even a reformed Second Chamber less immediately in contact with popular feelings and ideas might exhibit, while at the same time meeting the objections raised against single-Chamber government. The effect would be, of course, to transfer the veto from the Second Chamber to the people, while leaving to this Second Chamber the considerable power which the right of forcing an appeal from the Commons to the electorate will reserve for it. For in preparing any measure and in passing it through the Commons any Government would still have to consider its probable reception by the Second Chamber, and would be disposed to make reasonable modifications to meet anticipated opposition and to accept such proposed amendments as are not destructive, so as to avoid the trouble and the risks necessarily attendant on the popular voting. On the other hand, the opponents of the measure in the Second Chamber would be inspired by similar motives of moderation and concession; they would not care to kill or mutilate a Bill when the result of their violence might be to pass into law by the popular vote the original unqualified measure, which they might have modified if they had shown more forbearance. Thus the best fruits of the two-Chamber legislative method could be retained, though the ultimate act of ratification is taken from the Lords and given to the people.

D

A considerable argument in favour of this mode of settling differences between the two Houses is that it is the most reasonable method of applying that doctrine of the "mandate" which Mr. Balfour, Lord Lansdowne, and other defenders of the Lords' veto have adduced in support of the course taken by the Upper House. The House of Lords exists, they tell us, as a legislative body to ensure that no Bill of the House of Commons shall pass into law which has not behind it a clear mandate of the people. But the existing Constitution furnishes no method of obtaining a clear mandate for any single measure. The present contention of the House of Lords appears to be that it has the right to force a dissolution and an appeal to the country by rejecting a Bill like the Education Bill, the Plural Voting Bill, or even the Finance Bill. On this hypothesis we are placed in the following dilemma. Either a Liberal Government must dissolve every time an important Bill is rejected by the Lords and go to the country on this isolated issue, a condition obviously as impracticable as it would be unreasonable, or else it must wait until a number of important Bills have been rejected and then dissolve, placing before the electorate the question of endorsing these several Bills together with other prospective acts of policy. In this latter case, the actual case of a Liberal Government which goes to the country, what possible method does our general election, with its medley of measures, party cries, and personalities, provide for ascertaining whether a particular Bill or policy possesses a clear mandate? The least reflection makes it evident that, if it is a function of the Second Chamber to ensure that a Bill has a popular mandate, the only way of fulfilling this function is to submit the particular measure by itself to a separate popular vote. Here is a method of doing it which is the valid application of the constitutional power claimed as a prerogative of the House of Lords, but for the proper exercise of which no provisions exist in the present Constitution. The " right "

of the Lords to " test " the " mandate " can only be
exercised by providing a means of submitting to the
people the separate issues that are contested between the
Houses.

We are, of course, aware that there are those to whom
this doctrine of the popular mandate, though by no
means novel, is anathema. Ours, they say, is, or ought
to be, a purely representative system of government;
a House of Commons consists not of instructed delegates, but of Members empowered to use their free
judgment in passing such laws, and in performing such
other acts of government as they think most conducive
to the public interest. The party allegiance they profess
and the general statement of policy they make are not to
be understood as binding them to concrete legislative
proposals; they are not the vehicles of any such mandates as the theory of the defenders of the Lords implies.
But all practical politicians are aware that this is not a
correct presentation of our electoral methods of to-day.
Pure representation—*i.e.*, the election of the " best
man" on general grounds of imputed competency—does
not hold, perhaps never has held, the field. The strict
" party " method of election is itself a " mandate " of a
broad sort not leaving to the elected Member an unfet-
tered judgment. But in recent times specific pledges
are extorted, undertakings are given in order to win
the support of definite interests, which convey real
" mandates " of varying degrees of rigour. By formal
pledges, deputations, petitions, the electorate has con-
siderably qualified the representative system, ingrafting
a variety of sorts of " mandate." These mandates are
often illusory and ineffective, and in their present shape
they often undermine in an injurious way the independence of the Member. Worse still, they often enable
small minorities to exert an excessive influence upon the
structure of Bills, and even on the course of legislation.
In the present illicit or informal operation of the
mandate there is nothing to prevent Bills from passing

the House of Commons, by the votes of " pledged " Members, which have behind them not " the will of the people " but the pertinacious fanaticism of little organised groups representing a small minority of the electorate. This forms a serious and a growing danger to democracy. To substitute an open, full, and formal mandate of the people for this secret and insidious operation would be a distinct contribution to the honesty as well as to the efficiency of popular government. In other words, our system is not, and cannot be made, " purely representative "; the use in elections of " causes " and of single-issue leagues to " bind " elected persons exists and is growing; it implies, in fact, the insistence of a more educated and intelligent people upon taking a larger, a more direct, and a more continuous part in the conduct of public affairs.

All this is inherent in the growth of modern democracy. This instinctive demand for direct self-government is an wholesome sign of modern democracy. Its dangers and inconveniences arise from the defects of our present political machinery. It is important to provide safe and adequate instruments for its expression. If our contention is correct that the people will not be satisfied with those solutions of the problem which either retain a power of absolute veto for a permanently Conservative House, or else give unlimited power to a single elected Chamber, the most satisfactory alternative is to use the instrument of the direct popular mandate, which is a clean implication of modern democracy, in order to displace the veto of the hereditary House. Before discussing the other practical advantages and difficulties of this course one preliminary objection, however, must be met.

It may be urged that a Referendum, set in operation by the Lords, will leave a Liberal Government still at a disadvantage as compared with a Conservative Government. To bestow such a power upon an unreformed House of Lords would virtually be to concede to them

the claim made on their behalf by Lord Lansdowne.
Tory measures would go through unchallenged. Every
Liberal measure offensive to the interests or prejudices
of the Members of the Upper House might be referred
to the popular vote. Moreover, if our anticipation be
correct, a reformed Upper House, however appointed
or elected, would be likely to remain dominantly Conservative, and could use its Referendum power unequally
as between Liberal or Conservative administrations.
The real grievance here, however, would consist rather
in a tendency to pass without question Conservative
measures than to reject without good cause Liberal
measures. For to procure the popular endorsement by
a Referendum of a Liberal measure they disliked would
not serve their real interests, and the trouble and expense
occasioned by a frivolous appeal would strengthen the
popularity of the measure, besides damaging the opposition party in the Commons with the country.

What is required to secure substantial equality is a
power vested in a sufficient minority of the House of
Commons, concurrent with the power of the Lords, to
procure a Referendum. If 200 Members of the Commons were able to force the submission of a Bill to the
popular vote, it is exceedingly unlikely that the weapon
would be abused or frequently used. For any failure to
secure a negative reply from the electorate would
seriously discredit the minority and would damage their
chances of return to power at the next General Election.
There is, indeed, good reason to maintain that the
reasonable check thus afforded to the regular opposition
upon the tyranny of a majority would go far to remedy
an abuse of power illustrated by several conspicuous
examples in our time.

V

To substitute a popular voting, or Referendum, for
the veto of the Second Chamber, does not involve, as

is sometimes alleged, any abandonment of representative government. The full control of administration and finance, together with the initiation and preparation of all laws, would remain with the elected House or Houses; the ordinary course of legislation would run through the same forms as heretofore, Bills passing into law by the assent of the two Houses and the King; only controversial measures of great importance, proved by the sustained opposition of a majority of the Upper House or of a large minority of the Lower House to be of doubtful popular acceptance, would be referred to the popular vote. The frequent use of this expedient would neither be desirable nor likely to occur. It could not become, as seems possible at first sight, a serviceable weapon of obstruction, for the light use of it in the political game of party or faction, difficult enough under the conditions of a reformed Upper House, would, by affording a direct popular test of the weakness of the opposition, recoil against the latter, who would reap the added unpopularity of causing needless trouble and expense to the public. Even in Switzerland, where no such stringent regulations for the reference of laws exist as are here proposed, and where 30,000 citizens can, by signed petition, require that any law be submitted to the popular vote, this natural check upon abuse is so far operative that during thirty-two years of the existing Constitution only twenty-nine laws and resolutions were put before the people.

It would be reasonable, indeed necessary, to exempt certain sorts of measures from the operation of the Referendum. The most obvious exceptions are the Finance Bill and the related Appropriation Bill. For these, though legislative in their form, are in essence administrative acts, and both on this account and because of their intricate and multifarious character are improper subjects for direct popular control. General finance is in Switzerland excluded from the operation of the Referendum. It would also be necessary, here, as again in

Switzerland, to exclude certain measures of great
urgency as well as measures affecting foreign relations.
Bills, dealing with matters of small importance, or
affecting small areas of country or population, would
also be unsuitable for a national plebiscite, though in
many cases provision for a local Referendum might be
inserted in the Act, as is indeed occasionally done now.

Under the conditions here suggested the number of
laws actually submitted to the popular vote would be
far fewer and at considerable intervals.   The very
practical difficulty often raised by politicians against
the proposal, viz., the trouble and expense of its administration, would be likely to reserve its use for rare
and critical occasions, when the issue involved was
keenly and closely contested both in Parliament and
in the country, and when a direct and accurate measure
of public opinion was recognised as a prime condition
of final settlement.

But the actual operation of this new instrument will
afford no measure of the extent and value of its influence.   For the knowledge of the existence of this
popular court of final appeal will affect the whole course
of legislation, inducing both the Government and
individual legislators so far to conciliate the Opposition
in Parliament as to diminish the probability of a reference to the people, while all measures will be framed
with a closer consideration of the supposed wishes of
the majority of the electorate than is the case where a
Government possesses plenary powers of legislation. In
other words, legislation will be made more conformable
to the will of the people, though the specific expression
of that will through the popular voting may be seldom
given. Believers in popular self-government will deem
this a gain, though it will doubtless meet stout opposition among those who profess the view that elected
persons, knowing better than the people what the
people ought to want, should use their legislative powers
to put upon the Statute-book laws which, though not

acceptable to the people, are " good for them." Now, those who claim for the people the right to express their will in the acceptance or rejection of concrete measures of importance do so upon two grounds of even greater fundamental importance than that of finding a practical solution of the problem of the House of Lords. They hold that democracy is not effective so long as the representative system is liable to work in such a way that laws can be passed vitally affecting the public welfare which do not in fact possess the public approval. They resent the " we-know-better-what-the-people-want-than-they-know-themselves " attitude, not because of holding some abstract theory about popular government, but because they are aware that laws passed in such a spirit are not likely to be well administered and well obeyed. A people endowed even with a moderate measure of intelligence will recognise the advisability of deferring to the superior skill and knowledge of tried and trusted representatives upon · the technique of legislation, but they will not give to these agents a perfectly free hand over a term of years to pass any laws that seem good to them. They will insist upon retaining the ordinary customer's right to refuse " misfits." In a word, the fact that a law is acceptable to the body of the people is a prime essential to its " goodness," and there is no certain way of determining this fact unless an opportunity is afforded to ask the people. Experienced statesmen in this and other countries know, and detailed administrators know still better, that many laws, embodiments of excellent general principles and constructed with excellent official cunning, fail to " work " chiefly because of their unpopularity among the people whom they were supposed to benefit. The annals of factory, temperance, and education legislation are full of examples of this defect, due to the desire of superior persons, representative or official, to legislate ahead of the requirements of the people. The trust in the people which political Liberalism professes must imply some conviction that the people knows what it wants, and that it is better to give it what it wants than something "technically" better which it does not want, and will therefore misuse or neglect. This is no doctrine imputing any mystic virtue to the collective mind, or assuming that the people's will is always wise and just; it is merely the most obvious application of the maxim that good government involves "the consent of the governed." If the great body of the electorate is as ignorant and as foolish as it is often represented, it will sometimes make mistakes, accepting or rejecting the wrong laws when submitted to its vote. But this is a necessary incident in the education of democracy, as in that of the individual personality. If the people are not afforded the opportunity of making mistakes and learning from them, what sort of education are they getting, and what sort of progress can they make? It is here that we are brought to the very kernel of the case for the direct occasional participation of the people in acts of government. If it is desirable to work towards the idea of intelligent responsible democracy, a more real duty must be imposed upon the electorate than that of plunging into a sensational sporting contest once in six years and registering a single vote upon a medley of personalities and party cries. The demand that mandates shall issue from the people, determining the fate of important and disputed measures, is not only a reasonable way of settling issues that may arise between the two legislative Houses; it is the only sound method of educating the democracy for the work of self-government. The demand for specific popular judgments in concrete cases stimulates interest and imparts reality to politics. The "people," it is true, may not understand the full details of the Bills presented for their judgment, nor will they be competent to appraise the technical merits of the drafting. But they will find trusted advisers and exponents, skilled interpreters who will set forth effectively the substance of the Bills, and they will eke out their own understanding of the measure by the wisdom of accepted guides. The result will be a genuine though doubtless limited expression of the general will, and an education in practical politics that is of inestimable value.

The fundamental objection to the single-Chamber solution of the problem was that it poised the whole legislative fabric upon the narrow pedestal of a single dominant group within a single House. The proposal to retain a second reformed Chamber with real legislative influence, but to give the determinant voice in grave disputed issues to the people, broadens and strengthens the basis of sovereignty by distributing more widely the direct responsibility for legislation.

It will help to strengthen the respect for law, for people value more that which they have had a hand in making; it will also increase the stability of law, for Acts upon which the people have set the express seal of their approval present no opportunity for easy reversal on a change of government. These economies of legislative energy are attested by Swiss experience as attending the confirmation of critical acts of legislation by the vote of the people.

VI

Advocates of the Referendum as the best substitute for the veto of the Lords are not obliged to show that it is a flawless instrument. They need only show that it is better than an unchecked single-Chamber Government under our party system, and that it is more effective than any other check that is proposed.

To destroy the Lords' veto and to do no more is sometimes represented as if it were nothing else than the clearing away of an obstruction. But this is not the case. Such a course would confer upon the House of Commons a new and unlimited power not only to make laws but to alter the Constitution of the country.

This power, greater than any other single elective body in the civilised world possesses, the people of this country would not be willing to entrust to the House of Commons—that is, of course, to the majority for the time being of any and every House of Commons—when they understood what they were asked to do. They would refuse for three reasons—first, because they would hold it rash to dispense with a second judgment; secondly, because they would know that the real law-makers would not be the freely voting representatives of the people but a non-elected Cabinet; thirdly, because they are aware that a general election affords no opportunity of testing the popular will upon any single legislative issue apart from other issues. Any other real check that is proposed consists of a reformed Second Chamber endowed with more valid authority than the present House of Lords. The overwhelming majority of Liberals will be convinced, when they look closely into the various proposals for constituting such a Chamber, that under all of them it will possess a strong permanent conservative bias. Though they might desire to confer a consultative authority on such a Second Chamber, they would not leave it with a veto.

If these statements are correct, some sort of Referendum seems to present itself as the only alternative. In this event the defects and difficulties which critics point out in the working of a Referendum in this country may have some substance and yet may not dispose of its claim to be the safest and most feasible way out of the *impasse*. The Referendum will not do everything. If, as is sometimes urged, it is only put in operation when the two Chambers disagree, it seems likely to act at present as a one-sided weapon, for it fails to strike against the practical unicameralism that prevails when a Conservative Government is in office. It is held inequitable that the Lords should have a power to force a Referendum which they would only use when Liberals were in office. To this objection two answers can be given. The first use of a Referendum would be to force a reform of the Second Chamber through the existing House of Lords. But since even a reformed Second Chamber is bound, as we have said, to have a strong conservative bias, something more is needed. If, then, the Referendum is to be made an instrument of even-handed justice, it must be made competent not only for the Second Chamber but for a sufficient minority in the House of Commons to bring about the popular appeal.

But if either the Upper House or the full Opposition in the House of Commons can apply the Referendum, will not every contentious measure be put to the popular vote? The answer is, No. Several motives will counteract such a tendency. The first and chief is the unpopularity which would attend a light or frequent use; such abuse would recoil injuriously upon the popularity of the party practising it. Again, the existence of the popular reference would act as a peace-maker between the two Houses, especially when the Upper House was reformed. Critics of the Referendum fail to take account of one of the most valuable effects of that measure—its reaction upon the nature of the Bills that are constructed. The temper and discretion of the House of Commons would dispose it to frame measures which the consultative Chamber would accept, and to adopt the amendments of a body that had no power to compel adoption. The Second Chamber would cease to desire to be legicidal now that it had lost the power to kill. Still more important, as the experience of Switzerland shows, is the effect upon the structure of those measures which, from the importance of their character, are likely to be submitted to a popular vote. The result is an Act not made to suit the logic or the sentiments of some idealist reformer who claims to know better than the people what is good for them and what they ought to want, but an Act made to work, because it is framed as closely as possible in the image of the popular will.

In other words, a law which may be subjected to the endorsement of the people will be a different and a better law than one made in the present cloudland of our Parliamentary procedure, for the goodness of a law depends very largely upon its acceptability by the magistrates and other officials who execute it and by the citizens called upon to obey it. If, for example, we had one or two recently recorded judgments of the popular mind upon some salient aspect of the land or the drink problem, our Legislature would be far better qualified to frame a Small Holdings or a Licensing Bill that would work successfully than now. Even had there been no previous popular vote upon the particular subject for legislation, the necessity of framing a Bill likely to be accepted by the people would at once give more reality to the debates and would produce more practical and efficacious laws.

This will no doubt be disputed, but only by those Liberals who under a professed or real enthusiasm for a "representative system" conceal a deep-seated distrust of democracy. The representatives, they urge, are as a rule, somewhat wiser and better than those who elect them; they are more competent to legislate than the masses; the laws they pass are somewhat better than the people would at once be willing to accept. Now those who hold the Referendum essential to popular self-government do not deny the superior ability of the representative; they desire to use that ability in the framing of measures designed to express the popular will, but they insist upon the right of the people to have the opportunity of declaring whether certain measures do express the popular will. They wish to retain that liberty which every wise man retains throughout life in his dealings with specialists whom he invites to execute his orders—the right to refuse the article on the ground that it does not carry out the order. This does not imply a narrow construction of delegacy; the elected Legislature under a democracy will be entitled not merely to pass measures for which they may consider they have an express popular mandate, but others which have assumed importance since an election; their discretion will be real and their authority will carry weight, but they will not regard it as their duty to frame any law which they believe the majority of the people would refuse to adopt.

It is said often that the popular vote will be too conservative, that it will reject measures which are not only good but which if they were allowed to become operative would be generally recognised as good. There is some force in this objection; it is a defect of the " quality " of the Referendum. There is a certain inertia of the popular will that will retard the rate of progress, a conservatism if you will. But this is safer and better for democracy than the alternative " faking " of progress by pushing legislation ahead of the popular will. It is, upon the whole, far more profitable for reformers to be compelled to educate the people to a genuine acceptance of their reform than to " work it " by some " pull " or " deal " inside a party machine. Moreover, it is not true that such practical experience as is available shows that the " Referendum " is a weapon of conservatism. The Swiss people have during the last thirty years made by the use of it an advance in social and industrial legislation at least as great as that of any other civilised country in the world. The deduction from Swiss experience to the effect that the Referendum works conservatively because a few more laws are rejected than accepted is entirely invalid, for a Referendum is only demanded for those laws which it is held likely will be rejected; the great majority of laws are tacitly accepted by the people in the form in which they have been adopted by the Legislature.

It may, however, freely be admitted that when a nation possesses a fully and accurately representative system the Referendum might be needed only as a rare expedient for some sudden grave emergency when it was desirable to obtain a direct popular judgment. But the refusal even to consider the popular appeal, on the ground that we already possess such a representative system, is almost hypocritical. The real control of our legislation is in the hands, not of the body of elected representatives, but in those of a small Cabinet, selected mainly out of a little aristo-plutocracy with a leaven of successful lawyers, and of a powerful bureaucracy whose class sympathies are natural and notorious. The Referendum must be recognised not indeed as a substitute for, but as a necessary supplement to, representation in any nation aiming at popular self-government.

The fears that its adoption must damage the political calibre of the legislature are quite groundless. Only a minute fraction of the work of Parliament, in such a country as this, could be actually submitted to the popular vote, and even were it otherwise, the effect, as attested once more by Switzerland, would be to diminish the irrational fierceness of party and to secure a longer and a more continuous political career for well-known and competent politicians. For a Swiss citizen will support the election of a " tried " man though he may disapprove his views on one or two important topics, because he knows that the " Referendum " will enable him to correct any " misrepresentation " on these issues.

The objection that an adverse vote would shake the authority of a Government and force frequent dissolutions disappears before a closer inspection. The Minister responsible for a defeated measure might be driven to resign, though even that course does not seem inevitable. But when the final responsibility was undertaken by the people, as would be the case when a popular vote was taken, the responsibility of a Ministry would be proportionately relieved; their action in framing a difficult and doubtful measure on a matter of importance would be regarded rather as tentative and experimental, and not as one on which their entire reputation was at stake.   It is no doubt possible that the popular rejection of a measure of the first importance might once or twice in a decade so damage the Government that they deemed a dissolution advisable.   But it is not evident that this mode of selecting an opportunity for a dissolution would be contrary to the public welfare or particularly inconvenient.

It is, however, right to admit that the adoption of a Referendum, even for rare use, would probably produce some important changes in our unwritten Constitution, particularly as regards the collective responsibility of the Government.   I think it likely that reflection will lead to the conviction that these changes are likely on the whole to be salutary rather than the reverse.   The issue is, however, too large and intricate for profitable discussion here.   But those who express such timidity about the constitutional reactions of the Referendum may be reminded that their own proposals, simply to destroy the Lords' veto and confer complete autocracy not on the House of Commons but on the Cabinet would be fraught with constitutional consequences far graver.

One word in conclusion.   Advocates of the Referendum do not claim that it may not sometimes lead to the rejection of good measures and the adoption of bad ones.   But they affirm that these acts of judgment, with their good or evil consequences, are essential to the art of self-government in a nation as in an individual.   The summoning of the people to express a separate concrete judgment and to undertake solemnly the responsibility of a piece of political conduct is essential to the education of democracy.   It is not true that the people will be invited to disentangle and assess the intricate details of legal formulas.   Those who say this have not studied the working of the Referendum. Though the vote is taken on the merits of an entire bill, the education and discussion which precedes the vote are such as to inform the average citizen not merely of the principles but of the practical effects which the law is likely to produce, and thus evoke for legislation that general " wisdom of the people " which, whether it be great or small, sets the true limit upon the pace of popular progress through legislation or otherwise.

Chapter III

THE SWISS REFERENDUM

The presupposition of representative government is that the people are not able or willing to consider and determine concrete acts of polity, but that they are able and willing to select from among themselves persons competent to consider and determine on their behalf, choosing these persons not with particular reference to their supposed fitness for dealing with any one or several known issues, but for some general capacity applicable to the whole range of government that falls within the scope of their office.

Only certain simple issues of the ward, the village, or in some instances the city, it is held, fall sufficiently within the cognisance of the mass of citizens to be safely entrusted to their direct decision. As the area and population of the modern State expands, and the number, variety, and importance of public functions increase, it appears essential that the body of citizens should depend more and more upon the judgment of representatives for the making of laws and the general conduct of government. Regarded, however, as a mode of democracy, this representative system betrays serious defects, and in that country where it is most widely used the defects are gravest. The organisation of the party, which seems essential to the representative system, has led, in the United States and elsewhere, to the construction of party " machines " so strong and so ably operated that instead of the will of the people flowing freely upwards by processes of delegation and election, and thus finding expression in policies determined by men who are the genuine choice of the people, the will of the machine-politician, or his paymaster, is pumped down the machine from above and comes up again with a false and merely formal register of the popular will. For the party-manager is apt to let out the machine to the highest bidder, and those organised business interests which have most to gain by a successful manipulation of politics and most to fear from the free intelligent expression of the popular will, hire it and use it to secure that the chosen representatives shall be their creatures, and that their will shall obtain the popular endorsement.

The extent of this corruption of the representative system will, of course, vary widely with local conditions. In some States the crudest forms of bribery prevail and gross misrepresentation is procured; in others the arts of influence are subtler and less pervasive. The failure is everywhere relative; the popular will is not rendered impotent; even in States where the party boss and the machine are most powerful, known though ever-changing limits are set upon its management of representatives; any transgression beyond these limits arouses a ground-swell of popular feeling which throws out of gear the machine and lifts into power, or at least into office, men who are genuine representatives. But this safety-valve is unreliable and insufficient. For, as a rule, these popular movements are short-lived; it is a case of the weak, diffused interest of the many against the strong, concentrated and organised interest of the few. Wherever powerful business interests are founded upon or supported by legal privileges in the shape of charters, tariffs, or other concessions, wherever lucrative offices are available for party spoils, wherever public expenditure can be made a source of private profit through contracts, loans, and subsidies, this skilled manipulation of the representative system will continue.

How far these abuses of the representative system can

be remedied by schemes of proportionate representation tending to displace the two-party by the group system, or by slower processes of educating the electorate so as to weaken the dictation of the party-boss, are questions which cannot here be discussed with advantage.   For a deeper issue, coming gradually to the front of practical politics in modern democratic countries, demands priority of attention, viz., the tendency to question and to qualify the practice of unrestricted agency involved in a representative system which claims for elected Houses a *carte blanche* in legislative and other acts of government for a period extending over several years. With the development of explicit party programmes, election addresses, party and individual pledges, the theory and practice of unlimited agency have in this and other countries been subjected to such limitations as these methods of instruction admit.   In other words, the purely representative system is qualified by a loose and extremely unsatisfactory form of " mandate." Though the form of election in such a country as Great Britain still permits and presupposes that elected representatives shall be absolutely free to exercise their legislative functions during a period of not more than seven years, every Government more or less avowedly defends its concrete acts of policy as an interpretation of the national will, expressed either through a positive mandate given by a general election, or through such tokens of consent and approval as are afforded by bye-elections or by less formal expressions of public opinion.

A striking example of the growing acceptance of this modification of the representative system is afforded by the present defence of the legicidal actions of the House of Lords on the ground that they are the self-constituted defenders of the doctrine of a national mandate.

Now if it is desirable, or inevitable, that the representative system should be qualified by popular mandates, it is quite evident that such a method of conveying mandates as exists in Great Britain is utterly defective. If the assent of a majority of the electors be regarded as the qualification of a mandate, the proceedings of a general election, in which a heterogeneous mass of pro- posals is thrown down for popular judgment, quite evidently provide no means of ascertaining such assent. Even as regards the one or two measures which figure as predominant issues in an election, there exists no absolutely certain mode of determining whether a majority, still less what majority, of the electorate approves or rejects them; as regards those of secondary or tertiary interest, it is idle to pretend that any mandate can be thus conveyed; while other issues, sometimes of supreme importance, which come up unforeseen during the lifetime of a parliament, are not susceptible of any sort of genuine mandate. If then a popular mandate is to be a real factor in representative government, some method must be devised for taking a separate popular vote upon a particular issue, thus giving order and explicitness to a political force which is at present vague and irregular in application. Upon the working of this popular mandate Switzerland furnishes the only large body of modern experience. Of the nineteen full cantons and the six half-cantons comprising the federa- tion, nine possess an obligatory Referendum, and eight a facultative Referendum, enabling the people to exercise a veto upon any law, with certain rare exceptions; six others retain the primitive *Landsgemeinde* or State- Commune, in which all laws are submitted for sanction to the assembly of citizens; two cantons only, Fribourg and Valais, retain a purely representative government. Where the Referendum is facultative, a valid demand for its application requires the endorsement of a fixed number of electors, and the law submitted is accepted or rejected by a majority of those actually voting. An obligatory Referendum exists for all constitutional changes in the cantons, a majority of the actual voters finally determining the acceptance or rejection of the proposed change, with the exception of a single canton, Zug, where the majority of registered voters must tender an affirmative vote to secure acceptance.

Federal laws passed by the two Houses of Assembly, the Council of States and the National Council, must be submitted to a popular vote on the demand of 30,000 citizens, an absolute majority of recorded votes determining the acceptance or rejection. Changes in the Federal Constitution, general or particular, whether initiated by a demand of 50,000 citizens, or by a House of Assembly, are finally submitted to a popular vote, acceptance in this case, however, involving an affirmative vote both of a majority of the citizens actually voting and of the cantons.

Thus it appears that the people retains a power of veto upon all important constitutional and legislative enactments both in the cantons and in the confederation. While this Referendum is only a part of the machinery of popular sovereignty in Switzerland, it is much the most important part, and may legitimately form a subject for separate consideration. Historians sometimes trace its origins in the political history of the Grisons and Valais, or in customs prevailing in Berne and Zurich during the fifteenth and sixteenth centuries. Others lay stress upon the influence of Rousseau, whose *Contrât Social* must have deeply impressed his countrymen during the period when their old institutions were thrown by Napoleon into the melting-pot to re-issue in new rational moulds. But though ancient precedent and modern philosophic reflection may have exerted some conscious influence, the adoption of the Referendum and other accompanying checks on the newly-applied representative system must be attributed mainly to the self-protecting instinct of Swiss social democracy in provising a tolerably obvious set of checks upon what Whitman termed " the never-ending audacity of elected persons."

The history of genuine representative government

in the cantons and the confederation was not of long duration, perhaps not long enough fully to test its potentialities. Prior to the nineteenth century there was nothing that could rightly be termed a federal constitution, and the actual power exercised through the constantly changing federal league was slight; among the cantons which were genuinely self-governing the *Landsgemeinde* was the prevalent type, though in the cities and certain dominant cantons wielding power over subject territories the government was usually vested in representative bodies, often of an oligarchic character.

Although the Federal Agreement of 1815 which laid the basis for a stronger national union gave an impetus to the representative system in the cantons, that system continued until 1830 to be operated by local aristocracies with no real pretence of popular control. Thus it was not until the years following the French Revolution of 1830 that the Swiss entered on their experiment of representative democracy. Between 1830 and 1834 almost all the cantons set up single-chamber legislatures with no presidential veto, based upon universal suffrage and equal electoral districts. Full legislative powers were conferred upon the great councils t'ius elected, and the small council, forming the executive, was entirely nominated by the members of the great council. The makers of these constitutions threw themselves whole-heartedly into the logic of representative democracy. Since the people were to govern through agents the latter must enjoy all the powers and prerogatives of the former. The great council was, therefore, endowed with complete legislative power as regards all matters not expressly reserved by the federal constitution. It was also the sole source of executive and judicial power. No adequate safeguards against hasty legislation existed. A bill moved quickly through the council, even in those cantons where three separate readings were required, and passed into law without any external discussion or sanction. Administrative orders were even exempt from these slight restrictions or delays, so that the great council could, when it chose, govern by executive authority.

The results did not prove satisfactory to the people, who having stripped themselves of every shred of sovereignty, handing it over to an elected council, discovered that the latter developed, in its majority, a will which was not that of the people, but which operated independently of and often in antagonism to it. Interests re-established themselves in the seat of authority; ill-considered laws got into the Statute-book, and elected persons without the fear of the people before their eyes neglected or abused their trust.

The defenders of representation insisted that the only essential remedy was shorter parliaments, and they proposed to limit the duration of an assembly to one or two years, and in some instances to put in the hands of the people a right of demanding a dissolution. But the democrats refused to be put off with reforms which in their judgment were not even half-measures, and in all the cantons a prolonged agitation took place in favour of restoring to the people the right of initiating, discussing, and sanctioning their own laws. After a series of timid experiments in the late 'thirties and the 'forties, the German cantons came to adopt the obligatory or the facultative Referendum as their chief instrument of popular control, sometimes coupling with it the right of popular initiative which is to-day possessed by ten cantons. The French and Italian cantons fell slowly into line, until by 1880 all, with the exception of Fribourg, had adopted some form of Referendum for ordinary laws. In 1874 the optional Referendum was embodied in the new federal constitution.

Although this brief sketch of the movement in the cantons is historically important in showing the origins of federal democracy in the instincts of local self-government, it can hardly be pretended that a detailed

study of the Referendum in such tiny areas of government, where only in one instance dues the population
reach half a million, can throw much serviceable light
upon its virtues or defects as an instrument of national
democracy, which is the task we have before us.

What is of importance for us is the fact that for a
third of a century a European nationality, comprising
now three and a quarter millions of population, has
exercised a right of final veto over the legislative acts
of its elective assemblies in a federal State whose legislative power greatly exceeds in competency that of the
American Union.

The right is thus laid down in the Constitution of
1874 : " Federal laws, decrees, and resolutions can only
be passed by the agreement of the two councils.
Federal laws are submitted to the people to be accepted
or rejected by them if a demand be made by 30,000
qualified citizens or by eight cantons.   Federal decrees
which are of general application, and which are not
specially urgent, are likewise submitted upon demand."
(Art. 89.)

" The confederation shall by law establish the forms
and the suspensory intervals to be observed in the case
of the popular votes."   (Art. 90.)

It is evident that a mode of evading the popular vote
is here provided.   What is a law and what a decree, and
what decrees are "urgent" or of "special" application?
No definitions of these terms are provided either in the
constitution or in the law of 1874 regulating the procedure of the Referendum.   The determination of
these questions is conferred by the law of 1874 upon
the Federal Assembly, which is thereby enabled to
decide by a majority vote that a particular proposal is a
decree of such special or urgent nature that it shall forthwith come into operation without submission to the
popular vote.

Though no general rule determining the matters withheld from the Referendum has been laid down, certain

subjects have been reserved by custom. Of these the two most important are treaties with foreign States and federal finance, including under the latter Budget estimates and appropriations for war material. Other matters habitually reserved are : (1) Resolutions upon individual cases, as for instance decisions of administrative disputes; (2) resolutions voting subsidies for urgent public works such as protection of rivers and construction of roads.

The institution of the Referendum for ordinary legislation involves a certain machinery, not merely of voting, but of education. All ordinary laws and decrees, therefore, which have been passed by the Assembly are forwarded to the Federal Council, which publishes them and sends copies to the cantonal governments for circulation among the communes. Thus the people have brought directly to their notice the bills and decrees which are amenable to a Referendum. The method of demanding and applying the Federal Referendum is as follows.

As we have seen, this demand may be preferred by 30,000 voters or by eight cantons. The latter method is so difficult as to be virtually inoperative. The party or interest opposed to a law and desiring to defeat it on a Referendum must within ninety days secure the personal signatures of 30,000 active citizens. This of course implies organisation and canvass, and every signature must be attested by the communal authorities of the place where the demand is signed as a guarantee of validity. When the petition is sent in, it is submitted to examination by the Federal Council, which is empowered to cancel the votes when there is any informality in the declaration or the attestation. If the required number of valid signatures is obtained, the Federal Council organises the popular voting, fixes and announces the day, informs the cantonal councils and secures the prompt circulation of the law or decree to be voted upon. The bare text of the law is placed in the hands of every voter, with no report of the debates or other explanatory matter.

The voting takes place simultaneously throughout the whole country, and every male citizen over twenty years of age and qualified according to his cantonal law is entitled to vote. The voting paper simply contains the question : " Do you accept the federal law relating to (here the general title of the law), Yes or No?" The voter has simply to write his " Yes " or " No."

In order to save time and trouble it is usual for several votes to be taken at the same time and upon the same voting paper.

On the following page is a copy of a Federal Referendum taken in 1896, containing as its second item the important law on railroad accounts designed to lead up to the nationalisation of the railroad system.

After the voting each electoral district or commune draws up its report containing four columns, in which are recorded : (1) The number of registered voters; (2) the number of actual voters; (3) the number of those voting " Yes "; (4) the number of those voting " No." These reports are sent to be examined and corrected by the cantonal government, which forwards them within ten days to the Federal Council, which calculates the general result of the vote. If a majority of the voters have approved of the law or order, the Federal Council forthwith puts it into force, inserting it in the official Statute-book of the confederation. The results of the voting are in all cases published in the *Feuille Fédérale*, and the Federal Council reports them to the Chambers at the next session.

The Federal Referendum does not imply that representative institutions are destroyed, but that they are made supplementary to the direct action of the popular will, their functions being to relieve the people of a burden of public business too heavy for them to bear, to assist the popular will to attain adequate expression by providing discussion and advice, and finally to form a substitute for the people in matters of emergency and particularity.

Those unfamiliar with the working of the Referendum sometimes express alarm at the frequency of voting

BULLETIN DE VOTE

pour la

votation populaire du 4 octobre

1896

	Réponse :
I. Acceptez-vous la loi fédérale concernant la garantie des défauts dans le commerce des bestiaux ? - - - - - -	OUI ou NON ....
II. Acceptez-vous la loi fédérale sur la comptabilité des chemins de fer ? - - -	Réponse : OUI ou NON ....
III. Acceptez-vous la loi fédérale sur les peines disciplinaires dans l'armée suisse ? -	Réponse : OUI ou NON ....

Remarque. On doit répondre séparément à chaque question.

which it appears to involve. The tax upon the machinery of government and upon the time and trouble of the electorate is not, however, heavy. From the adoption of the Federal Constitution in 1874 up to June, 1906, the optional Referendum was applied to twenty-nine laws and resolutions, the compulsory Referendum to eighteen constitutional amendments. These forty-seven votes were taken in thirty-four separate votings, just over one per annum upon an average. Of the twenty-nine laws submitted to the Referendum, ten were accepted and nineteen rejected; of the eighteen constitutional amendments, twelve were accepted and six rejected.

The large proportion of laws rejected is sometimes adduced to support the view that the popular vote is in fact an obstacle to progress, inasmuch as it implies the refusal of a number of public measures which are endorsed by the two Houses of Assembly. The people, it is said, prove to be more conservative than their representatives, and it is suggested that this " conservatism " is injurious to the cause of national progress because of its unenlightened character. But though this " conservatism " of the people has an important meaning, very little light is thrown upon it by a mere appeal to the statistics of rejection. For it will be observed, first, that the people appear much more favourably inclined towards constitutional amendments than towards laws, though most of the amendments were really preliminaries towards the passing of some law which previously lay outside the legislative competence of the federation. Of these amendments twice as many were accepted as rejected. This is susceptible of two explanations. In the first place it is doubtless easier to get the assent of the people to a principle than to the particular law devised to embody that principle. So, for instance, the same people that had bestowed upon the Federal Government the right to legislate in a national accident and sick insurance scheme, rejected the particular scheme when it was presented in a draft law. A constitutional amendment generally adds a new function to the government, but the particular exercise of that function may quite reasonably be unpopular.

There is, however, another explanation of the discrepancy in the proportion of acceptances and rejections among laws and constitutional amendments respectively. The Referendum in the latter is obligatory, that in the former facultative. This means, of course, that only those laws and decrees are submitted to a Referendum which have evoked the opposition of a substantial body of citizens who conceive it possible that they may win the majority of the electorate to their view.

It is evident that this consideration completely disposes of the notion that the people are proved to be hostile to progressive legislation by the fact that they reject more laws than they accept. Of course they do, for only those laws which are likely to be rejected are put to the vote. In point of fact, between 1874 and 1906 no less than 246 laws and resolutions were passed by the Federal Assembly, almost all of which might have been put to the people, if the opposition to them had been strong enough to secure the qualifying number for the demand, and keen enough to press it to a vote. Where no Referendum was demanded it may be assumed that the people silently endorsed the act of their Federal Legislature, and that out of the total number of 246 laws and resolutions only nineteen met with their distinct disapproval.

The Referendum is in essence a veto, and it is therefore invalid to argue its destructive character from the fact that in a majority of cases where it is applied it causes rejections.

But if we direct our investigation to the two related questions, How does the Referendum appear to affect the course of legislation?—What light does it throw upon the operation of the popular will in politics?—we get some interesting information by examining the widespread impression that the Referendum works " conservatively."

That this " conservatism " is not inconsistent with a tolerably rapid development of the area and powers of the federal government and with the passing of many " advanced " laws is quite evident from the history of the last thirty years, during which the nationalisation of the railroads and of the wholesale trade in alcohol, the establishment of a federal bank, federal control of insurance, and a factory code more advanced than that of any other country, have been procured by the vote of the people.

Again, in considering the rejection of certain " socialistic " measures, such as the " Right to Labour " (1894), the Small Workshops Act (1894), the Federal Match Monopoly, as indeed in the recent rejection of the Federal Insurance Law, the States Right feeling with its accompanying distrust of central bureaucracy must not be interpreted as mere conservatism. In not a few instances it seems to signify, not a mere rejection of the principle or the policy of the law, but a preference for the canton over the confederation as an instrument of government.

That a certain amount of popular ignorance and prejudice is exhibited in the Referendum on issues which appeal to strong religious feelings (as in the passing of the famous anti-Jewish Slaughter House Law), or to the unimaginative parsimony of the peasant and the petty bourgeois (as in the rejection of the vote for Foreign Legations) must be admitted by the stoutest defenders of the Referendum. Indeed, apart from such special cases, there remains a residual truth in the imputation of crude conservatism to the people. Among the less instructed portions of the people there is a certain tendency to reject, implied in the very procedure of the Referendum. A peasant in a rural canton was asked why he and his fellow villagers always seemed to vote against the measures supported by the member whom they continued to return to the Legislative Assembly. " Well, you see," was the reply, " it is like this : If we say ' Yes ' it is nothing; but if we say ' No,' that is something for us." The adverse vote alone appears to be an exercise of power. Something, but not too much, must be allowed for this.

In general, it may be said that the Referendum discloses a truly serviceable strain of conservatism in the people. They will not vote for any large measure of centralised radicalism suddenly thrust before them. Their tendency is to prefer the canton which they know to the larger, vaguer entity of the federation. "My shirt is nearer to me than my coat," is their homely proverb. Moreover, they are not easily swept off their feet by some taking theory into giving large new powers to any sort of government. They want to feel sure how it will work out, especially as regards taxation, revenue, and local industry.

This sort of conservatism undoubtedly impresses itself upon legislation ; it must even be admitted to place impediments in the path of formally progressive legislation.

We are not, however, entitled to assume, as is commonly done, that the fact that the people reject a certain small number of advanced laws passed by the assemblies proves them to be less enlightened and progressive than their representatives. For, granted the existence of the Referendum, it must follow that in many cases representatives who would not be prepared to undertake the responsibility of giving validity to a doubtful new law by their vote in the assembly, will be willing to give that vote when the real significance of it is that it enables the issue to be determined by the Referendum, thus throwing the final responsibility on to the people.

But the more important issue lies deeper. Suppose it be admitted that the representatives are more enlightened and "progressive" than the people, does the Referendum diminish the pace of progress or damage its character? The plainest lesson afforded by investigation of the effect of the popular vote has reference to the structure of the laws that are passed. The draft of a law which is likely to be submitted to the popular vote must be more closely accommodated to the actual feelings and felt needs of various sections of the people than one which can become law by means of a party vote in a Legislative Assembly. In other words, the theoretically " good " law must be stamped with the sort of " goodness " required to secure the approval of the people. So much the worse for the " good law " ! it will seem to some. But here we touch the quick of the democratic theory. Is it better to get on to the Statute-book a theoretically good law accommodated to a people somewhat more homogeneous, more public spirited, more intelligent than the actual people is in fact, or a theoretically worse law which expresses the actual will of the people with some of its larger prejudices and other defects of intelligence and feeling impressed upon it? The issue is not easy to determine. Supporters of the representative system urge that sound representation will yield legislation substantially consonant with the national will, but often a little in advance of the conscious expression of that will; it will, in fact, reflect the superior wisdom of the representative over the represented. If such laws are put in operation, the public will by gradual experience come to recognise their merits and yield them a willing obedience. The presupposition of the Referendum, on the other hand, is that the kind of skill possessed by representatives is not a sufficient guarantee that the laws they pass shall in all cases be substantially consonant with the public will; the option of the Referendum is therefore essential to protect the people against acts of grave and injurious misrepresentation. It is further contended that a net waste in the art of government is involved by passing laws which are either in advance of general opinion or are insufficiently accommodated to sectional circumstances. The " goodness " of a law must always depend largely upon the efficiency of its administration; a " worse " law, well administered because it is acceptable to the people, will usually be more useful than a " better " law that is ill-administered because it is not acceptable to the people.

F

Now the Referendum ensures that a law is moulded into an acceptable shape, and can be successfully administered. The Swiss Law for the Federal Alcohol Monopoly well illustrates the point. There was a public widespread feeling of alarm at the growth of dram-drinking, strong enough to demand legislative interference but not prohibition; with this anti-spirit feeling was mixed a desire among the industries directly and indirectly interested in the production of wine, beer, and cider to secure protection and preference for these " home " industries; care must also be taken to exempt little local manufacturers of spirits from the operations of the law; the restriction upon spirits must not make it very difficult to get, or raise its price too high; finally, the regulation of the local trade must be left to the cantons, and the profits of the federal monopoly must be shared amongst them so as to afford a sensible relief of local taxation.

The result is a moderate law, with plenty of exceptions and special provisions directed to conciliate interests and abate prejudices, which has succeeded in reducing enormously the consumption of spirits, while at the same time dividing a considerable revenue among the cantonal governments. The chief maker and administrator of this law regards the Referendum as a necessary instrument for such legislation. The votes taken on the Constitutional Amendment and the Law enabled him not merely to test the general strength of public opinion, but to recognise exactly where and how strong were the different local interests and feelings which required consideration if the law was to be successfully operated.

Laws drafted with the knowledge that they may be put to the test of a popular vote are less rigorous in their form, and the practice of this art of accommodation ensures a process of investigation and discussion before the final form of the law is reached that is far more thorough than the procedure of a purely representative government with full legislative powers.

Again, a law which has received the direct sanction of a popular vote has a higher degree of stability than one passed by a party vote in a legislative assembly. There is no important instance of the reversal of such a law; the time and energy of Parliament is not consumed by constant repeals and amendments; the opposition in the country collapses before the *fait accompli*, and the knowledge of the irrevocability of the law not only imparts a confidence to its administrators and to the body of citizens that contributes to its sound administration, but helps to build up a general respect for a Government which thus visibly emanates from the general will of the people.

The sense of identity of the State with the people is the strongest ethical support for democracy, and in no other way is it better evoked and sustained than by imposing upon the people the responsibility of expressing direct judgments upon important acts of policy.

The experience of Switzerland discloses other economies of progress due to the Referendum.

Revolutionary action is thereby inhibited. Where each concrete proposal, either of constitutional or legal reform, requires the separate sanction of the people, there can be no possibility of rushing a large revolutionary policy through a legislative Assembly which contains a snatch majority of avowed revolutionists elected by a sudden swell of feeling in the electorate, or in which a revolutionist minority by skilful tactics compels a majority to execute its will. The practical and detailed working of Swiss democracy, obliging each step to be separately shaped and separately taken, imposes on the theoretic revolutionist a moderation which his German and French *confrères* have been much slower to admit.

Not less important, as a check upon wasteful methods of reform, is the fact that the Referendum furnishes a sharp indisputable test of the value of political catchwords. In such a country as England or Germany such an issue as " the right to work " or a " universal eight

hours " scheme may occupy the front place in the
radical movement for an indefinite period, because there
is no means of ascertaining with any degree of accuracy
how strong is the popular demand for such a measure.
In Switzerland it is competent either for the friends
or the enemies of such a scheme to demand and obtain
that it shall be submitted to a quantitative expression
of popular judgment.   If this test discloses the fact
that a strong majority is opposed to the measure, its
advocates recognise the futility and waste of progressive
energy involved in pressing it further for the present,
and relegate it to the list of reforms which require more
popular education before it is ripe for practical politics.
Thus the " Right to Labour " was brought to the test
by the *Grütliverein* and the Labour Union in 1894, and
was rejected by a popular vote of 308,289 against
75,880.   The result of such a vote is to divert the
emphasis and energy of the advanced sections from a
measure which, however desirable in itself, has evidently
no early chance of acceptance, to other measures which
may be urged with more chance of success.

These, then, are the three advantages claimed for the
Referendum in its effect upon the course of legislation :

(1) That it provides a remedy for intentional or
unintentional misrepresentation on the part of
elected legislatures and secures laws conformable to
the actual will of the majority.

(2) That it enhances the popular confidence in
the stability of law.

(3) That it eliminates much waste of political
energy by enabling proposals of unknown value to
be submitted separately to a quantitative test.

Most students of the Swiss system consider that these
economies more than offset the retarding influence of
Conservative inertia in the less enlightened orders of
citizen, and yield in the long run a larger net product
of progressive legislation than would accrue from a
purely representative legislature.   There is, however, one

grave theoretical and practical defect attaching to the Referendum regarded as a regular instrument of government, viz., that it enforces a separatist fragmentary treatment of policy. Each measure submitted separately to the people is almost of necessity taken entirely " on its own merits." Now when a law is a link in a chain of policy designed by some far-seeing statesmen, it can hardly be said to have separate merits, and to submit each link in such a chain for separate acceptance or rejection is to present an artificially-broken set of issues. It is true that in a legislative assembly each measure is separately discussed and determined, but there the authority of leaders and the discipline of party serve in some measure to enforce the wider consideration of organic policy.

It is difficult, perhaps impossible, to expect that the most intelligent electorate will approve a measure which, taken by itself, is unpalatable or inconvenient, on the ground that it forms part of a larger organic policy which they approve.

But this defect, grave as it appears were the Referendum used as the general instrument of legislation, is greatly mitigated when the use is occasional and confined to critical issues. For the heart of an entire policy is often contained in a single resolution or law; and if the doctrine of the mandate has any place in the theory of Democracy, it is applicable to these pivotal occasions. The issue, " Shall the Swiss people own and operate the railroads, acquiring them upon such and such a pecuniary basis, and managing them upon such and such a general plan?"; or the issue, " Shall the control of Hours of Labour and other conditions of employment form a subject-matter for federal legislation ?"—such issues are eminently fitted for popular determination.

The final and weightiest claim for the Referendum, as attested by Swiss experience, is the training in the art of government it gives to the people. It may indeed be questioned whether a people whose direct contribution to self-government consists in a single vote cast at intervals of several years, not for a policy or even for a measure, but for a party or a personality, can be or is capable of becoming a genuinely self-governing people. Some amount of regular responsibility for concrete acts of conduct is surely as essential to the education of a self-reliant people as of a self-reliant individual. To the intelligent Swiss democrat it never occurs to base his democracy upon a doctrine of infallibility of the people. The people, he is aware, make mistakes; the Referendum offers more opportunity to make mistakes, and therefore to learn from their mistakes than is furnished under purely representative government. But he holds that the obligation imposed on each citizen to take a direct part in the making of the laws he is called upon to obey is essential to the reality of popular self-government.

CHAPTER IV

THE RE-STATEMENT OF DEMOCRACY

The question whether we shall speak of a human Society as an organism, is, of course, largely one of convenience in language. If society is an organism it is not quite the same sort of organism as the individual body of an animal, and for some reasons, therefore, it might be best not to adopt the same word in describing them. But those who jump from this to the conclusion that it is a barren, unprofitable, academic question to discuss whether Society is essentially organic, are quite unjustified. The question is one of supreme practical importance, involving, among persons capable of practical politics, the complete re-adjustment of their conception of democracy and of the means of attaining it.

It is not here necessary to follow out in detail the biological analogy between the animal organism and Society regarded as an organism. It is sufficient to observe that recent biological researches strengthen the tendency to regard Society as an organism even on its physical side. The two gravest objections, put by Spencer and others, against the organic view were, first, that the separateness in space of the individual members of Society, their mobility and their power over their own actions, had no analogy in the cellular life of the units of an organism; and, secondly, that there was nothing corresponding to the sensorium, no central seat of conscious life, in a Society. Now modern biology tends to impair both of these objections, and so to make the conception of Society nearer to that of an animal organism. In the first place it shows that a cell is a more distinct, a more individual vital unit than was supposed, that it is itself of an organic structure, that it is not physically continuous with other cells, that it performs what may be termed free acts, giving out effort and even exercising choice in movement and in the selection of its food from its environment. Though most cells are tolerably closely fixed in local relation to other cells (*i.e.*, have status), others, connected with the work of digestion and protection against disease, are endowed with great freedom of movement. Modern psychophysics further tends to hold that this separate cellular life is accompanied by some degree of consciousness, in other words, that the specialisation of consciousness to the grey matter of the brain is not complete, but that some degree of cellular consciousness pervades the body.

The great German scientist, Virchow, recently summarised this view in the striking assertion that "The organism is not an individual but a social mechanism."

Nor can the other objection that there is nothing corresponding to the sensorium in Society be considered fatal. There are in fact two answers. Turning to lower forms of animal life we find composite beings, such as the myxomycetes and the sponges, which though consisting of almost undifferentiated units with no signs of a sensorium, can hardly be denied to be organisms. Indeed, the whole evolution of organic life is from forms in which there is no discernible sensorium towards forms which are more distinctly specialised in this regard. If, then, we could find no sensorium in Society, we are not therefore entitled to deny its organic nature, but only to conclude that it is as yet a low order of organism. This, indeed, is the conclusion at which some sociologists (*e.g.*, Professor Lester Ward) arrive.

But, regarding Society merely on its physical side, it is by no means clear that there is nothing corresponding to a sensorium in the highly-developed and differentiated life of the educated and actively-governing classes. The great mass of the people do no more real thinking, exercise perhaps no more real initiative, than the separate cells of the individual human body.

It is not, however, essential to my purpose to insist that Society is a highly-evolved organism in a physical sense, or even to insist that it is to be called a physical organism at all, though I think this view is justified and will obtain more and more acceptance.

The problem of Government with which I am concerned is primarily not a physical but a psychical one, and its solution depends upon the psychical relations between the members of a society. Now, whatever view we hold about Society on the physical plane as a collection of individual bodies living in some sort of union, it can, I think, be made quite clear that Society is rightly regarded as a moral rational organism in the sense that it has a common psychic life, character, and purpose, which are not to be resolved into the life, character, and purpose of its individual members.

It is easy to see why the organic life of Society is more easily admitted on the psychic than on the physical plane. Every man stands in his own skin, with an indefinitely big and expansible belt of inorganic atmosphere between him and any other man who is a member of his Society. Common sense is therefore disposed to insist that physically Society is nothing but a number of separate individuals. At first, no doubt, the same common sense is disposed also to insist that all the thinking and the feeling of these individuals is done separately by minds which are inside these bodies, and never get into any nearer contact with one another. But reflection and experiment oblige us to admit that the contact between minds is far more intimate and constant than between bodies, and that the inter-relations set up are far closer.

Turn to such a work as Maeterlinck's fascinating study, " The Life of the Bee." It is possible to deny the organic unity of the hive, or of the swarm, considered as a physical fact, or to regard it as a mere physical arrangement or organisation. But what the author terms " The Spirit of the Hive," the mysterious unity of instinct or conscious life, which minutely dominates the hive and the will and separate interests of the individual bees, is an example of organic psychic unity which cannot be denied. All through the animal kingdom we find examples of this common purpose of the herd, the drove or other social group, imposing itself upon the mind and conscious conduct of the individual animal, directing him to actions often opposed to his own interest or pleasure, not seldom demanding the sacrifice of life itself for the gain of the group or the continuance of the species.

This Spirit of the Hive or of the Herd is a true spirit of Society, a single unity of purpose in the community. Those who would cut the Gordian knot of this problem by saying that individuals alone are ends, and that Society is nothing but a means to these ends, will find it difficult to make their theory square with the facts of natural history in which the individual always appears as a means to the collective end of the maintenance of the race.

Those who would distinguish in kind this social or gregarious instinct of the lower animals from the individual reasonable consciousness in man have no warrant for their distinction. For there is ample testimony that the mind of man, in its feeling, its thinking, its will, is not the separate thing it seems at first to be.

Setting aside all the dubious and difficult evidence of direct intentional impact of one mind upon another by telepathy, and other similar methods, the growth and operations of a common mind or purpose formed by the direct interaction of many individual minds cannot seriously be questioned.

Even the fortuitous concourse of a crowd shows this : a mob in the streets of Paris or of London exhibits a character and a behaviour which is uniform, is dominated for the time being by a single feeling or idea, and differs widely from the known character and behaviour of its component members. Look at the effect of an orator upon a crowd, the power of a sudden panic, the contagion of some quick impulse to action; it is quite evident that the barriers which commonly encase the individual mind have given way, that the private judgment is inhibited, and that for a time a mob-mind has been set up in its stead, in which the reasoning faculties are almost suspended, and in which the passions of animal ferocity, generosity, credulity, self-sacrifice, malignity, and courage express themselves unrestrained.

A great personality, a great religious or political idea, a mere mis-statement invented by a lying Press, may weld into a common desire, a common will, the minds of a whole nation : the result is not intelligible as the added action of the same idea acting on so many separate minds : it is the inter-action of these minds growing by stronger social sympathy into fusion that is the real phenomenon. The mere fact of human beings living in proximity to one another produces a force of neighbourhood which for good or evil is a restraint upon all its members. There is not a school, a church, a club, even for the lightest and most recreative object, em-bodying some purpose or idea and the common pursuit of it, which does not impress a common character upon its members. The public opinion of any of these bodies is produced by some direct assimilation of the separate minds, and implies the formation of a common consciousness.

For political and social purposes in ancient and mediæval times, the City has been the largest and most convincing example of this real moral unity. The civic spirit was no mere phrase to describe the views of the average citizen : the City State of the Greeks is only intelligible as a moral unity, or as Mr. Bradley puts it, " The armed conscience of the community."

In modern times the wider social area of the nation has for many purposes displaced the City State. As a psychical organism it seldom presents so close a unity, but that the habit of common thought and action among the members of a nation can take place without creating and establishing a common consciousness, a common will and common obligations, cannot for a moment be admitted. Now, if the habits of thinking, feeling, and acting together among members of a nation thus bring their minds into a single mind which is dominated by thoughts and feelings directed to the ends of the whole body politic, then we have the clear admission of a social organism on the psychical or moral side.

This is the doctrine of the general will, as I under⁺ stand it, which Rousseau, among moderns, was the first clearly to enunciate, which has been developed on its political side by Hegel and his followers, and which in English finds its most masterly expression in Mr. Bosanquet's work, "The Philosophic Theory of the State." I have approached the matter from the psychological rather than from the philosophical standpoint, and in applying the term organism I go beyond the judgment of some of these thinkers. But what I seek to establish is the admission that a political society must be regarded as " organic " in the only sense which gives a really valid meaning to such terms as " the will of the people," " national duty," and " public conscience." The individual's feeling, his will, his ends, and interests, are not entirely merged in or sacrificed to the public feeling, will and ends, but over a certain area they are fused and identified, and the common social life thus formed has conscious interests and ends of its own which are not merely instruments in forwarding the progress of the separate individual lives, but are directed primarily to secure the survival and psychical progress of the community regarded as a spiritual whole.

To the common-sense objector who says, " A nation does not think, a nation does not feel, it is individuals who do these things," I would reply that if you could talk with a " cell " of the human body it would tell you it is not *we* who think and feel, but the separate cells, each of which is conscious in itself of such processes, but from the nature of the case is not and cannot be conscious of the feeling and thinking which goes on in the organism as a whole.

A nation does feel, and think, not so fully, so wholesomely, so happily as it should and will, when the process of forming a social organism has gone further, but within the limits of such conscious unity as it has attained.

The practical value of this thought consists in the material it yields for restating the doctrine of Democracy. It is quite evident that the conception of Society as a moral organism negates the old democratic idea of political equality based on the notion that every member of a political society had an inherent right to the same power as every other in determinating the action of Society. The idea of natural individual rights as the basis of Democracy disappears. Take, for instance, the formula of " No taxation without representation." From the standpoint of individualist Democracy this is understood to imply that, when the State takes away some of my property by taxing me, I have some right to earmark the tax I pay and to say what shall be done with it, or with a corresponding portion of the public funds afterwards. Now a clear grasp of Society as an economic organism completely explodes the notion of property as an inherent individual right, for it shows that no individual can make or appropriate anything of value without the direct continuous assistance of Society. So the idea of Society as a political organism insists that the general will and wisdom of the Society, as embodied in the State, shall determine the best social use of all the social property taken by taxation, without admitting any inherent right of interference on the part of the taxpayer. This does not, indeed, imply that " No taxation without representation," is an unsound maxim of government : on the contrary, it may be, and I think is, strongly advisable that those from whom taxes are levied shall watch and check the use which Government may make of them : but the worth of this practice is defensible not on grounds of individual right but of general expediency, because persons who have paid a tax will be found to be better guardians of the public purse than those who have not paid it.

So with the other individualist notion that political power belongs as a right to those who have " a stake in the country." When " a stake in the country " meant property or rank it brought class government. Democracy, taking over the phrase, insisted that a man's life was his stake, and that since every man's life was worth as much as every other man's life, political power should be equally divided amongst all. The popular doctrine, " One man one vote," is as a theoretical principle pure undiluted individualism. It rests upon a curious twist in the logic of Equality. Every man's life is worth as much to him as every other man's life. Society consists of all men, therefore every man's life is worth as much to Society as every other man's, and every man ought to have the same voice in directing social conduct as every other man.

Now there is very little meaning in the first proposition that all men's lives are of equal value to them; and there is no possibility of proving its validity. That every man's life is of equal value to Society, in the sense that it can yield equal social service, is not only false but absurd : and, if political power rightly varies with the capacity for public service, the case for equality of franchise utterly collapses. There is, of course, a sense in which the equal value of life for all is admitted, and is embodied in the equality of all men before the law. But this equality of all men as objects of social conduct does not imply a corresponding equality as agents in social conduct. The old individualist Democracy did not indeed often go so far as to maintain that every man was as competent as every other man to exercise a power

of government, though the American theory and practice, so far as white men are concerned, have gone mar-
vellously near to this position.   It rested partly on the
notion of an equal right in virtue of common humanity,
and partly upon an obscure notion that since each man
presumably knew best his own interest, or at any rate
what he wanted, the aggregate, which was what they
understood by " Society," knew best the general interest.
And this would be so, if Society were a mere aggregate,
an accumulation of human atoms, incapable of any really
organic action.

The organic view of Society entirely repudiates any
such equality as a theoretic principle.   Even J. S. Mill,
when he came to apply his utilitarianism to politics, left
a good deal of his individualism behind.   " In all
human affairs," he writes, " every person directly
interested, and not under positive tutelage, has an
admitted claim to a voice, and when his exercise of it
is not inconsistent with the safety of the whole, cannot
justly be excluded from it.   But though everyone ought
to have a voice—that everyone ought to have an equal
voice is a totally different proposition.   When two
persons, who have a joint interest in any business, differ
in opinion, does justice require that both opinions should
be held in equal value?"   Though few persons, on
mature reflection, are likely to admit the examination
test of political competence which Mill suggests, and
may not be prepared with any alternative measure of
such competence, they cannot deny the validity and
importance of his general admission that political power
ought to be distributed in proportion to ability to use it
for the public good.   The suggestion of individualist
Democracy, that the public good is simply a bundle of
private goods, and that every man ought to have a vote
in order that he may keep an eye on his particular contribution to the public good, was felt by Mill to be untenable when government was regarded as a joint stock
business.

Mill, in fact, was feeling his way to the true formula of political as of economic justice, " From each according to his powers." Once grasp the idea of the public as a Social Organism, or even as a Corporation administering a property corporately made, it becomes clear that no *right* appertains to any individual to administer any portion of this property, because as an individual he has made no part of it.

But while he has no *right* as an individual, he has a *duty* as a member of Society to contribute as best he can to the administration of the common property for the common good. His vote thus comes to him primarily as a duty, and the question of equality takes this form, " Is the duty equal in all cases?" Clearly not, for all have not equally the power to fulfil it. Knowledge, intelligence, strength, good-will, vary, and with them varies the ability to perform public duty. It is as absurd to demand the same contribution to the collective wisdom of the nation from all alike as to demand the same contribution to the collective purse. " From each according to his powers." Tom, Dick, and Harry have very little powers. Why should the State require of them what they have not got?

Does this imply that in a properly ordered State the more ignorant masses are to have no vote, no voice in the Government of the country? Are we to entrust all power to a Government of experts?

Let us see how far the fact or the analogy of organism carries us. From each member in a biological organism are demanded certain functional activities for the support of the life of the organism, the kind and quantity of this work being determined by the neural apparatus and regulated in accordance with the nature and strength of the several organs. So when a functional demand is made upon a particular organ, the work is delegated to its several parts, and is ultimately divided up among the countless cells which are regarded as the primary units of the organ. In a body which is in health and functions economically, every cell contributes to the life of the organism according to its powers. The direction, the demand for labour, at any rate so far as conscious actions are concerned, comes from a specialised governing centre. But this is only half the truth. " From each according to his powers, to each according to his needs," is the full organic formula. In a healthy organism the demand of functional energy from each member, from each cell, is accompanied by a continual replacement of tissue and energy conveyed by a just circulation of the blood. I use the ethical term " just " advisedly. Ruskin, in an eloquent passage of " Unto this Last," points out that the circulation of the blood is the true type of equitable economic distribution. It also gives the true significance to political rights. Each limb, each cell, has a "right" to its due supply of blood. It has a "right" to complain if it does not get it, and it does complain. It is to this right and habit of complaint that we must look for what in social politics corresponds to the franchise. So far as the conscious polity of the animal organism is concerned, the direct work of Government is highly centralised : a highly specialised portion of the nervous system issues the commands, it is the normal function of the several organs to obey, and in the ordinary course of nature they do so. They have had no separate voice in determining the organic policy, or in issuing the order which they help to execute.

Are the separate organs, the separate cells, then, politically powerless and destitute of rights? It is doubtless to the real interest of the organism as a whole to distribute blood in accordance with the needs of the individual members and their cells. But, even in the most highly-developed organisms, such absolute and unchecked power is not entrusted to the expert government of the cerebral cells. The entire afferent nervous system attests the contrary : the individual organs and their cells are continuously engaged in transmitting information to the cerebral centre and in

G

offering suggestions. This information and these suggestions are chiefly if not wholly self-protective in their purport. The ability of the local centres to transmit stimuli to the cerebral centres is of course essential to the politics of the organism. It is equally important to recognise that not merely is information thus given to the cerebral centres for their guidance, but by the same channels protest is conveyed against orders which injure or oppress the organ; the right to petition against grievance on the part of the organs and their cells is accompanied by an ultimate " veto," or the right of rebellion, which is the basis of popular government.

Nor are these the only "rights" exercised by the " cells." When a certain demand for functional activity is transmitted to the local centres, its distribution is determined by an elaborate system of local self-government, in which each cell participates, striving to throw off upon its neighbours any disproportionate strain, and they doing the same, until in a healthy organ the total strain is divided economically in accordance with the powers of the several parts. Understand that these rights of the members and their cells are not in any sense a qualification or denial of the truth that the good of the organism as a whole is the absolute criterion of conduct, and may in extreme cases require the complete sacrifice of an organ and its cells. But it is advantageous to the organism that these rights of suggestion, protest, veto, and revolt should be accorded to its members. Accept the view of Society as an organism, corresponding rights remain to its individual members, and a political machinery for enforcing them must exist.

There are those who would confine the direct political power of the people to a right of revolt against intolerable oppression. I have seen it seriously argued that the Czar's Government rests upon the will of the people, and is sanctioned by that will, because no general revolution takes place in Russia. But revolt is only the last of a series of " rights " ascribed to its members by a well-organised Society. The right continuously to convey information and advice, and by protest to assist the due distribution of work and food, requires the maintenance of a system of stimuli from the local cells to the central. The cerebral centres, the expert governing class, determine the organic policy, but the determination of this policy is based upon a mass of information conveyed from the members, while the detailed execution of the policy is again directed by the members and their cells, which distribute the work in accordance with adjustments of cellular self-interest that are not referred to the central power.

These considerations restore a good deal of practical liberty and equality which at first seem to disappear when the organic view of Society is accepted. If it is absurd to suppose that all classes and all individuals are equally wise and good, and therefore equally qualified to contribute by vote and voice to wise and good government, it is not absurd to suppose that every class and every individual knows more about the facts of his own situation than any other class and individual, and can say where the shoe pinches.

No one contends that miners, cabmen, or washerwomen know as much about foreign policy or the general art of government, as trained politicians, or even as members of the learned professions. But they do know more about the special group of facts which enter their life, and about the special way in which new legislation and administration will affect them : about these matters they are as competent to judge as the professional classes are about the matters which concern them. Nor are these more ignorant or less educated classes less important organs of the social organism than the better educated classes. It is quite as important to Society that the special conditions of the mining or the agricultural labouring classes should be faithfully recorded at the governing centres, and that the effect of legislation and administration upon their lives should be known, as in the case of lawyers or schoolmasters. Upon this ground, and upon this alone, the logic of the demand for Woman's Suffrage is unimpugnable.

This, then, brings us back towards equality. Equality of franchise and of representation is defensible by reason of a real equality of contribution towards government from the different classes and individuals who compose Society.

But I may be told that here I am reverting to an essentially individualistic view. Miners and lawyers, in exercising a franchise, are not only directing and safe-guarding the interests of their own classes, in regard to which they may be considered equal, but are helping to determine the general policy of the public, and here they are unequal in knowledge and capacity.

This may of course be met by arguing that the kind of mental training which the learned professions and the educated classes generally possess, and the sort of know-ledge which they own, does not appreciably increase their capacity to assist in governing a nation. Or it may be urged, even more plausibly, that any advantage they possess in knowledge or intellect is offset by strong bias of class interests, which will lead them to prefer the good of their class or their calling to the public good. Such bias is not, it may be urged, present to the same extent in individual members of the working classes who have less to gain by direct and special manipulation of politics. The directors of an American trust are far abler and better educated men than their employees, but in politics they are a far more dangerous force, because it is more possible and more profitable for them to handle politics for their private gain.

But though both these arguments may be forcibly employed to defend equality of franchise and of repre-sentation, a well-developed Democracy would not rely upon them in its assignment of equal voting power.

The real answer to the claim of lawyers, doctors and the educated classes generally to have more political power because they are better able to use it, is to deny the relevance of their education and ability. A developed organic Democracy will have evolved a specialised " head," an expert official class, which shall draft laws upon information that comes to them from innumerable sources through class and local representation, and shall administer the government, subject to protests similarly conveyed. The superior knowledge of general politics which lawyers and teachers and other educated classes claim will be no reason for giving them an extra vote; for this general knowledge, if it exist at all, will not be wanted, since it will be discarded as superficial amateur knowledge, whereas the public interest demands thorough professional knowledge. On the one hand, we should have a trained body of political specialists devoted to the public service, receiving gain and honour in proportion to these public services, who would take over much of the legislative work so badly done or so badly left undone by our elective assemblies of legislative amateurs. On the other hand, we should have the knowledge and desires, the will of the people, transmitted either directly or informally by public meetings, and other methods, or formally through elected representatives who would confine themselves to the work of representing, for which they were chosen and were competent, and not to the technical work of making laws, for which they are utterly incompetent. It is plain that when a rational Democracy is formed, laws, like hats, will be made by persons specially trained to make them, the people " ordering " these laws, directly or through their accredited representatives.

It may even be affirmed that the important question, whether such and such a law shall be made or not, will, in the first instance, be left to an expert political class. This doubtless could not be safely done in any country, until and unless a public service can be evolved which is both capable and honest, and which commands the genuine respect of a people enlightened, capable of testing results, and endowed with a real veto upon legislative failures.

A permanent legislative service commanding the trust of the people may seem a distant idea. But I regard it as an essential of a real Democracy, which must solve the question of conjoining legitimate authority and public use of expert politicians with a right and constant practice of instruction, suggestion and veto exercised directly or through representatives.

The possibility of attaining such an ideal depends chiefly upon the possibility of getting such a general or wide level of intelligence in a nation that they can safely use a specialised class of politicians. If a nation is incapable of developing this self-protective intelligence, so as to transmit accurate stimuli to the governing brain, and to exercise quick, accurate checks and vetos, the form of Democracy which seems truly organic would inevitably lapse into a bureaucratic tyranny. But this danger does not peculiarly beset the organic Democracy. Everywhere the individualist experiments in Democracy exhibit the same features of failure, except where they are safeguarded by the intelligence of a nation not too big to be bewildered by machinery of government. Everywhere a selfish and often a corrupt bureaucracy shares the power and gains of government with an industrial and social oligarchy. There is grave danger of bureaucracy under existing conditions. But this is no reason for supposing that real Democracy can dispense with a skilled official class. The chief danger arises where this official class is drawn from a small section of the people, and is thus identified with the interests of a few. The conditions of a really effective expert officialism are two: such real equality of educational opportunities as shall draw competent officials from the whole people, and such a growth of public intelligence and conscience as shall establish the real final control of government for Society in its full organic structure. Of all things this last is the most essential, the welding of public intelligence and morals into an effective general will. This brings me back in a completed circle to my opening statement. A true Democracy is only possible when Society, a true organism, becomes conscious in its intelligence and will, and thus is capable of that self-control which is the essence of Democracy, and which contains the only liberty and equality that are worth the names.

.

PART II
LIBERALISM AND SOCIALISM

CHAPTER I

THE VISION OF LIBERALISM

Bacon's saying that "adversity does best discover virtues" is of doubtful application to a political party. Twenty years of almost unceasing struggle against re-action have left their traces upon Liberal Parliamentarians in a strain of timidity and even of conservatism, which is evidently a source of moral and of intellectual weakness. There have always been voices ready to proclaim that the active mission of Liberalism was well nigh fulfilled, and that, for the present, at any rate, it was all-important to preserve what had been won, to regain what had been lost, and to do just as much or as little tinkering as was needed to maintain the fabric of our liberties. We do not for one moment suggest that this has been the conscious prevailing sentiment of the majority in the House, or in the country, and the strenuous warfare waged by the Liberal Government in many fields will appear to many a sufficient answer to such criticism. But without arguing the matter here, we cannot refrain from pointing out that almost all the important measures of domestic policy before this Parliament are, in substance, endeavours to recover, for the people and the State, liberties or properties or privileges which had within recent generations been lost or encroached upon by some class, trade, or other vested interest.

In this sense, the Trade Union Act, the Education and Licensing measures, and even the Government's land policy, in its essential features, are conservative. This admission by no means derogates from their importance, but it helps to make us comprehend why Liberalism appears in some quarters lacking in organic purpose and in free enthusiasm. While to Protectionists and Socialists politics are real, positive, and fervent gospels, stirring the imagination and evoking a fanatical energy, the zeal of Liberalism is everywhere chilled by doubts and difficulties. No sooner are we approaching such large issues of social policy as are involved in taxation of land values, pensions, unemployed relief, the House of Lords, than everywhere the atmosphere is kept abuzz with whispers about " sanctity of contract," confiscation, pauperisation, and those hints of popular indifference which take the heart out of reformers.

Does this mean that coldness and placidity of purpose belong essentially to Liberalism as a middle course, and is Liberalism committed to an embarrassing and disheartening opportunism? No such thing. But we have evidently reached a period when a more conscious organisation of Liberal energy is demanded. It is a time to follow Matthew Arnold's advice and ." Let our thought play freely upon our stock notions and ideas." The first result of such an operation will be to illuminate our commonplaces regarding the nature of that liberty to the service of which the party is devoted. The negative conception of Liberalism, as a definite mission for the removal of certain political and economic shackles upon personal liberty, is not merely philosophically defective, but historically false. The Liberals of this country as a party never committed themselves either to the theory or the policy of this narrow *laissez faire* individualism; they never conceived liberty as something limited in quantity, or purely negative in character. But it is true that they tended to lay an excessive emphasis upon the aspect of liberty which consists in absence of restraint, as compared with the other aspect which consists in presence of opportunity; and it is this tendency, still lingering in the mind of the Liberal Party, that to-day checks its energy and blurs its vision. A more constructive and a more evolutionary idea of liberty is needed to give the requisite *élan de vie* to the movement; and every cause of liberation, individual, class, sex, and national, must be recharged with the fresh enthusiasm of this fuller faith.

Liberalism will probably retain its distinction from Socialism, in taking for its chief test of policy the freedom of the individual citizen rather than the strength of the State, though the antagonism of the two standpoints may tend to disappear in the light of progressive experience. But it will justify itself by two great enlargements of its liberative functions. In seeking to realise liberty for the individual citizen as " equality of opportunity," it will recognise that, as the area and nature of opportunities are continually shifting, so the old limited conception of the task of Liberalism must always advance. Each generation of Liberals will be required to translate a new set of needs and aspirations into facts. It is because we have fallen so far short of due performance of this task that our Liberalism shows signs of enfeeblement. We must fearlessly face as our first, though not our only question, What is a free Englishman to-day? If we answer this question faithfully, we shall recognise that it comprises many elements of real liberty and opportunity which have not been won for the people as a whole. Is a man free who has not equal opportunity with his fellows of such access to all material and moral means of personal development and work as shall contribute to his own welfare and that of his society? Such equal opportunity at least implies an equal access to the use of his native land as a workplace and a home, such mobility as will enable him to dispose of his personal energies to the best advantage, easy access to that factor of capital or credit which modern industry recognises as essential to economic independence, and to whatever new form of industrial power, electric or other, may be needed to co-operate with human efforts. A man is not really free for purposes of self-development in life and work who is not adequately provided in all these respects, and no small part of constructive Liberalism must be devoted to the attainment of these equal opportunities.

But all such distinctively economic liberties are evidently barren unless accompanied by a far more adequate realisation of spiritual and intellectual opportunity than is contained in our miserably meagre conception of popular education. For education in the large meaning of the term is the opportunity of opportunities, and the virtual denial to the majority of the people of any real share of the spiritual kingdom which is rightly theirs must remain for all true Liberals an incessant challenge to their elementary sense of justice, as well as the most obvious impediment both to the achievement and the utilisation of every other element of personal liberty. It is this truth that also underlies the great struggle against militarism and Imperialism which assumes so many shapes upon the stage of politics, and which, driven to its last resort, will always be disclosed as the antagonism between physical and moral force, as the guardian and promoter of civilisation. The practical interpretation and realisation of moral and intellectual liberty for the people as the most urgent and fruitful of all tasks of Liberalism, though standing first in order of importance, cannot, however, be detached in political endeavour from the other more material liberties. It is the peril, as it is the glory, of Liberalism that it is required to drive several teams abreast along the road of progress.

Finally, though Liberals must ever insist that each enlargement of the authority and functions of the State must justify itself as an enlargement of personal liberty, interfering with individuals only in order to set free new and larger opportunities, there need remain in Liberalism no relics of that positive hostility to public

methods of co-operation which crippled the old Radicalism.   When society is confronted, as it sometimes will
be, by a breakdown of competition and a choice between
private monopoly and public enterprise, no theoretic
objections to the State can be permitted to militate
against public safety.   Just in proportion as education
guides, enriches, and enlightens the will of the people,
and gives spiritual substance and intellectual power to
democracy, the presumption which still holds against
the adequacy of public as compared with private co-
operation will be weakened, and Liberalism will come
more definitely to concern itself with the liberation and
utilisation of the faculties and potencies of a nation and
a municipality, as well as with those of individuals and
voluntary groups of citizens.   It surely belongs to
Liberalism to think thus liberally about its mission and
its modes of progressive achievement.   Not, however,
of fulfilment.   For it is this illimitable character of
Liberalism, based on the infinitude of the possibilities
of human life, in its individual and social aspects, which
affords that vision without which not only a people but
a party perishes, the vision of

> "That untravelled world where margin fades
> For ever and for ever when I move."

CHAPTER II

EQUALITY OF OPPORTUNITY

What speciousness attaches to the charge of Socialism which is freely flung to-day against the latest developments of Liberal policy is due to the fuller and more positive interpretation of personal liberty slowly forced by pressure of events upon the Liberal party. And not upon the Liberal party alone. In a recent indictment of the " Socialism " of the present Government, Lord Hugh Cecil named three crucial instances, the Old Age Pensions Act, the Development Bill, and certain provisions of the Finance Bill. But the two former measures have received the sanction of all save a small section of Conservative politicians, while the "Socialism" of the Budget (if the attempt to exact an increased contribution from certain "socially" created values merits that description) involves no new principle in English government, but merely an application of a taxing and rating principle already applied by the Governments of Conservative States like Germany.

That the end of good government is to furnish individual liberty and opportunity is so firmly rooted in our habits of political thought that it is perhaps difficult to conceive the easy displacement of this principle by that of " the good of society " or any similar abstraction. The modern enlargement of the functions of our State in the direction of Factory and Public Health Acts, Education, the extension of municipal public services, has always been advocated primarily as a defence of individuals against evil conditions of work or life imposed upon them by the superior economic strength of landlords, employers, or private monopolies, aided and abetted by their own folly, ignorance, and lack of forethought. Every one of these measures, whether or not regarded as Socialistic, has been mainly directed so to improve the physical, moral, and intellectual or economic condition of individuals as to secure for them a larger measure of liberty in the disposal of their lives.

The phrase in which this reform movement is most succinctly expressed is equality of opportunity. Like most general phrases it has its ambiguities, but none the less it furnishes the best opening for an inquiry into the nature of the fuller and more positive liberty to which the Liberalism of the future must devote itself. This inquiry will best take shape in an attempt to give a simple dogmatic answer to the question, " What are the equal opportunities which every Englishman requires to-day in order to secure real liberty of self-development?"

It is, I think, plain that in the front of this charter of individual liberty comes the right of every man to an equal share with every other in the use of the land and of the other natural resources of his native country. This right, if it has been alienated or compromised, must be restored. That the bulk of the land of any nation should continue to be the property of a few thousand persons who are thereby legally empowered to determine to what use it shall be put, or whether it shall be put to any use, and to determine whether large numbers of their fellow-citizens shall be free to work and live in the village or the countryside where they were born and bred, is a manifest infringement of this doctrine of equality. The legal status of a landless man in England to-day lacks the elements of personal liberty : upon enclosed land (virtually all the land); he may not trespass so as to obey the primeval law bidding him earn his bread in the sweat of his face; upon the public

H

thoroughfares he may not rest, and moving on continually he becomes a rogue and vagabond. In order
to live at all in his native land he must succeed in making
a bargain with some owner, who has a " right " to refuse
him this right to live. Competition between owners
in some part modifies the rigour of the landless status :
it never cancels the lack of liberty.

Now what does equality of opportunity demand in
relation to the land? Evidently not that every man
shall have an equal sized parcel of land assigned to his
exclusive use, for that would be impracticable, even were
it otherwise desirable, in a country so thickly and so
unevenly peopled as ours. If every one wanted to
return to the soil, there would not be enough, however
intensive the cultivation. What is required is that any
man who wants the use of a bit of land which he is fit
to work shall have an equal chance with every other man
of getting and of keeping it, on terms regulated by a
public authority and not a private owner; and that every
man can on similar terms get a fixed home to live in
without the liability of being turned out at the will of
another. These conditions cannot ultimately be
achieved, as is sometimes fondly imagined, by the
intervention of public bodies hiring land from private
owners : no settled equity is possible until by degrees
private ownership in urban and large portions of rural
land has given place to public ownership.

Apart from this equal access to natural resources for
individual use, the axiom of equality requires that,
either by means of public ownership, or by taxation,
the annual values of land, as distinct from its improvements, shall become a public income to be expended for
the equal advantage of all members of the community.
An equal stake in the valuable uses of the land, with
publicly guaranteed security of tenure for those who
want to work or live upon a piece of land, is now a
generally accepted principle of land-reform among all
grades of thoughtful Liberals.

So important is equal access to the land as a basis of individual liberty that it is not unnatural that many reformers should call a halt at this point, insisting that all the elements of practical freedom are present, if every man is free to apply his labour to the land, and no one is permitted to monopolise the sources of all material wealth. But most persons, on reflection, will perceive that full liberty of self-development involves other opportunities, some of which are not related even remotely to the ownership or use of land.

First let us take one form of modern liberty which is in part a land question. The right to move unhindered from one place to another is as much an element of freedom as the right to stay where you are. If a man is to make the best use of his faculties, he must be free to take himself and his belongings from where he is to where he wants to be. Mobility is more and more essential to freedom in our modern industrial system, where local industrial conditions are continually changing, and where every one must be able to follow his trade and to open up new markets for his personal skill or his products.

That this mobility belongs to individual liberty is indeed embodied in the most hallowed maxim of the individualist philosopher, *laissez-faire, laissez-aller*. But to tell a man he has this right, this liberty *to go*, is not to give it to him. The freedom to walk along the high road is not the real mobility required for modern life. Effective liberty to travel involves the use of railroads, which in substance are our national highways. Now an ordinary labourer, obliged to bargain with a private company for carriage, and disabled by his narrow means from moving easily, quickly, or far at a time, is in fact deprived of an opportunity essential to his full liberty of choice in life and work, and society is also the loser by this limitation of his power. Most civilised nations have already become aware that it is the business of the nation to be the owners and managers of its highways, and that they cannot safely be left either to the wasteful competition or the vexatious combination of private profit-makers. In this country the issue of nationalisation of the railways is just coming into the arena of practical policy, and it is important to dissociate it from any general Socialism, recognising it as a reform warranted by the most accepted principles of individual liberty. A dividend-seeking company is justified, indeed may be compelled, to discriminate in rates so as to favour foreign importers as against British producers, to shower advantages of cheap and rapid service upon thickly peopled centres, while starving outlying and more sparsely populated regions, and in various ways to help rich localities and persons and injure poor ones in freight and passenger rates. A truly public high-road policy, designed to give equal opportunities to all parts of the country and all classes of the people and so to develop in the fullest and the farthest-sighted way the national resources, can only be pursued by a railroad system owned and operated by the nation. Absolutely free transit may not be attainable or advisable, but a national railway system, which, by its cheap rates and quick frequent service, enables every man to move to and from his work without waste of time or money, and to follow his economic opportunities wherever they may lead him, is necessary to-day to " free " men in a " free " country. And what holds of persons holds of the produce of their labour. A public railway system will tend towards an equalisation of rates such as prevails in the postal system for the carriage of letters, telegrams, and small parcels, the purpose and result of which would be to facilitate access to markets for local industries in all parts of the country, and so to contribute to equality of opportunity for the persons dependent on these industries.

Then comes another issue of modern liberty which also has its roots in Nature and man's equal access to natural powers. For most purposes of organised industry the use of some non-human energy is necessary: civilisation more and more implies the liberation of the muscular and nervous powers of man from heavy routine work, and the substitution of mechanical energy. In large provinces of industry the time has come when the success or failure of a man to establish himself in business, and to make a living wage or profit, depends upon the terms upon which he can get cheap and reliable access to this energy. Hitherto steam has been the dominant power, and the wide distribution of our coalfields and the competition of the numerous mines have maintained over large industrial areas a substantial equality of access to this power. But it is tolerably evident that we are on the eve of a new industrial revolution, which is destined rapidly to displace steam by electric energy as the main instrument of production. If all our factories and workshops are to be dependent on the supply of electricity, which may, by improved economy of distribution, decentralise many trades, perhaps reviving large numbers of home industries; if, in addition to this general industrial use, traction, lighting, and other local services become entirely electric, it is evident that the question of the generation and distribution of this new power is of supreme importance. Should the control of this agent be allowed to pass into the hands of great profit-making companies, possessing virtual monopolies of electric supply over entire districts, the ordinary man of business and the body of citizen-consumers will find themselves confronted with a new industrial tyranny even more oppressive than the so-called land-monopoly or railroad-monopoly from which they may have liberated themselves. That serious attempts are being made by far-sighted business men to fasten this new yoke on the necks of this and other industrial nations, before the full significance of the age of electricity is grasped by the larger public mind, there can be no manner of doubt. Whether patents of secret processes, superior access to coal, water, or other sources of power, monopoly of copper or of some other dominant factor in electric processes, are made the instruments of the new control, the peril of allowing such power to be utilised for purposes of private profit will be apparent to any moderately thoughtful person.   If every big or little manufacturer and every ordinary citizen has to make his separate bargain with the local branch of some huge electric syndicate for leave to work his mill, to turn his lathe, to light his shop, to cook his dinner, it is clear that we shall enter a new *régime* of extortion and discrimination far worse than is exhibited by any railway in this country. For the electric-supply companies will hold the keys of industry, and on their policy and rates will depend the prosperity and ruin of whole towns or trades, while the biggest manufacturing concern may be a mere pawn in this profitable game.   The menace is a very serious and a pressing one : it is one of the chief tests of public intelligence in our day whether our Parliament and our local authorities will, out of ignorance, apathy, or corrupt connivance, permit a new economic despotism to arise which will cost a mighty struggle and immense expenditure of public money to " buy out " when its oppressive power has grown intolerable.

Since it is possible that the new physics and chemistry may in the early future disclose new mineral sources of energy in radium or other form available for industrial uses, or may furnish a practical solution to the difficulties which at present preclude us from utilising the direct power of the sun or the tides for generating mechanical energy, the modern State should safeguard society in advance against new possibilities of economic tyranny. This could be done by means of an enactment reserving to the Crown such mineral or other sources of power as are as yet unrecognised or unutilised.   It would be sheer madness to hand over to the owners of our foreshores the right to rack-rent the community for the use of tidal energy, or to permit the monopolists of spots of land rich in pitchblend to " hold up " the national industries in " an age of radium."

Liberty of trade demands the public ownership and operation of industrial power for sale on equal terms to all who want it.

The use of capital on fair and equal terms is in this country essential to every man who wishes to live, not as a wage- or salary-earner, but as an independent producer or trader. For such purpose credit is capital, and no man is " free " to use his business skill unless he can get a reasonable amount of credit upon easy terms. There are two purposes for which a worker or a small business man wants an occasional advance of money. One is to meet some unforeseen emergency in his business or his private life against which adequate insurance is impossible. Every one is liable to such misfortunes, and a small man working and living with no margin is obliged, when they befall him, to have recourse to the money-lender. It is not too much to say that next to war and pestilence the greatest single source of human misery in world-history has been the oppression of usury forced on peasant cultivators of the soil by bad harvests. No serious land reformer here, or in any other country, can hope to set agriculture on a sound basis without finding some way of rescuing the peasant from the clutches of the money-lender. But it is not the peasant only who is subject to this peril. Everywhere in our industrial towns, for lack of reasonable credit, the poor become entangled in debt to money-lenders, shop-keepers, or other richer persons who can take advantage of their extremity of need to drive hard bargains.

The other need of credit is, not to meet an emergency, but to seize an opportunity. It is sometimes supposed that only a big man with large resources can set up in business to-day with any reasonable prospect of success. But this general supposition is unwarranted. Even in some of the staple manufactures it is often possible for a workman who has got a practical understanding of some branch of a trade to set up for himself with a good prospect of doing well, if he can get a little business capital on reasonable terms. At present, as a rule, he must either forego the chance or else put himself entirely in the hands of some " trade-furnisher " or machine-making firm which can squeeze him as it likes. Our ordinary banking system, falling more and more into the hands of a few great amalgamated companies with innumerable local branches, and virtually compelled to run its loan business by strict regulations as to security, does not attempt to meet the needs of these small men. Even manufacturers and traders of fair position feel more and more the lack of any cheap elastic credit system, and are often driven to borrow upon usurious terms and under conditions which enslave them to some bank. The machinery of credit and finance is the dominant factor in our modern capitalist system : more and more of the practical control over industry, as well as of the profits, belong, not to the manufacturer, the merchant, or other trade-capitalist, but to the financier. I am convinced that if a close scrutiny into the distribution of wealth were made, it would be found that in every advanced country a rapidly growing proportion of the wealth was passing into the possession or control of that small class the manipulators of fluid capital. Recent statistics showing the exceedingly high average rate of interest upon paid-up capital in British banking companies bear striking testimony to the truth of this conjecture.

What this restriction of credit means for the ordinary man is this. If he has got a bit of land, and knows how to put it to advantageous use, he requires some money to get manure, stock, or farm implements : though he may have good personal credit he cannot get the money upon fair terms. If he is a small artisan with a good idea, a shop-foreman or an agent, anxious to set up a little business of his own, he is in fact deprived of the opportunity to apply his ability by the absence of all access to credit. This is a grave practical barrier, not merely to individual advancement, but to the growth of national wealth, for it shuts out great numbers of able enterprising men from contributing to industrial progress. So far as agriculture is concerned, some recognition of the difficulty exists and some remedies are in course of experiment : governmental loans have for some time past been made to distressed landlords to assist them in improving their estates : Irish and now English Small Holdings Acts make some provision of public loans of capital for specific purposes. In various countries, as is well known, local co-operative banks have succeeded in organising a system of cheap credit, not only among farmers but among industrial groups of town workers. Whether private co-operation is competent to solve the problem in this country, or whether a public system of loan banks is required, is a question too intricate to be discussed with profit here. It is enough to insist upon the prime importance of devising a bank system which shall enable any person who can show that he can make good use of capital, giving personal or other security, to obtain it upon the easiest terms. Personally I believe that the credit of the State is of necessity so much better than the credit of any private banker or money-lender as to indicate that the whole of the money-lending business from the pawnshop up to the largest discount operations will in time pass into State control. Most of the objections raised by business men to such a proposal are based either upon the greater elasticity of private enterprise in banking or upon the supposed necessity of secrecy in matters of loan-credit. Now the first of these advantages is rapidly disappearing under the modern branch-bank system : the second, the secrecy, is not an advantage at all, for though the interest of the individual borrower lies in secrecy, that of society lies in publicity.

These considerations, however, are too nice for us

here to pursue. I can only repeat that credit is an essential element of liberty and of equality of competition in modern business, and so becomes an item in our charter of opportunity.

If a man has his fair use of the land and other natural resources of his country, and of the national highways, can get industrial power and financial power upon equal terms with any other man, he has made large strides along the road of liberty. But he is not really free—because he is not secure, and the sense and the substance of security belong to a free man. A working man, a clerk, a small shopkeeper or his assistant, in fact, the great majority of the population in our rich and civilised country, are conscious always of standing in a precarious condition. They and their families may be plunged into poverty and its attendant degradation and disease at any time by the ill-health or other disablement of the bread-winner, by the failure of an employer, by some change of public taste, some shift of market, some introduction of improved machinery, or some trade depression. Few of these emergencies can be foreseen; against the graver ones no adequate provision can be made, even by the best-paid grades of workers. Among the middle classes, especially among the professional and commercial classes of our towns, the competitive struggle is fraught with growing hazard: it is rarely possible to see far ahead, and the complexity of markets and of price-changes baffles the keenest foresight. Though such men may make some fair provision against destitution, they cannot ensure a standard of comfort for themselves and their families, and the wear and tear of anxiety is an increasing cost of production in modern industry. The business of insurance has sprung up to deal with these conditions, and is grappling manfully with some of them. But then insurance itself so often is not sure, and this applies particularly to the societies to which the working classes have recourse. An enormous proportion of the savings of the workers, made often at the expense of some element in their personal efficiency, goes in competitive expenses of management, contributing nothing towards insurance, while the system of weekly retail collection involves the maximum trouble of collection. It is quite evident that if there is one form of enterprise where the State has an advantage over private profit-making companies, it is insurance. The intelligence of civilised nations in all parts of the world is coming to a clear recognition of this truth, and Governments are everywhere assuming the new responsibility. Organised Society must do for its members what they are unable, either as individuals or as loose co-operative groups, to do for themselves, viz., to obtain such security of employment and of livelihood as is necessary to give them confidence and freedom in their outlook upon life. No man, whose standard of life lies at the mercy of a personal accident or a trade crisis, has the true freedom which it is the first duty of the civilised State to furnish.

How very imperfectly this prime duty of the State is yet performed appears in the administration of justice. We are in the habit of accepting the dictum that " all men are equal in the eyes of the law," as if it were equivalent to the statement that " every man equally enjoys the protection of the law." Now this latter statement is notoriously false. Freedom and equality of access to public justice do not exist in this country. Neither in a criminal nor in a civil suit does a poor man stand upon a level with a rich man. So long as the preparation of a case, the feeing of counsel, the expenses of witnesses, court fees and other costs of public justice are charged against private litigants, the owner of the long purse has an evident advantage, and can beat down, choke off or wear out his poorer adversary. This iniquity is still more monstrous where, under the false name of public justice, the Crown with all the public resources at its call, in a court of its own selection, assails the life or liberty of a poor and ignorant defendant, who has neither the wit to defend himself nor the money to fee skilled counsel and to state his full defence. That some courts have power to provide counsel for persons suing or defending *in formâ pauperis*, and to remit certain fees, I am aware, but such provision is utterly inadequate to meet the demand for equal justice. The result is that in classes of cases where heavy expenses are involved in hiring counsel, calling experts and in appealing to higher courts, justice to all intents and purposes is sold to the highest bidder. Nor are these by any means the only inequalities of law that need redress. The substance of whole departments of our law is still biassed in favour of real property, the whole scale of penalties is weighted by class interests and prejudices, and still worse the bulk of the administration of the law is entrusted to incompetent and untrained amateurs, drawn almost exclusively from the possessing and employing classes. Under such conditions justice must remain precarious, and the general implicit confidence in justice which is the spiritual foundation of a State is grievously impaired.

I cannot here enter into discussion of the precise remedies required, but must content myself with formulating a demand for the free and equal access of all men to public justice. This can only be achieved by relieving private litigants from all expenses in the preparation and conduct of criminal or civil cases, and the removal of all such work from a private to a public profession. The defence of life and property from internal attacks must be put on the same footing as external defence. Because the special interests of individuals are involved in law-suits, that is no reason for leaving half the work of justice to private enterprise under conditions of such inequality as I indicate. These cases are undertaken in the interests of public justice, and the public should pay and provide, taking what precautions are necessary to safeguard itself against frivolous or otherwise unwarrantable litigation.

A man might have all the equal liberties which I
have named, access to land, facility of travel, industrial
energy, credit, economic security and justice, all these
things might be freely distributed throughout the community, and yet true equality of opportunity might be
lacking: a society where all these liberties were won
might be sunk in the stagnation of conservatism, or
might even breed new forms of inequality and tyranny.

For there is one opportunity upon which the efficacy
of all the others, as instruments of self-development and
of social benefit, depends: equality of access to knowledge and culture. Without this every other opportunity is barren for the purposes of personal or social
progress. Education is the opportunity of opportunities. We, therefore, who are concerned not with
liberty to stagnate but with liberty to grow, must set the
nationalisation of knowledge and culture in the front of
our charter of popular freedom. It sometimes seems as
if this great secular struggle for popular enlightenment
were won, in principle at any rate. Everyone, we are
told, believes in opening wide the gates of knowledge
that anyone who will may enter: everyone believes in
personal culture, in the extension of general and technical
education, in free libraries and cheap literature: most
persons admit that the State must take, as it is taking,
an ever larger part in the education of the people. But
the battle in this country, at any rate, is far from won.
For consider what equal opportunity of knowledge and
of culture implies. It implies that neither poverty, nor
ignorance of parents, nor premature wage-earning, nor
defects of teaching apparatus, shall keep any person
from any sort of learning which will improve his understanding, elevate his character, and increase his efficiency
as a worker and a citizen. Now we have hardly begun to
realise these essentials in our system of public education,
where not 5 per cent. of the children of the working
classes get anything beyond the barest rudiments. No
serious endeavour is yet made to bring within their

reach any appreciable fraction of the great world of literature or science, or to bring home to them through history that knowledge of social institutions and popular movements without which the formal rights of citizenship are little better than an idle toy or even a perilous tool.

What is needed is not an educational ladder, narrowing as it rises, to be climbed with difficulty by a chosen energetic few, who as they rise enter a new social stratum, breathe the atmosphere of another class, and are absorbed in official and professional occupations which dissociate them from the common life of the people. It is a broad, easy stair, and not a narrow ladder, that is wanted, one which will entice everyone to rise, will make for general and not for selected culture. I am well aware that all will not equally avail themselves of the opportunity for culture, but, unless the door is held far wider open than it is at present, an intolerable wrong is done and an immeasurable waste of national efficiency and progress is incurred. The individual culture and the social efficiency of every man and woman are the two related aims of national education. Such an education must be free, so that poverty be no impediment, open to all from the primary school to the university, disinterested in its aims and management. These are the main essentials of intellectual economy. We are very far from having secured them. At present popular culture in this country is crushed between the upper millstone of public parsimony and the lower millstone of theological intrusion. We do not believe in ideas as we believe in force, as an instrument of national security and progress. Otherwise we should not find it so easy to add ten millions of yearly public expenditure on warships, so difficult to find one million for the higher education of the people. Yet any truly intelligent public financier, looking ten or twenty years ahead, who merely concerned himself with the provision of future public revenue, would recognise his wisest policy to lie in sowing knowledge broadcast in the common mind, to ripen afterwards in industrial efficiency. And this is but the lowest plea for national culture. But short-sighted parsimony, proceeding from a lack of faith in ideas, is not the gravest peril to our free education. Disinterested culture is what we need. Now this is not attained when a church, an academic caste, or a social class, directs or dominates our schools or colleges. Popular self-government is as essential for education as for any other province of public conduct. So long as clergymen are permitted to tamper with education, or military patriots are allowed to inject their poison into the minds of the young, or authorities from the older seats of learning are allowed to impose obsolete intellectual standards upon the rising popular culture, the free intellectual life of the people will be heavily impeded.

One particular peril which immediately confronts us I cannot forbear to name. It lies in the temptation to rely upon the financial patronage of rich men, millionaire endowments, for the means of establishing universities and colleges for the higher education of the people. Now for any nation to turn to private charity for the performance of its public duties is a degradation and a danger. Education sustained by such means will never be really free, or fully disinterested. The history, the economics, the ethics, even the biology, taught in these privately bounty-fed institutions, will carry in various subtle but certain ways the badge of servitude to the special business interests that are their paymasters. If rich men can afford this bounty, the State can by taxation obtain from them the public income needed to sustain the intellectual needs of the nation. If intellectual liberty in the sense of free access to disinterested culture is to become the common heritage of all, public ownership and control of the instruments of this education is indispensable.

I am particularly urgent in this matter because, not

merely is this intellectual and moral franchise essential
to the effective operation of the other opportunities, but
it is essential to their winning.   We have not yet got
the land, the railways, the public credit, the free justice,
and the other opportunities.   A cluster of special interests
stubbornly defends each stronghold of monopoly.   The
success of the popular demand depends upon the intelligent use of the franchise and the instruments of government, so as to form sound judgments, to express them in
valid legal forms, to press these demands through the
legislative machinery, and to secure accurate, even-
handed administration of the laws.   Now an ignorant,
dull, capricious people, more interested in drink, sport,
and gambling than in anything else, easily diverted from
pressing their "rights" by some artful appeal to
military or commercial Jingoism, and broken into contentious factions by any specious promises of present
gain, is incapable of a sustained, energetic, and well-
directed effort to realise Democracy.   Skilled sophists of
the law, the Press, the party, aye of the pulpit and the
lecture-room, become the conscious or unconscious tools
of reaction and obstruction, denouncing the illegality,
the immorality, the unreason, and the futility of the
popular demands.   The greatest of immediate needs,
therefore, is the training of popular leaders with the
intelligence, the knowledge, the discretion and the
confidence required to break down these sophistical
defences, together with that broader general intelligence
which will enable the people to choose able leaders, to
resist scares and bribes, and to form sober judgments on
the broad issues of public policy submitted to them.

These are reasons why "free education" in the fullest
sense of that term must rank as the first and most urgent
issue of our time.   By this I do not mean that other
demands should be postponed.   The field of progress is
best ploughed by driving many teams abreast.   I only
mean that important as is access to the land and to other
economic liberties, the intellectual and moral liberty

which comes with the cultivation of the mind is more valuable, not only on its own account, but because without it none of the others can be won, or if won can be securely held. That the charter here drafted contains the full tale of human rights and liberties, or that it exhausts the political reforms which an enlightened modern State should strive to compass, I do not profess. But I would invite serious consideration of these two questions. First, is there any one of these great lines of advance here indicated which would not contribute to the positive enlargement of personal liberty, and which, by redressing some present inequality of opportunity, would not secure the better development and more advantageous use of the energies of individual citizens? Secondly, is it not evident that these reforms belong to Liberalism and are involved in that saner, more positive and progressive conception of liberty which identifies that word not with absence of restraint but with presence of opportunity?

It is true that the attainment of this practical equalisation of opportunities involves a larger use of the State and legislation than Liberals of an older school recognised as necessary or desirable. But the needs of our day are different from theirs, and the modern State is a different instrument. There is nothing in Liberalism to preclude a self-governing people from using the instrument of self-government for any of the measures I have named : on the contrary, to refuse to do so is to furnish the mere forms of liberty and to deny the substance. Moreover, there is not one of these great positive liberties that has not been acknowledged and in large part secured for the people by some advanced State in Europe or in our colonies. Free land, free travel, free power, free credit, security, justice and education, no man is " free " for the full purposes of civilised life to-day unless he has all these liberties.

CHAPTER III

COLLECTIVISM IN INDUSTRY

A contemptuous neglect—sometimes a boastful repudiation—of principles or theories of social reform is a characteristic attitude of most " social reformers " in England to-day. Rejecting the " scientific " claims of Social Democracy upon the double ground that its analysis of economic problems is radically defective and that it fails to apply practically to the future the conception of historic evolution which it recognises in interpreting the past, English " progressives " present no alternative analysis or theory, nor do they recognise the need of forming any. Not a few among them have passed through a period of half-intellectual, half-emotional Utopianism, dreaming dreams and seeing visions, but they have come out at the other side, and pride themselves upon having sloughed all hallucinations and settled down to the practical work of detailed reform. Most of them frankly admit that along with their early hallucinations they have shed all " theory " or " principle " as awkward encumbrances which impede that facility of compromise by which alone they deem each separate measure of real progress can be achieved.

Many earnest workers in the cause of that expansion of Municipal and State activity, which is termed Collectivism, are especially impressed by this conviction of the futility of theories and ideas. Progress is for most of them purely a matter of detailed experiment, which shall concern itself only with the special circumstances of each case. Such work, they hold, is best entrusted to men with no particular intellectual principles or broad convictions, or who, if they have any, will be careful not to seek to bring them into application. Mazzini, indeed, has told us that " principles alone are constructive," but our practical reformer is sure that he knows better : he sees how very apt principles are to get in the way and to clog the wheels of progress. Whatever may be true of France or Germany, English history, as he reads it, proves that progress is not governed by the conscious operation of ideas. This revolt against ideas is carried so far that able men have come seriously to look upon progress as a matter for the manipulation of wirepullers, something to be " jobbed " in committee by sophistical motions or other clever trickery. Great national issues really turn, according to this judgment, upon the arts of political management, the play of the adroit tactician and the complete canvasser. This is the " work " that tells : elections, the sane expression of the national will, are won by these and by no other means.

Nowhere has this mechanical conception of progress worked more disastrously than in the movement towards Collectivism. Suppose that the mechanism of reform were perfected, that each little clique of specialists and wirepullers were placed at its proper point in the machinery of public life, will this machinery grind out progress? Every student of industrial history knows that the application of a powerful " motor " is of vastly greater importance than the invention of the special machine. Now, what provision is made for generating the motor-power of progress in Collectivism? Will it come of its own accord? Our mechanical reformer apparently thinks it will. The attraction of some present obvious gain, the suppression of some scandalous abuse of monopolist power by a private company, some needed enlargement of existing Municipal or State enterprise by lateral expansion— such are the sole springs of action. In this way the

Municipalisation of public services, increased assertion of State control over mines, railways, and factories, the assumption under State control of large departments of transport trade, proceed without any recognition of the guidance of general principles.   Everywhere the pressure of special concrete interests, nowhere the conscious play of organised human intelligence! Yet the folly of thus ignoring ideas and the enthusiasm they can evoke, and of trusting entirely to the detailed pressure of felt needs and grievances, can be made manifest even to the practical man by pointing out how such an expansion of Collective action by redress of known long-standing grievances not merely implies a waste of Collective energy in the past, but involves the grievous expense of compensating vested interests which a wiser regard for " theory " would never have permitted to grow up.

My object here is to justify the practical utility of " theory " and " principle " in the movement of Collectivism by showing that reformers who distrust the guidance of Utopia, or even the application of economic first principles, are not thrown back entirely upon that crude empiricism which insists that each case is to be judged separately and exclusively on its own individual merits.

There are certain middle principles and sober hypotheses which are serviceable half-way houses, built by legitimate generalisation out of past experience, to which it is reasonable to appeal.   The student of recent economic history finds a plainly marked development of the structure of business, which throws a clear and powerful light upon the true paths of progress in collective enterprise.

" The Wealth of Nations," written upon the very brink of the industrial revolution, contains a most instructive passage in which Adam Smith assigns what he held to be the necessary economic limits to joint-stock enterprise :

" The only trades which it seems possible for a joint-stock company to carry on successfully, without an exclusive privilege, are those of which all the operations are capable of being reduced to what is called a routine, or to such a uniformity of method as admits of little or no variation. Of this kind is, first, the banking trade ; secondly, the trade of insurance from fire and from sea-risk and capture in time of war ; thirdly, the trade of making and maintaining a navigable cut or canal ; and fourthly, the similar trade of bringing water for the supply of a great city."*

Now in the first place it will be observed that all these " trades " which in the later eighteenth century Adam Smith saw ripening for joint-stock enterprise, together with their allied branches of business, have passed right through the phase of joint-stock enterprise, and are in various places and at various paces visibly moving towards the condition of public businesses. Not merely in America, but all over the civilised world, the growing use of credit-money and the speculative processes of modern commerce are driving home the dangers of private banking, and the support which various governments are practically forced to give to private firms in financial emergencies is everywhere strengthening the conviction of the necessity of a firm national control of currency in all its complex forms, which is the normal development and adjustment to modern conditions of one of the earliest and most general functions of the State. Closely related to the trade in money is the Insurance trade. With the growth of credit on a basis of banking has grown a number of risks against which provision must be made. As Adam Smith truly foresaw, this work has proved suitable for joint-stock enterprise; but in several countries private joint-stock is giving way before public joint-stock. The most pressing risks of old age poverty, disablement and death, are passing under schemes of State insurance, voluntary or compulsory; the habit of

---

* Book V., chap. i., part 3.

" pooling " risks of fire and life among formally competing companies, so as to eliminate genuine competition, is rapidly preparing the way for a wider recognition
in this country of the economies of State insurance. The
" navigable cut or canal " was the first fruit of large
capitalism in the transport industry and involves in its
development of structure that large department of
industry which takes national shape in railways, postal
service and steamship companies, and municipal shape
in tramways, omnibus companies, local telephones and
railroads.   This whole vast transport trade has fully
ripened under companies : the mightiest member of
this industrial class, the railroad, has in most countries
been established by or fallen under State management;
or, as in the United States, is either drifting out of
private into public hands from the pure pressure of
economic circumstances,* or is organising its hitherto
competing members into vast monopolies wielding a
dangerous dominion over the industry of whole States.
The fourth of Adam Smith's trades, that of Water
Supply, is likewise the index and forerunner of an ever-
increasing series of industries for the supply of common
municipal needs, including gas, electricity, etc., which
are being municipalised in all parts of the civilised world.

Now, the first lesson contained in these facts is the
plain testimony to a natural course of growth by which
certain large classes of industry are seen to pass from
individual into joint-stock business, and again from
joint-stock business into public business, the limit of
Collectivism being determined by the specific character
attaching to each work. So wide and so multifarious is
this movement, that it cannot fail to impress all
observers with that feeling of inevitability which is the
characteristic of the operation of " natural " laws.
Many even among those who both in principle and
practice have set themselves in most stubborn opposition

---

* In 1894, 192 railroads, containing nearly one-fourth of the aggregate mileage
in the United States, were in the hands of Official Receivers.

to this current of events are compelled to bear regretful testimony to the overpowering force of the stream.

Some, again, have been so powerfully impressed by the volume of this movement that they derive from it a general law which they seek to impose upon all industrial growth. All businesses, they urge, pass from small simple types into larger and more complex types, outgrowing first the bounds of individual or family control, then, taking on the joint-stock or voluntary co-operative structure, so increase in size and strength as to develop a monopoly character, which ultimately compels the State, as agent for the interests of oppressed consumers, to " take them over." According to this view, all industry alike is moving along the same road, at different paces, towards the same goal of State Collectivism.

Is this a just interpretation of the facts? If not, what limits are to be assigned to the operation of this law? To find the answer to this question, let us turn to the pregnant criticism of Adam Smith. The common character of those businesses which in his day were suitable for joint-stock enterprise he marks by the word " routine." This furnishes a crucial test. Trades which are susceptible of " such a uniformity of method as admits of little or no variation," which can be reduced to " routine," are visibly, and in some cases rapidly, moving along the prescribed road to Collectivism. " But," it has been said, " cannot all industry, sooner or later, be brought under ' routine ' conditions and worked collectively?" This question is intimately connected with another relating to the limits of machinery. The machine has been continually encroaching upon the domain of handicraft, and has executed by mechanical " routine " methods the work which formerly required the exercise of individual skill. Can all work be brought under the control of the machine? The vital connection of the two questions is marked by the fact that the growing application of machinery, especially to the manufactures and the transport industries, has been the most potent agent in driving these industries towards joint-stock enterprise and towards Collectivism. If, then, it appears that there are certain kinds of work which cannot be done by machinery, which do not require large capital, which are essentially and eternally incapable of reduction to "routine," such work seems likely to resist the movement to Collectivism. Are there such kinds of work? For answer, turn to the consumer, for the satisfaction of whose needs the whole of industry primarily exists, and whose "effective demand" controls alike its quantity and character. There are certain needs which nature or custom has imposed alike on all members of a community, or upon large sections of Society in cases where economic resources are unequally apportioned. There are general human needs which are satisfied by the production of large quantities of goods of common quality and common shapes and sizes. Such "routine" wants can be supplied by "routine" industry, and the very economic nature of these wants, as we have seen, drives the industries which are engaged in their satisfaction towards Collectivism. It is, of course, this principle, which has collectivised the high roads of all civilised countries, placing them under national or local control according as they supply the common need of the nation or of the locality; and the demand for nationalisation of railways involves no new principle of policy, but merely an adjustment of the mechanism of transport to the modern conditions of the "consuming" public. Almost all the means of transport, whether for persons, messages, or goods, in populous countries tend to pass into the condition of "routine" industries. The whole work of conveyance along common routes is of a "routine" and mechanical nature. It is true that what is called "routine" may consist with great complexity, and with some irregularity of demand. But when we are dealing with a wide common demand this complexity may be copied by complex machinery, and this irregularity discloses its own laws of fluctuation. The conveyance of men and goods is not more irregular than the conveyance of letters and telegrams.

But many of the needs of ordinary material consumption are of a " routine " character, for the whole or for large sections of a community. Because all citizens use water and gas, and because there should be only one sort of water and gas in use for all, namely, the best and purest that is attainable, these industries tend to pass into collective forms. It is not quite Utopian to look forward to a time when it may be considered as important that one sort of milk should be consumed by all, and when the general demand for bread may be brought within such narrow limits of difference that these industries shall be added to the services of municipal supply. So far as the body of the public are dominated in their needs by common elements of humanity, whether on the material or the mental plane, mechanical and " routine " methods which tend to take on collective forms will be more and more adapted to their supply.

In proportion as a genuine levelling up of the standard of comfort for the masses of a population takes place, the number of industries which can thus be regulated economically upon the largest scale for the satisfaction of wants which, once only common within a narrow " class " range, have now extended to the whole population, will be constantly increasing. Thus an incessant growth of Collectivism is indicated by the essential facts of common progress.

But those who fix their eyes ecstatically upon this movement often ignore the other side of the case. If this law of progress covered all the needs of man, then no limits could be set upon Collectivism. But man is not only one with his fellows, but also one by himself, not only a partaker of common humanity but an individual with nature and conditions which evoke tastes and needs that are his own and his alone. Now such tastes, such needs, can never be satisfied by "routine" industry, which for its essential economy depends upon the production of large quantities of similar goods for the satisfaction of common un-individual needs. The needs of an individual nature can only be satisfied by the conscious activity of an individual producer. Here emerges the radical antithesis which utterly destroys the validity of all ideals of complete Collectivism. It is the antithesis of "routine" and "individual" work, of machine production and art. A machine can be made capable of satisfying all or any of the needs which we have in common with all, or with a large number of our fellow-men : if those needs are for material commodities, steam-driven arrangements of iron can be devised for making them; if they are for intellectual goods, they can be turned out cheaply from the factories of "schools," "churches" or "presses" which are contrived for the wholesale production of common intellectual or æsthetic wares for the consumption of those who will consent to merge the individuality of their demand and consume these common articles. But if I stand out for the satisfaction of those wants in which I differ from my fellow-men, I require not a machinist but an artist to satisfy me, one who by the conscious exercise of some individual skill of his own can mould the material on which he works to the satisfaction of my individuality. Now the whole gist of the matter lies here. Is the Collectivism of the future going to impair the multiplicity and force of those needs and tastes which mark off one person from another? Is individuality to be swallowed up by humanity? Few even among the most advanced or fanatical Collectivists admit this tendency; most are prepared to stake the value of their Socialism upon the single test of its active promotion of individuality, the increase of the satisfaction of those needs which mark off each from his fellow. Though the absolute number of common needs

capable of routine supply will grow, though much of the.
higher satisfaction which comes to individuals will
be derived from the individual use of opportunities
which are accessible to all, " of joys in widest com-
monalty spread," they are few who do not eagerly insist
that a chief object and result of such Collectivism will be
to enable individuals more fully and freely to cultivate
and satisfy their individual aspirations. Now if this is
so, and it seems incontrovertibly true, any growth of
Collectivism based upon the most economic use of
routine activities of nature and of man must be progressively outweighed by the growth of human activity
devoted to those kinds of work here broadly designated
Art. Under this term will come all handling of material
or intellectual " stuff " which involves individual skill
and attention in the worker imposed by the need of
executing an individual order. The Fine Arts of course
yield the plainest examples of such work, but, as
Ruskin has so admirably shown, there is no material
which does not admit a genuine artistic treatment, provided there exists some true public appreciation of the
excellence of the product. Metals, wood, stone,
leather—every form of matter—will afford infinite scope
for a handicraft which shall exhibit the truest and most
noble character of Art in places where there live lovers
of beautiful form and colour. There are few who will
not admit that the progress of civilisation in a nation
implies a constant rise in the discriminative character of
work and enjoyment. Now if this is so, it implies a proportionate diminution in the quantity of effort devoted
to routine or common work as compared with that
which is individual in its execution and in the enjoyment
it furnishes. This, of course, does not mean that the
enjoyment of a great picture by a wide class of the
community is inconsistent with true progress, but that
this enjoyment, though common to many as enjoyment,
will be more discriminative, that is, more individual,
in the appreciation and satisfaction it affords.

Now, there is no evidence from the tenor of recent history to show that the fine arts, or any of those arts which, not so fine, are yet engaged in satisfying individual tastes, tend to pass from small into large businesses moving towards the goal of Collectivism. The chief economies of great industry, the adoption of mechanical processes of production and routine management, do not equally apply to them. Dependent as they are for the most part upon close constant individual care of execution, and not upon that minute division of labour which goes hand-in-hand with machine-production, most of them do not even take the first step of entering large business shapes. Though a work of art in tailoring or millinery, as in statuary, may be erected upon a basis of rough mechanical work, the finer processes which constitute the art commonly defy the economy of division of labour. " There is no fit—there can be no fit—in a coat made by the machine and by sub-divided and unskilled labour," writes Mrs. Sidney Webb, in dealing with the London tailoring trade. So, again, of the best kind of clocks, a trade which still maintains its primitive form in London, we are told : " The work of making a clock is conducted under one roof, both by hand and by machinery. The men learn to make a clock throughout, and whatever their particular work may be, they do it with conscious reference to its bearing on the action of the whole clock." Here even in the production of a mechanism survives the principle of unity and individuality. Not only a poem and a picture, but a well-fitting coat and a well-made clock, is an individual, retaining the distinctive character of a work of art, and imposing upon the industry a corresponding nature. Thus the two closely-related forces, machine production and division of labour, which conspicuously favour the big complex business tending towards Collectivism, are inoperative where industry consists in the satisfaction of nicer individual needs. Not only in the most skilled branches of such trades as cutlery, bookbinding, and cabinetmaking do we find the healthy survival of domestic industry or small workshops, but even in trades where some of the worst features of sweating have appeared, the best work still remains in businesses of a primitive type, *e.g.*, boots and handmade ropes. It is not, however, always the individual taste of the consumer which imposes the character of art upon an industry. A close investigation of the structure of the textile trades will show that the nature of the raw material, as well as the size and uniformity of the demand, determines the character of the industry. The silk trade and some branches of the woollen trade have failed to attain the full economies of machine production, as much from a certain irregularity or individuality in the raw material, which requires care and judgment in its treatment, as from the irregularity and qualitative character of the demand. Sometimes individualism will inhere not in the material, but in some condition of the work. Taking the example of street transport, we find that whereas trams and 'busses are almost everywhere in the possession of large companies, the cab business is for the most part in small businesses, though in London and other large towns, where the demand for cabs is larger and more regular, the " company " is gaining ground. Applying the " routine " principle, we easily understand how trams and 'busses, which run with regularity of routes, times, and prices, are far more amenable to collective control than cabs, more dependent for their business upon the will of individual " fares."

It is true that where skilled work plays a comparatively unimportant part in the aggregate of processes, and in general wherever there exists a large and steady demand for goods not widely differing in character, the industry passes into large capitalist shapes, the small survival of skilled workmanship being a mere appendage to the big routine business. But it is important to recognise that a sharp and genuine antagonism exists between industries engaged in the satisfaction of quantitative demand and those engaged in satisfying qualitative demand. Whereas the former can utilise to the full all the economies of machinery and division of labour, the latter cannot. The chief forces which are visibly making for Collectivism in material industries are weak just in proportion as the elements of skill and art are strong. If, therefore, we admit that social progress will express itself in increasing taste, refinement, individuality of consumption of material goods, we admit a slackening of the very forces which have hitherto been driving these industries towards fully-developed Capitalism. Though it is probably true that in a progressive society the tendency to seek expression for individuality in ordinary articles of material consumption might not be widely prevalent, while fashion and the irregularity of demand which comes from unbridled caprice would be weakened by education and an approximate equalisation of material resources, we cannot fairly regard the whole of material industry as subject to a set of economic forces driving irresistibly towards the goal of routine work and Collectivism. It is, of course, probable, as Socialists would urge, that a *rapprochement* would come from the other side, that a State or Municipality, confined at first to the control of the most routine forms of industry, would become by experience qualified to enter businesses where the routine was less rigid and to manage them successfully. Such an expectation has a certain *à priori* validity and some backing from experience. But this admission does not negative the main principle of demarcation between industries which at any given time are essentially Collective, and those which are not. Though the signification which each society and each age may give to the term " routine " will differ in degree, it is not the less true that a State which is best equipped for Collective control and unimpeded by vested interests from the exercise of such control will nevertheless limit that direct control to industries which are relatively of a routine character.

Our illustrations have been drawn from industries engaged in production of material wealth. But there is no essential difference here between the production of material and non-material wealth. If our reasoning is sound, it applies equally to State education, to State enterprise in art, science, or literature, as to transport and manufacture. Historic forces are not driving these activities wholesale under Collective control, though everywhere the State is encroaching and organising by social machinery the lower stages of these " arts." As we have already recognised, there is in the " arts " themselves a routine basis, certain work which is relatively common or unskilled, and which can be conveniently executed by machine methods. Such education as is directed to the preliminary training of those faculties which belong to common humanity, physical, intellectual, and moral, the communication of that great social heritage of knowledge which is the rightful intellectual possession of all citizens, the provision of colleges and technical schools, art schools, museums, theatres, and the completest machinery for the best education of our common life—these things will be recognised as properly belonging to the routine department of intellectual production. This " Collective " work will always remain the relatively " ruder " work, though much of it be far in advance of the present conception of " routine " education in a nation which does not understand education, or even understand that it is a thing to be understood. The finer intellectual work in science, in the fine arts, in literature, will never be directly controlled by Collective machinery. Whatever progress Collectivism may make in its capacity of skilful, energetic, and disinterested management, its methods must always continue to be more mechanical than those of private enterprise, and less successful in directing the more individual elements of effort to the satisfaction of individual needs.

This principle to which we have addressed ourselves,

the antithesis of quantitative and qualitative consumption, of routine and art industry, in reality covers the chief lines of advance to which Collectivists appeal. Professor Marshall has summed up a remarkable investigation of the conditions of great industry by declaring that " there is *primâ facie* reason for believing that the aggregate satisfaction, so far from being already a maximum, could be much increased by collective action in promoting the production and consumption of things in regard to which the law of Increasing Returns acts with a special force."* Now what are those goods which in their production and distribution conform to the law of Increasing Returns? They are " routine " goods which go to satisfy the common needs of large numbers of consumers. These are the things, which, because there is a large and constant regular demand for certain common forms and qualities of them, can be produced and distributed more cheaply on a large scale than on a small scale. Elaborate machinery and sub-division of labour are most fully utilised in keeping down the cost of making them, while wholesale buying and selling, and large advertising assist in cheapening their distribution, and last, not least, expenses of direction and management are most fully economised. These economies of cost are the very forces which we have observed driving " routine " business along the road to Collectivism. This judgment of Professor Marshall, taken with the careful evidence upon which he bases it, is a most important testimony in favour of the practicability of the Collectivism of " routine " industry. Professor Marshall also recognises, though not so fully, the relation between this tendency and the theory of monopoly. The polemics of Collectivism are largely concerned with the insistence of the need of Collective control as a protection of the interests of the consumer against monopolies. Now monopolies (using the term in its

---

* "Principles of Economics." Vol. I., p. 537 (Ed. 2.).

broad sense to signify all industries in which prices are not regulated by " free competition " of sellers) are of two classes; those in which the monopolist power is derived from control over some source of supply restricted in quantity by nature or by law, and those in which the power comes from the superior economies of the big over the little business. Most of the strongest monopolies conjoin these two powers, resting partly upon monopoly of land or raw material, partly upon size of capital, as in the case of railways or of such a trust as that of the Standard Oil Company. But the difference in source of power, though both are dangerous to the community, suggests clearly that the defence of Collective interests will adopt a different attitude to the two kinds of monopoly. Where size of capital, underselling competitors, and narrowing the area of effective competition until some syndicate can be formed to obtain sole control of the market, is the source of power, we are dealing with a routine business taking advantage of the operation of the law of Increasing Returns to establish a private monopoly. All around us in the most highly-developed industry such forms are crystallising, often not completely shaped and not absolute in their monopolist power. They are not, as sometimes is pretended, the mere product of tariffs, though tariffs have often helped them to mature. They are the normal necessary issue of competition in business where machine-economy and widening markets make size and strength chief constituents of success, conditions under which competition must finally give way to the private monopoly of the biggest and best placed competitor. The demand for public protection against the powers which these monopolies exercise over the consumer, and over the labourers whose employment and subsistence they hold in the hollow of their hand, is a growing force in modern politics. In England and upon the Continent of Europe there are perhaps no industries which can be considered to have reached the form of perfect

K

monopoly, from which direct competition has permanently disappeared. But there are many cases where the dominion of organised capital exercises a serious restraint upon competitive prices, and where the monopolist power differs only in degree from that of the perfected " trust." It is consistent with the historical tenor of progress that the practical pressure of these dangers and grievances should be more potent forces in the growth of Collectivism than any conscious recognition of the natural ripening of this class of business towards a Collective form, or of the ability of the public to undertake such businesses. The contention of theoretical Collectivists, often sustained by arguments of general utility or of humanitarian import, to the effect that the State should at any rate control those industries engaged in producing the necessaries of the life of the people, harmonises with the general policy impressed by these structural considerations. For those industries which, by operation of purely economic forces, tend towards private monopoly, will generally be industries engaged in supplying the commonest and most universally-consumed commodities. These "necessaries" will be in the largest regular demand, will be " routine " commodities, and since an exercise of monopolist power will have the least effect in reducing their consumption, it follows that monopolies in the sale of them will be most profitable to the undertakers. Thus the demand for a Collectivist policy along the line of increased public control over " necessaries " is in general accord with the wider principle upon which we base the Collectivist advance. This recognition of the natural historic growth of private monopolies imposes Collectivism as the sole substitute. The only alternative to private monopoly is public monopoly. For when a private monopoly is the product of economic forces restricting competition, it is futile to endeavour to break up forcibly by law the monopolic form, that competition may be re-established. It is impossible to turn back the hand of the dial. A private monopoly built upon legal privilege may be resolved by rescinding the legal basis, but a monopoly evolved out of competitive conditions admits no other remedy than Collectivism.

In those industries where elements of "natural" monopoly chiefly express themselves, we do not find a general movement along the same lines. The question of large and small culture still remains to be fought out in different departments of work upon the soil and in different social and racial conditions. In some large industries the "niggardliness of nature" seems to yield before the employment of machinery and capitalism, bringing agriculture, too, under the law of increasing returns. Where this occurs, as on the great Bonanza farms, agriculture is brought into line with the great manufactures, and becomes a routine industry. But where small culture survives (and the strong individualism which soil, climate, position, and other natural facts impose upon land indicates a wide survival), the tenor of our argument does not place agriculture among the mere routine industries. This seems to indicate a bifurcation of collective policy according as we regard monopolies established by the operation of the law of Increasing Returns and those established under a law of Diminishing Returns. While the former tend to pass under directly collective management, the latter may remain under private control, the collective policy being confined to securing for collective use those economic rents due to the special values which public needs assign to funds of natural supply.

A policy built upon a recognition of these principles of collectivist development is of course in no sense a compromise. It claims for collective action all work which the community can profitably undertake; it recognises that the absolute area of that work is constantly growing in two directions, first and foremost by the ripening of "routine" industry into the form of private anti-social monopolies, secondly by the growing capacity of public management which experience should evoke in public bodies. But it also recognises that since the direct object of collective action will be so to economise the claims which Society shall make upon the Individual as to leave him an ever-increasing proportion of his energies for self-expression, the amount of energy which is organised directly for collective work will be a diminishing proportion of the aggregate energy of individuals, and that therefore the field of private enterprise in all departments of effort will grow faster than the field of Collectivism.

These are no new principles, and this is no new presentment of them. If practical workers for social and industrial reforms continue to ignore principles, the inevitable logic of events will nevertheless drive them along the path of Collectivism here indicated. But they will pay the price which short-sighted empiricism always pays; with slow, hesitant, and staggering steps, with innumerable false starts and backslidings, they will move in the dark along an unseen track towards an unseen goal. Social development may be conscious or unconscious. It has been mostly unconscious in the past, and therefore slow, wasteful, and dangerous. If we desire to be swifter, safer, and more effective in the future, it must become the conscious expression of the trained and organised will of a people not despising theory as unpractical, but using it to furnish economy in action.

CHAPTER IV

SOCIALISM IN LIBERALISM

The charge of Socialism brought against the Liberal and Progressive Party by their Conservative opponents is commonly resented as a merely tactical device to shift the strain of political controversy from the Tariff issue and to blacken an enemy with a vituperative epithet. An effective technical answer is afforded by an appeal to the party of avowed Socialism which still continues to designate Liberals here, as upon the Continent, a party of capitalists. But motives and technicalities apart, there is enough substance in the charge, as applied to the section of Liberals committed to advanced social reforms, to demand a fair examination. For the first time in the history of English Liberalism, leaders with a powerful support of the rank and file have committed themselves with zeal and even passionate conviction to promote a series of practical measures which, though not closely welded in their immediate purport, have the common result of increasing the powers and resources of the State for the improvement of the material and moral condition of the people. These measures, aiming to secure the use and the value of the land for the people, to obtain for municipalities and other public bodies increased ownership or control of local services, to strengthen governmental supervision of private industries, to enlarge the public machinery of education, to afford increased public assistance to the young, the sick, the aged—such measures and the policy of public finance which they involve are correctly designated as " socialistic " in their character.

It is true that each measure is urged upon its separate merits, that the pace of its advancement and the spirit of compromise which dogs its footsteps hide the logic of the revolutionary process even from many of its active agents. For revolutionary in one sense it is. Not that it involves any violent breach of continuity with Liberal traditions, still less any such sudden dangerous disturbance of public order or of property as is commonly associated with the term. But the general underlying meaning and motive of the social policy, struggling now for the first time into clear consciousness, is the intention to use the popular power of self-government to extirpate the roots of poverty and of the diseases, physical and moral, associated with it. This process of practical reform, if it is to be effective, assuredly demands an interference by Government with existing rights of private property and private business enterprise, and an assertion through taxation of public rights of property, so novel in character and so considerable in size as rightly to be considered revolutionary. The real revolution is in the minds of men. The recent Parliament contained some scores of men passionately moved by a sense of social wrong, of undeserved poverty and riches, of baneful waste in the resources of the commonwealth, and eager to apply large organic remedies. It is the strength of these men's faith and the size of the remedies they are willing to apply that distinguish their social policy from the tinkering devices of the earlier programmes of the Liberal Party. Experience has taught them the profound truth of John Mill's saying : " Small remedies for great diseases do not produce small results : they produce no results."

Will this policy of social reconstruction go forward? The last century has shown several epochs of ebullience of the reform spirit in our nation. The 'thirties and 'forties were seething with constructive Socialism of a swift, idealist order. The Christian Socialism of a generation later was the sentimental utterance of popular protest against the new miseries of city poverty. The Radical Party of the late 'seventies and early 'eighties gave in their programmes a dim fragmentary reflection of demands in which the new teaching of Henry George and of Continental Socialism found vigorous expression. But these movements achieved almost nothing; their fervour was soon spent, their forces dissipated. Will it be the same with our Parliamentary party of social reform and the popular enthusiasm which swept them to the fore? Have they the principles, the strength of conviction, and the grit of character demanded for the task of constructive Liberalism assigned to them? The answer to this question we think depends upon how clearly the larger body of the party can be led to realise the grave historic nature of their task. Let them plainly recognise the truth that this is the last chance for English Liberalism. Unless it is prepared for the efforts, risks, and even sacrifices of expressing the older Liberal principles in the new positive forms of economic liberty and equality along the lines indicated in the programme of its advanced guard, it is doomed to the same sort of impotence as has already befallen Liberalism in most of the Continental countries.

We believe that what we term the advanced guard is well aware of the historical crisis which confronts them, that they are willing to make the necessary effort and to undergo the necessary risks. But can they succeed in rallying round them the genuine support of the Liberal "centre" in Parliament and in the nation? This "centre" is, alike in sympathy and in formal policy, more advanced than it has ever been before. But upon the critical issues of social reform it lacks passion and principle, and is continually disposed to enervating compromise. In Parliament it consists largely of well-to-do men whose social policy is weakened by fears of high taxation and of encroachments upon private profitable enterprise; in the country this same large class, well but not vigorously disposed towards social reforms, stands halting in opinion, fearful of the Socialistic movement, not because of any definite individualism or abstract theory of the limits of the State, but because certain spectres and phrases have got upon their nerves. Holding, as most do, a difficult and slippery footing in some business or profession, they are nervous about attacks on property, disturbance of business, bureaucracy, corruption, mob domination. Though not opposed to social experiments, they are not prepared for efforts or for risks, and their genuine desire to see improved conditions for the people is invalidated by an excessive belief in the possibilities of narrow forms of self-help, a survival of the *laissez faire* Radicalism of the Victorian age.

Unless a sufficient proportion of these men can be won over, their objections met, their fears dissolved, their sense of justice stimulated, the Liberal Party as the historic instrument of social reform is doomed to failure. For a small band of " righteous men " will not save a party; they must carry with them the majority of solid Liberals in the centre if the reform policy is to be substantial. Let it be clearly understood that this policy cannot consist in mere economy, in good administration at home, peace abroad, in minor legislation for education, temperance, or even land reform. The volume, the direction, the pace, and the substance of the positive measures for improving the economic condition of the people must be adequate, and these conditions involve a larger provision of public income than is yet recognised by most politicians, a larger development of interference with existing landed and other economic interests than is yet admitted.

Whether a sufficient Liberal Party can be brought to face this task, with its risks and difficulties, depends upon the education of this " middle " section in the principles of social reconstruction. For their real difficulties are mainly of principle. Any Radical social policy must, of course, involve a shedding of Whigs, even of a few honest Radical individualists, and of some Liberals whose business interests too closely based on privilege will dominate their policy. It is with the large remainder, probably a majority of the Liberal Party, that we are concerned. The situation, as we understand it, is this: Their mind is at present impeded for effective co-operation in the great work of social reconstruction by certain doubts and fears and difficulties, which are real in the sense that they are honestly held, and are important in that they rest not on points of practical detail but on deep-seated notions respecting the meaning and effects of social reconstruction.

These doubts and fears relate, some to Socialism, some to democracy, and are due in large degree to the spirit and the forms which social democracy have taken in the programmes of the Socialist parties, on the Continent and here. Though Marx and the philosophers of Socialism have been little read in this country, certain characteristics of their criticism, its materialistic interpretation of history, its crude assertion of the rights and functions of " labour," its wholesale repudiation of the legitimacy of rent, interest and profit, and its doctrine of the absorption of all industry by the State, have become accepted formulæ and have naturally been adopted as the authoritative exposition of the movement. While this hard-cast revolutionary Socialism has softened even on the Continent and never had much vogue in this country, the milder and more opportunist brands suffer from excessive vagueness. If the Radical policy of social reconstruction is to be effective in this country this lack of intelligible formulation of principles must be remedied. The real difficulties must be met; the right limits of State and municipal collectivism must be laid down; the questions, how far brains, how far " labour," are makers of wealth, how far freedom of private profitable enterprise is essential to secure the work of " brains "; whether efficiency of labour can be got out of public enterprise; whether the tyranny of bureaucracy would become unendurable; whether the tendency of such Socialism will be to dwarf individuality and to make for a dead level of humanity; whether the general result of impaired productive motives will lead to so great a diminution of wealth as no improvement in distribution can compensate—these and other not less radical questions which beset the wavering mind of our "centre" Liberals demand thorough and impartial consideration. Then there is the group of not less serious questions relating to taxation, condensed in the charge that " Socialism " consists in taking away the property of the rich and giving it to the poor, a policy alleged to be unjust in itself and disastrous both to the receivers and the tax-payers. The timidity of the Liberal centre is based primarily upon fears engendered by these questions which imperatively demand intelligible answers, if the Liberal Party hopes to press forward with energy and confidence along the path of social reconstruction to which it is formally committed, and upon which its future existence as a party depends.

CHAPTER V

THE PSYCHOLOGY OF PUBLIC
ENTERPRISE

The most serious difficulties in State Socialism are connected with the political structure of the State. Can a government conduct a number of large complex business operations with the requisite economy, efficiency, and honesty? Though the competition of private profit-mongers may involve much waste of power by needless duplication and the friction of industrial war, while a sweating economy may injure its employees, the normal conduct of such businesses, it is maintained, will be energetic and economical and the public will get most of the gain of industrial improvements in a fall of prices. Even when the virtual monopoly of one large company or combination has displaced competition the desire of the management to earn high profits will maintain most of the former incentives to efficiency and progress, and in many instances, at any rate, considerations of maximum net profits will induce the management to supply a sound article at a low price.

But when the State has taken over such a business, though it may be theoretically possible to maintain many of the former stimuli to efficiency, the vital question whether they will actually be maintained will be one of political integrity. Will it be possible to ensure that the public managers, upon whose personal control the efficiency of the business operations will chiefly depend, will do their duty to the public with the same honesty and zeal which they displayed when working in the interests of private capital, and will they secure from the rank and file of the public employees an efficiency nearly equal to that obtained from ordinary wage earners? In an ordinary joint stock company engaged in trade the body of shareholders in proportion to their respective interests exercise the right of electing directors : these directors control the general policy of the business and appoint the management, making it responsible for the detailed efficiency of the business structure, and enforcing this responsibility by the power of dismissal. Underneath this form of business democracy a practical oligarchy often exists, one or two directors with the manager virtually determining the conduct of the business, with very little interference from the body of investors. But taken as a whole this business system has worked well, securing honesty, economy and efficiency: there is sufficient conscious identity of interests between shareholders, directors, management, and employees to support an effective co-operation of activities.

Take a railroad or an electric engineering works from this business form and put it under the operation of the State or Municipality. The nominal structure undergoes very little change. Instead of the shareholders you have the body of taxpayers or ratepayers, the electorate is responsible for financing the business as the shareholders were before : they elect representatives to sit in Parliament or in the City Council, part of whose business it is to see that this railroad or engineering works is properly managed in the public interest : these representatives, or a Committee of them, appoint the management and act as directors; the permanent officials who actually administer the public works are public servants whose duty it is to run the business for the benefit of the body of citizens.

Why should not such a public business be as efficiently managed in the public interest as the company was in the interests of the shareholders? Theoretically, there is no necessity why the State should equalise the payment for all sorts and qualities of workers, or should cease to apply the stimuli of personal gain in salary and position which are found effective under private enterprise. But practically, it is contended, these stimuli will not be so effectively applied. The removal of the profit-making motives will in various ways slacken the human energy which drives the organism (or mechanism); there will be less efficient co-operation between the parts, and definite corruption may set in, introducing motives of secret illicit gains.

Such is the charge against State Socialism. Let us examine it in the light of known facts and probabilities.

Though, as we see, there is an analogy between the structure of a public and of a joint stock business, certain differences must be recognised. If an electric lighting business is taken over by the Town from a Company, it is true the citizens become the shareholders, taking their gain not in dividends but in good and cheap lighting; the Committee of the Council take the place of the Board of Directors, representing the interests of the civic shareholders : the management is under the general control of the Committee, as formerly under that of the Directors, and the ordinary worker in the business holds his appointment and receives his pay in the same way as before.

But when we regard the operation of the business as a complex arrangement of motives operating in the wills of the various co-operating agents, we note the following changes. The shareholders who elected directors had a power of election strictly proportionate to the number of their shares and the gain they expected to receive : those with a considerable stake at issue would command a majority of votes and could elect directors in whom they placed confidence, and could determine the large issues presented to them at the yearly or half-yearly meeting. These men with the large personal stake would give some close study to the conduct of the business: some of them would become directors, or would have had other experience in this line of business. So far as the nature of the business enabled control to be exercised by the shareholders, that control would be wielded by those possessing a substantial interest and some amount of business knowledge and skill. When the business was municipalised, the control of the citizen-shareholders would be differently distributed. There would be no individuals among them with an incentive of personal gain corresponding in strength to that of the large shareholders. Though cheap, good lighting would confer more gain upon some than upon others, all would have an equal voice in electing the Council that appointed the Committee. Nor is the popular control apportioned with any regard to the amount contributed to the upkeep of the business through the rates. A big ratepayer has one vote along with the little ratepayer. Thus on the appeal to material self-interest there appears a greatly diminished security for effective control on the part of the shareholders. There are no shareholders to whom the efficient management of the lighting means a considerable increase of their personal income, and the few large consumers who stand to gain or lose any substantial amount by the good or bad management of the public lighting are fully aware that their votes count for very little among the general body of the ratepayers; to most of them the difference between dear and cheap, good and bad, electric light is not a matter of great urgency. Moreover the issue is only one among a large tangle of issues presented at an election, so that at no time is the real intelligence and interest of the body of ratepayers focussed upon the question of lighting policy.

There is one other factor of considerable importance in municipal and state Socialism. If the whole profit or product of the public undertaking, *e.g.*, the municipal lighting, were divided among the rate or tax payers, even upon an equal basis, all members of this public would have some personal interest in its economical and efficient management, the interest represented by their rates and taxes. But, it is contended, part of the profit or product, the use of the public lighting, goes to people who pay no rates or taxes. Although these latter may have no votes and no voice in public management, the part of the public product which *r*oes to them for nothing is *pro tanto* a diminution of the gains of the citizen-shareholders and diminishes their incentive to improve the public work. If 40 per cent. of the citizens pay, or think they pay, virtually the whole of the rates which support street-lighting, the benefits of which the other 60 per cent. enjoy as much as they, will they be disposed to pay for so good a lighting system as if they were going to get the whole benefit themselves?

Bearing in mind these differences between shareholders as dividend-receivers and as citizen-ratepayers, we cannot fail to recognise that a transfer from private to public enterprise involves some loss of effective control on the part of those for whose benefit the business is run, so far as selfish personal interest is a motive force. Unless, therefore, some public spirit and intelligence can be evoked and educated to counteract this loss, a waste of efficiency in management accrues.

So much for shareholders. Now for directors. Will the Committee of the Council set to control the lighting do it as well as the Board of Directors under the private régime? *Primâ facie* it is unlikely that they will, if we confine our attention to the play of interested motives. In the first place, there is a substitution of unpaid for paid services, and although many paid directors do little for their money, the payment must be considered a real stimulus to the output of effective energy, and the substitution of unpaid Councillors would seem to indicate a loss. When we add that, in the case of a company, the chairman, and sometimes other directors, do often make the affairs of the company the chief concern of their working hours, while it is rare that the chairman or other committee members under the Council can afford to give their full time and best energies to work which after all must usually be supplementary to the profession or business by which they earn their livelihood, we appear by municipalising a business to have weakened appreciably the control exercised by the elected representatives of the shareholders. This loss, however, is not essential to the Socialistic system. There is no reason why the chairman and even the committee should not be paid on the same scale as that on which the directorate of the company was paid. So far as chairmen or vice-chairmen are concerned this is sometimes done, as the history of the London County Council testifies. This economy belongs to the larger issue of the payment of representatives. Here, however, the substitution of public spirit for private gain, as a motive for effective work, is easier and has been more manifest than at the lower stage which we discussed.

There are various kinds of public and private motives which in many departments of municipal and state work do visibly evoke industry and energy of mind from Mayors, Chairmen of Committee, and many other elected persons taking a responsible part in the administration of important public businesses.

These motives are not always clean, and some, as we shall see, are subject to grave anti-public distortions: but they do often yield a far more effective power of public government than is consistent with a purely self-regarding theory of business economy.

It is often urged, and with much force, that in these arts of government, as in all the finer and humaner arts, the very best creative and progressive work is got by appealing to the unselfish disinterested love of work and of humanity, an appeal which is actually blurred and enfeebled when under a private profit-making company great personal gain is held out as the main incentive to all effort. Moreover, it may be maintained, that in public elective institutions there is some considerable chance of getting into the Council, and from the Council into the Committee, any man out of the whole population who is willing and able to contribute some such great disinterested service—a better chance than if the business were kept in the restricted circle of a group of private investors.

In London government we can very easily illustrate this consideration. If, for instance, the technical and elementary teaching professions in London had been left to competing private enterprise, it is exceedingly unlikely that such able, enlightened and essentially creative minds as those of Mr. Sidney Webb and Mr. Graham Wallas would have been able to make the large steady contribution to the progress of our great Metropolitan community which they have made.

Every considerable city has its history brightened by not a few similar instances of able public-spirited men who, as citizens, have given better services than could be bought by a private profit-making company. But under our present system of competitive industry there can be, and are, very few who are in a position to afford to do such work. It will be one of the chief tasks of progressive policy to secure such conditions for an expanding proportion of the population as shall enable these disinterested social instincts to become operative in the public service.

At present, keeping closely to our analysis of the structure and working of a Municipal Lighting Committee, or other public business, it must, I think, be acknowledged that some loss in technical efficiency of control is incurred by substituting a Committee, appointed as most Committees are appointed, for the directorate of a company. Even setting aside all questions of corruption or jobbery, less regularity of attendance, less energy, less knowledge of the business in question may usually be expected in a committee than in a directorate. There are cases, however, where this may not hold. Most railroad directors in this country know less of railroading than would a Standing Committee appointed by Parliament. But an industrial director generally knows more about his business than does a Committeeman. If this is so, it will have some necessary reactions on the permanent officials to whom the real concrete and detailed conduct of the business is entrusted. As a result of the substitution of a political for a distinctively economic system of control, they will " have a freer hand." Their masters in the Committee of the Council will be less able to "interfere" than the directors under whom formerly they served, for both the incentive to interfere will be less and the knowledge making interference effective will be less. This will rest, not merely on the considerations already named, but upon the fact that the personnel of the Committee will be much less stable than that of the Directorate, shifting with party and other expediencies. If, as often happens, a different chairman comes into office every few years, the control of the Council over the permanent officials is necessarily weakened. This virtually means that instead of the Council controlling and directing the permanent officials, the latter "manage" the Council, suggesting or imposing the policy which is best or most convenient for them. This may mean a very efficient and enlightened policy, if an able, public-spirited or ambitious man gets into the saddle as head of the permanent staff. So many a town owes much to a masterful Town Clerk or a go-ahead Borough Surveyor. But it is an uncontrolled or inadequately controlled bureaucracy, subject to all the dangers which attend this mode of government : the essential defect being that no *real* part is taken in this department of policy or administration by the people or their representatives.

Normally the condition I have described will mean that the Borough Surveyor and the manager of the

Electric Lighting Works will have their own way with a minimum of control from the Council: not only current details of management but policy of development and its finance will be largely in their hands. A very important factor in the situation is that these high officials will be securer in their office and their salary than under a company, where, if dividends went very wrong, they were in danger of displacement. So long as they do not get violently at loggerheads with the Committee and the Council or commit some very flagrant act of indiscretion, their tenure of office, with a rise of salary not closely related to economy of management, is tolerably safe, safer than any post in the ordinary business world outside.

In our preliminary discussion of incentives under public enterprise we assumed that this security with other loss of direct selfish stimulus would tend towards torpor, conservatism, and slackness. This, I think, will be the normal result. But there will be exceptions where it will seem to act in the opposite direction. Where an ambitious borough official gets the bit in his teeth, he may seek free scope for his energy and ambition by a reckless go-ahead experimental policy, which he enjoys and for which the town pays. This peril of bureaucracy is confronted on a larger scale in great State departments. A magnificent bureaucrat, with a masterful, expansive, and resourceful personality, seeing the chance of translating his inspirations and aspirations into concrete realities at the public expense, may plunge into all sorts of dubious novelties.

If it be admitted that these risks of undue conservatism and torpor on the one hand, or reckless experimental plunging on the other, flow from an insufficiently controlled bureaucracy, it is evident that their consequences will be felt all through the public business, affecting in various degrees all the employees and their capacities of effective co-operation in the public service.

In considering the relative efficiency of officials under

private and public enterprise, however, one point of considerable importance must not be ignored. The assumption that the profit-seeking character of private enterprise will lead to a better selection of administrative ability requires qualifications. Where private capitalism has attained its highest structural development, efficiency of administration is often notoriously injured by an abuse of patronage in appointments and promotion of officials and even of subordinate employees. This is particularly true of those great branches of industry where amalgamation has gone so far as to exclude effective competition. In our railways and great banks, for example, the influence of directors and large shareholders is habitually used to procure appointments and to obtain promotion. If these services were nationalised our civil service examination system would certainly raise the level of ability among the higher grades of employees, and if this system of appointment were extended to our local Civil Services a similar gain might attend the socialisation of some at any rate of those municipal services which remain in private hands.

But, bearing in mind the manner in which most public appointments are " jobbed " by Town Councils and other local elected bodies, we are not entitled to make large present claims on this account as any set-off against the " patronage " system under private enterprise.

The general trend of this analysis of the structural changes of industry involved in socialisation indicates several perhaps considerable wastes in controlling and co-ordinating power due to the working of the political method of control of the productive forces, and suggests that this net waste might be disastrous, unless the new public possession generated a new public spirit and new methods of popular control which should counterbalance or prevent this loss of social energy.

But all this is closely connected with a graver charge against Socialism which must now be discussed. " Substitute public for private enterprise : a double process of corruption is generalised. The dishonest use of political power is made possible and profitable in innumerable ways: party politics will be rapidly adapted to purposes of private gain, and an elaborate system of ' graft ' will spread over the whole body of the public industries. Socialism will be a vast spoils system: the struggle between capital and labour which now goes on will be transferred from competitive industry to the political arena where it will rage more destructively than ever with organised bodies of public employees using their votes, not as citizens for public purposes, but as wage-earners to extract higher pay and superior conditions of employment for themselves and their particular trade. Candidates will be returned to Parliament and to other public bodies not as independent persons, not even as party delegates, but as ' kept ' politicians tied to a particular trade, and primarily devoted to seeing that this trade improves its ' pull ' upon the public purse." You have, it is suggested, the beginnings of this vicious system already operating, in the organised pressure brought by unions of teachers, postal employees, arsenal workers upon Members of Parliament and the Government to get preferential conditions of employment for themselves at an increasing expense to the taxpayers. Even now, where the organisations are strong enough, they are constantly trying to interfere with the most economical administration of the public work in which they are engaged, endeavouring not merely to raise their wages, shorten their hours, and to secure pensions which make their conditions of individual employment preferable to those in private businesses, but also to secure an excessive amount of employment for their particular branch of the public service, and practically to insist upon a permanency of work and salary for the maximum number of employees. The influence of Members of Parliament and of other political bodies is used to secure appointments, to obtain advancement, and to prevent dismissals. The worst effect is seen in the appointment and promotion to the higher and more important administrative posts of men chosen for political reasons who are not fully competent.

If these evils are visible in a State where not more than $2\frac{1}{2}$ per cent. of the workers are public employees, what will be the case where the proportion has advanced to 10, 20, or 40 per cent., where all the railway servants, miners, dockers and other large groups of organised workers are put upon the public roll? The great mining districts of the North, the Midlands, and South Wales; such railway towns as Rugby, Crewe, and Derby, would no longer return Members of Parliament to assist in the general work of making and administering laws in the general interests of the nation; even the interests of party would yield place to the narrowest form of trade individualism, and knots of men would sit in Parliament pledged to devote themselves to the supreme end of securing for the workers in a particular industry a bigger pull upon the public purse in pay, pensions, or other advantages. As Socialism advanced further, politics would more and more degenerate into the cockpit of sectional industrial strife, each national trade seeking to advance itself at the interests of the nation as a whole. Every town would be a Chatham or a Plymouth, and the public good would disappear in favour of a number of competing private goods. Incidentally the re-alignment of political forces and issues would lend itself to a fiscal policy of Protection, as politics became more and more a game of pulls between groups of producers, each of which would be urgent to maintain for its members the largest volume of employment at the highest wage and would insist on taxing or prohibiting imports which might impair this policy.

In this indictment of progressive Socialism there are two chief counts which, though connected, are distinguishable. That upon which I have dwelt presupposes the working of party politics upon lines with which we are familiar in this country. Great organisations of public employees, by political pressure, might exert a tyranny over the general body of the public, exacting an excessive pay for an insufficient service. But there is another even graver danger, illustrated in the spoils system of America, where the entire structure of the democratic institutions of the nation has been perverted by the dishonest disposal of public offices. A chief business of an American Congressman or Senator in the eyes of his constituents is to secure assistance to local interests by tariffs, contracts, appropriations, or other grants of public money or special measures of protection : in the eyes of the local members of the party which elected him his chief business is to secure for them lucrative offices. This habitual use of the public resources to feed local, party, and personal interests has so corrupted the party organisations and the entire machinery of democracy in America that the intelligent will of the people does not flow upwards from the electorate, expressing itself in legislation and administration based on sound public policy : it is pumped down from above by party " bosses," themselves the creatures of great business corporations, who mould the government of the country in accordance with the will of their paymasters, disposing of the public offices to evoke the necessary party activity out of the rank and file of the minor party politicians who manipulate in detail the popular votes. Though the people reserves some "kick," some power of independent judgment, expressed in occasional revolts against the tyranny of the machine, this constitutes a very real and grave evil in American democracy. Now, though the system by which in America the great majority of offices change ownership with every change of party government, might not be adopted here (and is certainly inconsistent with efficient Socialism), it is evident that advancing Socialism must leave large numbers of new offices at the disposal of Government and great opportunities for securing the good will of large bodies of voters by improving the conditions of their employment.

The individualist represents that any party government under a popular franchise must succumb to these temptations, and that here, as in America, the party system will become a highly elaborated machine financed by capitalistic interests seeking a protective tariff and other large spoils for themselves and using the socialised services as instruments for assuaging discontent and buying votes. The forms of democracy will survive : the spirit will have disappeared : a vast system of public corruption will have been established for which the unorganised non-socialised consumers and taxpayers will have to pay.

Such is the charge. What is the reply ? In the first place, an appeal to facts turns somewhat the edge of the attack. Do our existing socialised services display these terrible corruptions ? Are our postal employees and public teachers able to exert this tyranny, plundering the public purse for their private gain, and are these services administered ineffectively by reason of political pull ? It is evident that they are not, and that the unions of these employees do not exert the injurious power which in theory they might appear to possess.

Again, supposing, as is doubtless the case, that there is a tendency for the State, after taking over a private industry, to yield to the representations of the employees and to raise the wages and otherwise improve their conditions—such improvement of conditions, as we have seen—is not necessarily, or even normally, a public loss. On the contrary, within certain limits it is a public gain. The claim that the State should be a " model employer " does not merely rest upon the view that it should set a good example and can afford to do so because it has the public purse out of which to pay. It rests on the economic principle that sweating, or any terms of employment injurious to the worker and the efficiency of his family, are a social injury entailing waste in the economy of public resources. Put concretely, it may be said that a large part of the higher wage bill under Socialism would be a public profit, not a loss, a wise economy and not a dole or bribe.

But, it will be retorted, granting the validity of this margin for levelling up, the demands of public employees will not stop there. They will be continually asking for more and will use political pressure to get it. So long as they are numerically a small proportion of the electorate they cannot tyrannise much. But if the State employed 20 or 40 per cent. of the workers, many electoral districts would be entirely in their hands: they would become the dominant force in party politics and would work the machine for their private gain.

It is no use meeting this objection by imputing to the groups of socialised workers a new and lofty spirit of social morality which will enable them to resist temptations to abuse their power. That spirit must be a slow growth; we cannot assume in advance its effective operation. It is safer to admit that they will try to use their power to get for themselves all they can. But how much can they get? Let us assume that Socialism was advanced so far that 10, 20, or even 40 per cent. of the workers were employed by the State, in a variety of public industries, the members of each of which sought to get as much as possible for itself out of the public purse. Either the several public industries would form separate unions, each playing for its own hand, or they would federate and form a single force in politics. In the former case it is evident that their power would be strictly limited. Even the largest public industry, say the railway workers, would form a small minority in the whole electorate, and though through their predominance in certain centres they might bring strong pressure to bear, where political parties were closely balanced, any attempt to raise their economic position much above the level of other public workers would arouse resentment among the latter as well as among the general public who would have to pay for the " favouritism " accorded to the railway workers.

Those who think such jealousy would be a negligible factor can know very little of the workers of this country. There is more force in the suggestion that a powerful combination of employees in the various public services might use their voting power with great effect to extract excessive pay and other advantages for their collective enjoyment by manipulating party politics. This in truth is a grave menace in a socialising State which has not developed its representative system along truly democratic lines. Under our present artificial party system (artificial in that it represents no clear actual cleavage of thought, sentiment, or even interests), it is possible for a very small compact energetic minority in a constituency, devoted to some single issue such as temperance, anti-vaccination or the like, to extort a pledge from one or both party candidates to support legislation : if a sufficient number of successful candidates have given such pledges, the course of legislation in a so-called representative assembly may be vitally influenced by what is the will, not of the public, nor of a majority, but of a small minority.

Small groups of keen politicians have in this manner often exercised an influence quite disproportionate to their numbers in matters where their policy is dictated by purely disinterested motives. Will not local and national groups of miners, railway men or municipal employees utilise this flaw in our representative system far more keenly and effectively in order to extort legislative or administrative measures fraught with direct material advantage to themselves? It would be idle to assert that public spirit, or contentment with the good conditions of their employment, will deter them from such a profitable course.

Some practical Socialists are so alive to this danger as to advocate the disenfranchisement of all public employees. But that is to remedy one disease by introducing a worse one. The larger the adva· ·e of Socialism the graver the injury such disqualificatiᵘ vould inflict upon democratic government. That 10 or 20 per cent. of the citizens should be deprived of the right and duty of contributing to government because they were paid public servants would be a mutilation of the representative system. The fact that they will indisputably tend to use their voting power more for their private advantage, if they find that they can do so, than for the public good, is no reason for disenfranchising them. It is, however, a reason for so reforming the representative system as to deprive them of the power effectively to abuse the franchise. The real danger which we have described consists in the power of a compact minority to obtain a representation which is excessive, to impose its will as if it were the will of a majority, upon an elected assembly. A sufficient remedy consists in proportional representation, accompanied in certain cases of critical importance by a referendum. Proportional representation is no mere fad, not a mere improvement of our existing mode of representation : it is the only method by which the " tyranny of Socialism " can be averted. Under our present misrepresentative party system the danger of an organisation of the public services using the public as their milch-cow is a very real one. Well-organised unions of miners, railway workers, postal employees, etc., would, when they got practice, use the party machines to get far better wages and far softer jobs than fall to the body of outside employees; and such capitalistic interests as still survived (for remember I am not dealing with a completely Socialistic State) would buy their support for their own political designs through the party bosses.

But once set our systems of election upon a properly proportionate basis, no body of public servants, owning special interests, could impose upon the Government a policy unduly favouring these interests. If railroads and mines were nationalised, strong centres of these industries would return some members chosen chiefly to safeguar these special interests in ways which might sometimes conflict with the wider interests of the nation. But it is right and proper that these important interests should be given a fair amount of this direct representation, that there should be some men who can speak with authority and experience of the special needs of special groups of workers. Even if Socialism had gone so far that 20 or more per cent. of the electorate were public employees, this would not give them any of that power to work the party machine, and so to loot the public purse, which would be possible, and I think probable, under the vicious system of representation which prevails at present in this country.

The real peril of advancing Socialism, the fear of a corrupt use of political power, is not a vice of Socialism itself, but one which Socialism discovers in our crude realisation of democratic methods. The individual voter must be educated and trained to use his individual judgment by the larger choice of candidates and the liberation from party trammels which a rational reform of electoral methods will bring.

There is no other way of making Socialism safe than by making democracy real, i.e., by securing representative assemblies which are just and accurate reflections of the will of the electorate and by testing through direct appeals that general will in all important cases where representation fails.

PART III
APPLIED DEMOCRACY

.

CHAPTER I

POVERTY: ITS CAUSES AND CURES

During the last few years we have been deluged with facts and figures attesting the great material progress of the working classes of Great Britain during the last three-quarters of a century. Higher money wages are paid to all classes of regular labour in town or country; falling prices enable these higher wages to secure in most articles of food, clothing, and other goods a still greater rise in the standard of working-class comfort; a larger proportion of the workers are engaged in skilled labour at the higher standard wages; hours of labour are shorter than they used to be; increased opportunities of free or cheap recreation and education are open to most workers; the modern development of city life, the co-operative activities of the workers themselves, the charitable liberality of the richer classes have all contributed to lighten many of the burdens which lay heavy on the workers and to awaken and supply a variety of needs unknown to their ancestors. This general picture of working-class progress is verified by details showing the increased expenditure of workers upon flour, tea, meat, and other necessaries and comforts, and the growth of working-class savings.

No one who reads the history of the "hungry forties" or studies "the condition of the people" as set forth in Engels' *Condition of the Working Class in* 1844 and the Report of the Poor Law Commission of 1834, can question seriously the reality and size of the improvement which has taken place. It may, I think, be safely said that there is no class of regular wage-earners in this country that has not made steady and substantial progress in its standard of material comfort during the last two generations.

There are many who take these general admissions of working-class progress to mean that poverty is disappearing by the process of natural causes, that we need not, perhaps ought not, to endeavour to hasten this natural process: the only duty that devolves upon the more prosperous classes is to alleviate the misfortunes of "the deserving poor" by means of charity, which should be so carefully and charily bestowed as not to injure the spirit of self-help by which all persons of character and industry can lift themselves out of the mire.

The general effect of this blend of optimism and indifference is to induce the public mind to shirk the grave issue which modern poverty presents. Until recent times poverty was regarded as the natural and necessary destiny of a great mass of the people of every country. But two great changes have come over modern life which have shaken this fatalist creed.

The first is a change of sentiment, of moral attitude, the conviction that the good of the people, not of any special class, creed, or interest, must dominate all public arrangements, the tacit general acceptance of the democratic principle that government, both political and industrial, exists to secure " the greatest good of the greatest number."

The second is an economic revolution, the vast extension which modern science has brought about in man's command over Nature for the production of wealth. This command over Nature means the possibility of material comfort for all. It is these considerations that give new force to the pressure of the problem of English poverty to-day.

For, in spite of all the general advance of the working classes to which I have borne testimony, there remains in this land a vast amount of grinding poverty. Mr.

Booth's investigations in London, corroborated by those of Mr. Rowntree for York, indicate that about 30 per cent. of the town populations of the United Kingdom are living in poverty ; that is to say, under material conditions inadequate to maintain them as healthy human beings capable of efficient work. Thirty per cent. of the general population will mean, of course, a much larger percentage for the working classes taken by themselves : it will stamp with poverty more than one-third of the town working population. Several recent inquiries into the conditions of agricultural villages point to the conclusion that the proportion of poverty is even larger in the rural parts. Agricultural labour, at any rate in the southern parts of the country, has shared less than any other class of regular workers in the rise of wages. The broad conclusion warranted by these researches is that fully one-third of the working classes are " poor " in the sense that they are ill-fed, ill-clad, ill-sheltered, living under conditions injurious to health and physical efficiency. Some of this poverty is due to misuse rather than to insufficiency of money income; even this misuse, rightly understood, ranks as a result of poverty, not merely as a cause : such is the vicious circle.

It may be true that a smaller proportion of this poverty than in former times approaches the actual starvation point, but it none the less remains a deplorable and an amazing fact that a third of the working class in the richest country ever known in the history of the world should be living in this state of physical and moral degradation.

For when we survey the actual resources which science and art place at the disposal of a modern civilised people, we recognise that poverty is no longer inevitable, that we now no longer wait for its slow mitigation by natural processes. An intelligent people, confronting the actual causes of poverty and guiding its conduct accordingly, can abolish poverty.

M

There are two fundamental causes of poverty, related in their nature, but here distinguished for convenience of argument:

1. Waste of human power.
2. Inequitable distribution of opportunities.

1. We produce as a nation an annual income of material goods and services estimated at about £1,800,000,000 per annum, and this amount of money income is distributed as wages, profits, interest, rent, etc., to those who own labour-power, business energy, land, or capital, which contributes to this output. This sum of wealth (some of it, alas, is " illth "!) sounds big, and is complacently compared with the much smaller national income of a generation ago. In reality it is very little compared with what we could produce if we applied intelligently and economically our existing powers of production.

Economists are fond of dwelling upon the delicate and elaborate mechanism of industry and commerce, working by intricate adjustment of parts to make and distribute commodities over the face of the earth. In point of fact the machine works very clumsily, with countless dislocations, innumerable wastes of power, and almost intolerable creaking.

Much of this waste is visible. Wherever we look we find during long periods of time great quantities of capital and labour lying idle—unemployed, underemployed, or mis-employed. Everywhere the waste of duplication, new factories built where the existing plant is excessive, new shops arising to divide the custom of established shops, the endless multiplication of agents, branches, commercial clerks, and travellers, the constantly growing proportion of human energy drawn off from effective production to wasteful competition. I do not say all competition is wasteful: our present system requires competition. But where six competing grocers in a neighbourhood do the distributing work which could be done by two, the work of the other four is costly waste. This is the normal state over large areas of manufacture and of commerce.

But the invisible wastes, due to a failure to apply existing funds of knowledge to the actual work of production, are still greater. Anyone acquainted with the sciences of chemistry and mechanics, who knows what is being done in various parts of the world by an intelligent application of these sciences to the arts of manufacture, by improved machinery, utilisation of waste, economies of power, will perceive that lack of efficient education, ignorance, and apathy, absence of keen direction and bold experiment, weigh down enormously the productivity of our nation. Take the conspicuous example of agriculture : read Kropotkin's " Field, Factory, and Workshop," see what is done in a score of different lands by putting brains into work upon the soil, in France, Belgium, Switzerland, nay, in China and Japan, you realise how wealth is stopped at its very source by failing to bring modern science to bear upon that which must ever remain the most fundamental of industries.

Is it not pretty clear that if England could stop these visible and invisible wastes, could organise her actually available resources for the production of wealth, she could treble or quadruple her output of material wealth without any increase of human strain?

It is evident that poverty is not any longer necessary because the nation cannot make enough wealth to " go all round."

Indeed, it is probable that this analysis of waste appears to some readers irrelevant to the main issue. " What has all this talk about insufficient production to do with poverty? There is plenty produced; poverty is obviously due to bad distribution of the wealth that is produced." Now, no one is more fully alive than I am to the defects of distribution; but I nevertheless hold it to be of the first importance to realise the mistake of fastening the responsibility of poverty upon bad distribution as the sole sufficient cause. No doubt it might appear a simple cure for the people of this land to force the Government to distribute the £1,800,000,000 equally in incomes for all the population : this levelling process would yield some £180 per family, luxury for nobody, but no poverty. But then those wise defenders of things as they are readily explain to us how such an attempt to level incomes would so impair the stimulus in the professional, employing, and other brain-working classes that they would no longer do their best work for such a pittance : so the total income would fall far below £1,800,000,000, and perhaps everybody might after all be brought to poverty. Now, nobody really proposes this exact equalisation of incomes, nor does it need serious discussion. I mentioned it in order to lay stress upon the central truth to which it gives prominence. The quantity of wealth available for distribution chiefly depends upon the stimulus afforded to the productive energies of man : this stimulus in its turn depends chiefly upon the opportunity open to every member of the community to do his best work.

The main cause of poverty is inequality of opportunity, because such inequality implies a waste of productive power upon the one hand, bad distribution or waste of consuming power upon the other.

" Equality of opportunity " as a cure for poverty is a familiar enough form of words, but to many it sounds vague and barren. I want to make its meaning plainer. But in explaining poverty as due to inequality of opportunity I must first brush aside one widely prevalent fallacy to which the personal vanity of lucky or successful men gives vogue.

Poverty, these are never tired of telling us, is due to personal inefficiency. Go down among the poor, what do you find? Most of them are ignorant, untrained, feeble, shiftless, thriftless, shirking hard steady work—often drunkards, wastrels, cadgers upon

charity. There is, they tell us, no real lack of opportunity. Opportunities abound for energetic, honest,
and industrious persons : the schoolmaster is abroad—
emigration is cheap—willing, responsible workers can
always get good work and a chance to " rise "—and
then actual instances are cited of capable and steady
men who have risen from the lowest grades of labour
into comfort and independence. In personal efficiency,
education, moral elevation of individual character lies
the slow but only cure for poverty!

Now, while it is quite true that no cure for poverty
will be really effective unless it raises personality, it is
most unprofitable to identify degraded personality as
the cause of poverty.

For such analysis ignores the roots and the soil of
personal efficiency. The factors of personal efficiency,
industry, sobriety, energy of will, quickness of intelligence cannot be got out of ill-born and ill-nurtured
children.

The slum-child who personifies the problem of
poverty, born with low vitality, reared by ignorant and
poor parents on bad food, breathing bad air, exposed to
countless degrading influences, physical and moral, such
a child growing to manhood or womanhood has
commonly lost the power to grasp those opportunities
which are said to lie within its reach. Except in rare
instances of favoured stock, personal efficiency cannot
grow in such a soil. Bad seed sown in poor earth will
not grow into flourishing and fruitful plants, even if
carefully watered, pruned, and protected as it grows.
The material conditions of poorer working-class life are
hostile to the attainment of personal efficiency : they
not merely stunt physical and intellectual growth, but,
still more detrimental, they maim the human will,
sapping the roots of character.

This moral injury is the greatest sin committed by
society against the poor.

But we must go further. Granting his attainment of

a fair standard of personal efficiency, it is not true that an ordinary worker has a reasonable security against poverty.

Individual efficiency cannot produce wealth. The "self-help" commonly imputed to individuals, the ability to earn "an independent livelihood" when closely inspected, is seen to be illusory.

Economically, no man liveth to himself : we are all members of one another. Put in its simplest terms, this means that the worker requires the use of land, tools, and plant, the co-operation of other labourers, and the skilled organisation of industry to give any value to his individual efforts.

Poverty arises from the unfair terms upon which he gets these things. If he enjoyed *equal access* to all these requisites he could get his fair share of wealth, and his poverty, when it occurred, might be imputed reasonably to some personal defect or misfortune on his part.

Practically he has equal access to no one of them. Take, first, land, "the mother of wealth." Not merely is he born in a country the whole of which is marked out as "private property," but he cannot even buy or hire land in order to put his labour into it, except at a prohibitive price, and upon terms which give him no security that he will get the good of his labour. The English land system is the worst in the civilised world : excluding the ordinary labourer from advantageous work upon the land it is a perpetual breeder of poverty. If a poor man wants land, either to work it or for a dwelling, he must always bargain for its use with an owner who is economically stronger and can rackrent him. Decade after decade the burden of housing falls heavier upon the working-class population of our towns, and is a main factor in city poverty. In our villages the housing question is not less serious, for there the land-monopoly gives to one man, or a few, the power to determine whether men and women shall live at all in the place where they are born and bred, or shall be driven out to sojourn among strangers.

The use of some capital is another essential to economic independence. No man can work for himself either on the land, in a handicraft, or in any other business, unless he can get on easy terms some small capital or credit when he needs it. Everywhere for lack of cheap credit the poor are entangled in debt to money-lenders, shopkeepers, or other richer persons, who can take advantage of their extremity of need to drive hard bargains. Again, the ordinary labourer, untrained in business life, cannot set up for himself in any business, or co-operate with his fellows to produce goods which he can sell at a profit in the general market. He cannot buy the services of an organiser or business man so as to utilise his labour-power for his own gain, but is practically obliged to sell his labour-power piecemeal at a " sacrifice " to a business man to be used for profit to the latter.

The labourer, then, cannot get high personal efficiency, and must sell his low efficiency cheap. Poverty, of course, is primarily due to the terms of sale of the labour-power, which is the only means of living for the great mass of the people in countries where there is no " free " land. The worker who sells his labour-power for a living ordinarily bargains for its sale at a disadvantage : he must sell it or he and his family starve; the employer who buys it will not starve, but only lose some " profit " if he fails to buy it. This difference between starvation and loss of profit means a perpetual handicap to the worker in bargaining for wages. He is a weak seller of a perishable commodity, which he must sell continuously in a fluctuating market.

As he sells his labour-power at a disadvantage so he buys the goods he needs at a disadvantage. Free Trade, with its cheap loaf and its more or less cheap meat, mitigates and hides this truth. But it is none the less true that the general fall of prices which has taken place since 1870 has benefited the poorer grades of the working classes less than any other grade of the community, the high prices of shelter, fuel, dairy, and vegetable produce in the towns taking a larger share of their small incomes than in the case of the well-to-do classes. The very poor notoriously pay the highest prices for the worst qualities of goods, compelled to buy in small quantities, and often " tied " to certain credit shops.

The great mass of the low-skilled workers and their families still lie on or below the margin of poverty, subject to conditions of the labour market which preclude them from any reasonable hope of comfort, security, or independence. The " Iron Law of Wages," slightly abated in its rigour, still holds them down.

This natural weakness of a " proletariat " has been alleviated by organisation among the more skilled workers, those whose conditions of employment have thrown them together and laid the basis of effective association in working-class movements.

This organisation has taken two chief forms directed to remedy the two weaknesses on which I have just dwelt.

In order to strengthen the selling-power of labour, workers have formed Trade Unions which, though they serve other useful purposes, are primarily engaged in substituting collective for individual bargains in the sale of labour-power. The general effect of Trade Unionism has been to diminish the superiority of employers in buying labour by increasing the loss or inconvenience they suffer if they over-reach themselves, and to enable a group of workers to refuse to sell at a low price by amassing resources sufficient to keep them for a time without employment. In improving the conditions of employment this Trade Union organisation is materially assisted by the network of Truck, Factory, Employers' Liability and other laws designed to remove particular disadvantages in labour contracts.

As Trade Unionism seeks to improve the selling-power of workers, so the Co-operative movement in its main branch has been directed to improve the buying power of their wages by releasing them from credit shops and the enormous and ever-growing cost of a distributive system which continually absorbs a larger proportion of retail prices in the profits of traders and other middlemen.

Now large sections of the workers have so materially improved their condition by these and other forms of working-class organisation as to induce enthusiasts to hold out hopes that the problem of poverty can be solved by free, voluntary co-operation.

I confess that to myself this notion appears chimerical. It is, indeed, *conceivable* that groups of skilled workers might by private co-operation secure land, credit, education, and business organisation for themselves, and so form independent, self-sufficing, economic societies within the nation. This idea from time to time has floated before the minds, captivating the imagination of reformers; occasional experiments of such free working-class communities have been made, never with durable success. It has sometimes been suggested that the great genuine success of the retail and wholesale Co-operative movement in this country, gradually extending through the various productive and transport processes, might eventually build up a full economic independence for large masses of working-class producers and consumers. Upon this speculation I cannot profitably dwell, but will only remind you how far remote such possibility stands from the actual attainments of the present. Great and worthy as the progress of Co-operation has been in this country, immensely beneficial to large numbers of town workers, its advance has been almost wholly confined to the distributive processes. I am well aware of the successful businesses in productive Co-operation, too often dependent upon outside capital, established in various trades to the great advantage sometimes of workers, sometimes of consumers, sometimes of both.   But proud as co-operators have a right to be of their achievement, they must bear in mind that the great capitalist enterprises of our modern life in mining, and staple manufactures, in transport, banking, and finance, are scarcely touched as yet by Co-operation, and it is hardly conceivable that working-class savings can grow large enough to enable them to be the real owners and controllers of these fundamental forms of modern business.

The large and growing profits of the Co-operative movement, amounting to some nine million pounds last year, form about one two-hundredth part of the general income of our nation.

Moreover, we must not forget that Co-operation and Trade Unionism have been successful movements precisely in proportion as the more extreme forms of poverty have already been got under.   The poorer floating or sinking populations of our great modern cities, the weak agricultural labourers of our villages, cannot and do not help themselves by Trade Unionism or Co-operation.   Their weakness, ignorance, inefficiency, render vigorous, continuous organisation for such purposes impracticable.

The idea that the poor can help themselves, either as individuals or collectively, without mastering and using the public organisation called Government, can only be maintained by those who refuse to analyse the conditions of poverty.   For the evil conditions which preclude the poor from gaining personal efficiency, which oppress them when they seek to sell their labour-power, and when they seek access to land or capital or skill or knowledge, are fastened upon them by *laws* relating to the ownership and use of the material and intellectual resources of the nation.

Those who share or support the monopolies, vested interests, or superiorities of bargains, which I have named, usually deride the notion that changes of law can do much for the poor. Do not be deceived by this depreciation of politics and laws. If it is true, as I maintain, that most of these inequalities of opportunity which oppress the poor are produced or sustained by unjust and unprofitable laws, it is folly to suggest that any effective remedy of poverty can come without alteration of these laws. It is true, that State action in changes of law will not in itself cure poverty, but it can enable poverty to cure itself by securing liberty for all to use their powers to the best advantage for their own gain and for the common good.

There is something pathetic in reading the history of the great Chartist movement to recall the enthusiastic confidence of the workers of that day in the immediate efficacy of mere political machinery. Give us, they said, shorter Parliaments, ballot, etc., and the will of the people will find free expression in legislation for the common good. Most of the six points of the Charter, not all, have been won, but now we need a new People's Charter with six new points :—

(*a*) The value and the use of land for the People. Public ownership or full control of the city by the citizens, the village by the villagers, and powers for local government to acquire agricultural land at reasonable prices and to let it to small holders with fair conditions of tenancy.

(*b*) Public ownership of the effective highways of the country, railways, tramways, canals, and suppression of the abuses of " shipping conferences " controlling transport on our waterways.

(*c*) Public organisation of credit and insurance, essentials of modern business. The largest of our national wastes is the waste of public credit, and the practical abandonment of the monetary business, which rightly forms a State function, to private profitable enterprise.

(*d*) Full freedom of education : equal access for all

to the social fund of culture and of knowledge. The right of the community to secure for every citizen the fullest and best use of his individual gifts and powers should be enforced even against the alleged rights of parents to keep their children in ignorance or to drive them prematurely into wage-earning.

(e) Equal access to public law. The entire cost of justice to be defrayed out of the public purse, and the machinery of the law courts free to all citizens. At present, whenever an issue arises between a rich and a poor man, the former enjoys a great advantage in utilising the machinery of the law, the result being that " justice " is bought by the longer purse.

(f) The assertion of the popular power to tax or control any new form of monopoly or inequality which may spring up in the changing conditions of modern communities. This point covers those changes in the machinery of government required to depose the existing " class government " and to substitute an effective democracy. It may be called " socialisation of government " to correspond with the " socialisation of law " which was just named.

No improvements of individual efficiency by education, temperance, technical instruction (important as these things are), no private co-operation under the existing political-economic system, can extirpate or greatly reduce poverty—except so far as it helps in working for political and legal reforms which shall secure the essential conditions for evoking individual efficiency and for supporting it by social opportunity.

This equal opportunity of self-development and social aid, so as to live a good and happy life, is practicable Socialism. It differs from what may be called full or theoretic Socialism in the following respects :—

It aims primarily not to abolish the competitive system, to socialise all instruments of production, distribution, and exchange, and to convert all workers into public employees—but rather to supply all workers at cost price with all the economic conditions requisite to the education and employment of their personal powers for their personal advantage and enjoyment.

There is, of course, no economic or moral finality in such proposals; even if secured they would not bring a heaven upon earth. But they seem to me to represent the measure of reform to which those primarily concerned to stamp out poverty in England in this generation should address themselves.

It is right to add that, not even so interpreted can this charter stand alone. Opportunities proverbially belong to the young. There is a mass of poverty which is past the age of opportunity, but which no wise or humane nation can ignore.

For this reason the curative policy here expounded needs to be supplemented by palliative measures which cannot be defended as organic reforms, but which belong to the realm of public charity. Those who realise, not merely as a sentimental phrase but as a scientific truth, the responsibility of society for poverty, will not grudge the most generous outlay of public money for dealing gently and humanely with the debilitated and often demoralised lives which form the social wreckage of our nation. There are many who cannot stand even in the stream of equal competition, and who are too feeble to grasp opportunities. The aged and the infirm among the poor should be well cared for; the shirker, the loafer, the tramp, and the criminal, must be regarded from the newer, truer standpoint of social responsibility. The degradation of our Poor Law, the brutality of our casual ward, the damnable mechanism with which our prison system seeks to deal with the most delicate problems of human character must all give way to more humane and more intelligent modes of handling our battered types of humanity. With one tithe of the energy and the money, I will not say the science, which goes into our armies and navies and engines of destruction, this work of human preservation might be made to yield noble benefits. We are rich enough to take care of our weaklings, our unfortunates, our physical and moral invalids, and to give them some taste of the real fruits of civilisation from which as wanderers in the wilderness of city poverty they have been precluded. We need not be afraid of pauperising them with public charity: they have a right to claim this alleviative treatment at our hands; if *they* do not so understand this to be the case *we* do, and have no call to make a favour of what, rightly interpreted, is a meagre tardy restitution of opportunities withheld and social benefits denied at times when they might have sufficed to prevent the human decay we are now seeking to arrest.

But urgent as is the need for thoughtful palliatives, we require to set our minds with even more persistency of purpose to the application of the organic remedy for poverty—equalisation of opportunities.

Once realised, this condition brings not only a better distribution of existing wealth, but a prodigious increase of national productivity. Closed opportunities mean torpid minds, slack effort, routine activity: open opportunities stimulate energy, rouse initiative, stir progress. We boast of the pace of modern industrial progress, but this pace is slow compared with what it would become if every man had a full stimulus applied to evoke his best thought and liberate the spark of talent which lies hid in every soul. Here is the great waste that would be saved by securing for every man a fair chance in life. Equality of opportunity would not merely stir individual energy, it would fertilise with fresh accessions of science and of skill large barren or backward tracts of industry.

One final word needs to be said. This equality will not be won without fighting for it. We would that this were not so: gladly would we compass the ends of justice by methods of persuasion or peaceful penetration. But though reason and moral appeals are in the long run the true force of progress, they cannot operate except through a preliminary stage of political and economic struggle. We can only cure poverty by an attack upon the sources of riches. Every rich man—though he seldom knows it—makes many poor: reaping where he has not sown he devours the needed subsistence of many sowers. For riches can only come in one of two ways: either by " sweating," " grinding the faces of the poor " in buying their labour cheap or selling goods to them dear; or by converting to his private use and profit some public property which is needed for the support and enrichment of the common life of society. To discover, to assert, and to achieve the claims of economic justice, this is the only radical cure for poverty.

CHAPTER II

THE HIGHER TACTICS OF CONSERVATISM

If we consider the essence of human progress to consist, not in the increasing control of man over his material environment, but in the increasing realisation of reason and justice in the conduct of human affairs, it is not evident to all men that progress is attainable, or that, if it be attainable, the moral aspirations of mankind play any real part in determining its pace or course. The sceptical view is commonly based upon an economic interpretation of history according to which the acquisition and enjoyment of class or personal power based on property is the one continually dominant factor, all social institutions being moulded and directed by economic considerations, all the ideas and sentiments of religions, politics, art, literature, and morals being ammunition in the hands of warring economic interests. The independence of the higher ideal aspirations is but illusory : examine closely the critical events in the history of any nation, their religious reformations, their political revolutions, nay, even the rise and fate of their architecture or drama, these are but aspects of a conflict expressing a disturbance in the balance of economic power.

" If we examine the hidden mysteries of the social mechanism," writes an exponent of this doctrine, " we shall, I think, be free to admit that the sentimental element surounding all great social revolutions is after all but an illusion."*

This mirage of beckoning ideals, reason, liberty, and justice, is indeed needed often to impel the activities of

---

* Loria, " Economic Foundations of Society," (Sonnenschein,) p. 285.

men, but the real ends and the real motor-power lie in the pressure of economic processes.

This explanation of progress as the mere drive of a *vis a tergo;* physical necessity, is philosophically—even biologically—untenable.

But it would be idle to deny that it contains a sufficient element of truth, when applied to modern social politics, to cause many to doubt the possibility of achieving popular progress by any form of reasonable concerted action.

So far, at any rate, as the politico-economic structure of Society is concerned, history appears to show that the preponderant possession of property, and the control over the lives of men given by property, passes from one class or order to another, from king to barons, landowner to capitalist, from merchant to manufacturer, from entrepreneur to financier, in accordance with changes in the relative importance of certain economic functions. In English history, it is the scarcity of labour following the Black Death, the rise in value of work and the debasing of currency under the Tudors, the power of the new merchant class in the Stuart revolutions, the rising power of the manufacturers of the eighteenth century, the substitution of corporate for individual capitalism, and the growing dominion of finance over industry in our own time—of such nature seem to be the critical events determining ever and anon a fresh shift in the balance of power among the powerful classes, a fresh composition of the political and industrial control. Nowhere are considerations of abstract justice or reason, or greatest happiness of greatest number, real determinants in these changes; one interest, grown more powerful, asserts itself against another grown more weak : king, pope, barons, squirarchy, capitalists, entrepreneurs, financiers, each uses all the power afforded by new circumstances to obtain the largest control of property, and moulds the forms of political and economic government to further the maintenance and increase of its power,

N

If any progress in the nature of extended liberty and wider diffusion of material property comes this way, it is incidental and unintended, a dole or a concession from the possessing or ruling classes, and in no sense a product of the reasonable, intelligent co-operation of the people.   The people cannot help themselves; the have-nots are powerless against the haves.   If the people possess the name of political power through the forms of a liberal constitution or a democracy, it is because the possessing classes have discovered ways of checking, controlling, and dividing public opinion, which render the forms of public government innocuous.   How can it be otherwise?   The class, or classes, in control of the material resources, have leisure to organise methods for conserving their property and power, they can buy men of picked brains or strong bodies to defend their interests with laws or guns, and to confuse or coerce their enemies.

We say that, when the people get education and become intelligent, they will be able to organise and overpower their masters.   " Mighty men may thrash numbers for a time; in the end the numbers will be thrashed into the art of beating their teachers."* But is this true?   The sceptic replies : The means of popular education, the machinery of popular organisation are themselves created, financed, controlled by the possessing classes; the church, the press, the school, the party machinery do not, and cannot belong to the people, for each of these educative organs involves the maintenance of a profession and a plant which are not provided out of the pence of the people, but out of the guineas of the well-to-do and the cheques of the millionaires, and those who pay the piper call the tune. How, then, is it possible that the people shall be allowed to get such education as shall furnish the intellectual and moral sinews of an effective revolt against an oligarchy of vested interests?

---

* Meredith, " Beauchamp's Career,"

Is it not always open to the makers of public opinion to curb, direct, or dissipate the forces of popular discontent before they enter politics, or else to employ them in a futile rotatory action inside the machine, as they do in the democracy of the United States and of Great Britain? Or where the popular temper and institutions of a country are refractory before such acts of management, it is always possible to revert to force, to suspend the forms of popular liberty and to reorganise the machinery of government by a *coup d'etat*. This is the interpretation of the history of South Africa during the last decade of the nineteenth century. Is it inapplicable here? In the last resort the armed forces of the nation are at the disposal of the possessing classes, whose political and economic power represents that public order and safety of the commonwealth which it is the function of an army to safeguard.

Or turn from the political to the industrial arena. "Labour," we are told, "is the basis of all wealth. Let the workers organise so as to present a united front to the employing class, they can enforce their demands for their full share in the product of industry." Can they do this? Is this menace of a general strike a feasible and a logically efficacious policy? In the first place, it may be urged, if the capitalist classes recognise the danger, they can prevent the general organisation of the workers for simultaneous action. By the superior organisation which their smaller numbers, greater ability, and ampler resources furnish they can out-general the workers, harrassing them in detail, corrupting their leaders, sowing dissension between the several trades and localities, buying selected groups by profit-sharing and other preferential schemes of employment, procuring fresh legislation and adjudication favourable to their defence through lawmakers and administrators bound by social and economic bonds of sympathy and interest to support their domination. But if such a general organisation of labour for simultaneous action were feasible upon a national, or even an international scale, a contingency scarce thinkable, its economic command of the situation is by no means obvious. Were Government merely to " keep a ring," preserve public order and leave capital and labour to fight to a finish, the great bulk of the existing stocks of food and other necessaries of life would be the legal property not of the workers but of the employers by virtue of present ownership and command of money: this stock could be increased by the labour of the capitalists and their entourage of servants and unorganised dependents: to this must be added such " free " labour as is in all times available. The straits employers would be placed in would doubtless be serious, but nothing as compared with those of the workers, if these latter kept within the law: for their actual command of food would be infinitesimally small, and they could have no recourse to the machinery of industry to supplement it, for this machinery belongs to the employing class. The whole body of organised workers would be starved into submission —such at any rate is the strict logic of the situation. In no large actual strike have the workers won on the strength of their own saved resources; they have always drawn largely from the funds of other Trade Unions and from the general sympathetic public, from both of which resources they would be excluded upon the hypothesis we are considering.

If it is replied that the workers would not keep inside the limits of the law, but would seize the workshops and instruments of production in order to utilise their labour-power, the struggle at once ceases to be economic and becomes political, or rather, military, a conflict between the armed trained forces of the State defending the interests of capital and an unarmed, untrained rabble. About the issue of such a conflict there can be no doubt.

On the assumption, then, from which we started,

that economic interests are the really dominant, and, ultimately, determinant factors, it seems as if the sceptics had an impregnable position, and that substantial progress in the sense of an increasing power of reason and justice over the direction of human affairs were impracticable. The progress seems to involve a vicious circle; popular progress is only possible by means of popular organisation, organisation requires intelligent direction, intelligent direction depends upon education, and the machinery of education is in the control of interests opposed to popular progress.

Such is, in large outline, the sceptical position. But is it sound? Is progress really illusory, the progressive forces dissipated by this perpetual movement in a closed circle? The very simplicity of the reasoning is entitled to arouse suspicion. Nowhere else does nature present any instance of purely rotatory movement. Everywhere we are confronted in our analysis with the same apparent antagonism between the *vis inertiæ* of the existing order, the vested interests, and that power which we conceive pulsating through nature, and seeking to lift some form of matter to a more complex and highly adapted shape through *variation*. All evolution in inanimate and animate nature, is expressed in terms of this conflict, and nowhere does the conflict resolve itself into the futility of mere rotation. Are we to suppose, that when this conflict is raised to the plane of conscious human life and social forces, the result is different? . . . . .

" But," it may be said, " these fundamental considerations are beside the point, no one seriously disputes the reality of progress in general. The question is whether we are not confronted with an *impasse* in that sort of progress which is involved in the realisation of social justice." We may have every sort of progress that is consistent with the maintenance of a selfish class government in politics and industry, and yet the overthrow of that oligarchy may be unattainable.

But if we test this hypothesis by an appeal to actual history, it certainly appears to break down. Admitting the continuance of class ascendency in politics and industry in modern civilised states, it is easy to show an expansion in the political liberties of the peoples and a corresponding shrinkage of more direct and forcible control by the political and economic rulers: the life of the average citizen is safer and larger, his command over commodities and services is increasing, his intellectual and moral life freer and better nourished. It may, indeed, be replied: " These liberties are concessions of the ascendant classes, the old slave and serf systems no longer pay, the modern domination is subtler and more direct, it requires a higher standard of material comfort, a larger circuit of liberty and a higher intelligence on the part of the helots: but this improvement of the general life of the people does not really diminish the real subjection in which they are kept or realise social ideals opposed to the interests of the master-class." It is not easy to disprove such a contention. Yet the argument really contains in itself an admission of positive progress, for the elevation of the nature and instruments of domination is itself progress: to enforce control by laws is an advance upon the use of naked swords, to govern by working political machines an advance upon open menace. This is indeed the natural course of progress; the vicious circle as it first appeared is no closed circle, but an ascending spiral. The spiral is rightly accepted as the mechanical symbol of social progress, implying the natural course of a more powerful force deflected from a straight upward movement by resistance meeting it transversely. The spiral form explains also the illusion of the sceptic who, falsely identifying the outlook at the several elevations, fails to recognise the gradual ascent.

The most conclusive evidence of the growing power of popular ideas and sentiments is the fact that the vested interests base their defence more and more upon appeals to the supreme court of reason and of morals.

But do not, therefore, let us be misled into supposing that the present immediate object of strife, the question of victory, is higher education or some elevation of the moral standard of the people. Before a really effective demand for the higher forms of wealth, the nobler means of life, can be evoked, sufficiency and security of the material basis of personal efficiency must be won. Economic reforms must take precedence in time : problems of housing and of food, of regular remunerative employment, of access to the land, of greater leisure, of ease and comfort in old age, everywhere stand as barriers to a higher life for the people. Now the real solution of every one of these practical problems involves a successful attack upon vested interests : economic liberty can only be won by the rasing of the fortresses of monopoly. The new shift is not an alteration in the objective of the campaign, but in the methods of conducting it. It is not merely the abandonment of the revolutionary appeals to physical force; the more thoughtful leaders of popular reform perceive that even the weapons of the franchise and legislative power cannot yet be used with much effect. What the present pressing interests of progress demand is the organisation of the intelligence and moral energy of the people for the definite work of economic reform by the overthrow of vested interests and the establishment of economic equality of opportunity, within the nation.

This enables us to understand the new tactics of defence adopted by the possessing classes. Their supreme object is to prevent the popular organisation on a basis of intelligent appreciation of the problem of social progress. There are two chief ways of doing this.

The first is to deny the existence of social-economic problems and to urge the claims of individual moralisation as the only valid and effectual path of progress.

If enough individuals separately win salvation society is saved. The second is to foster the combative competitive instincts of the lower nature of man by urging the necessity and utility of industrial competition within the State and military competition with other States. Thus the moral cohesive forces which would vitalise an organised democracy can be diverted to lower activities and rendered innocuous.

In order thus to divide and degrade the moral and intellectual forces of democracy, an informal sociology is required. Those who watch carefully the influences exercised by the possessing classes over our Universities, churches, political parties, press, and even our literature, art and drama, can see how this body of social theory is consolidated for its defensive work. It is not indeed a consciously constructed or consistent system of thought that is evolved, but rather an improvisation of social theory out of the floating ideas and sentiments of the age.

To this sociology of the vested interests Biology, Psychology, Economics, Ethics, Philosophy, Religion, are all made to contribute special aids. But the staple consists in an illicit extension of certain teachings of biology and a falsification of certain premises of economics. Space will not permit me to describe in detail the composition of this sociology, but only to indicate a few of the concepts and formulæ drawn from the several sources.

From biology as the science which first formulated the modern conception of the evolution of man, the central doctrine of the individual struggle for life as the test of fitness and the means of progress transplanted straight into sociology, has been used to defend the necessity and social utility of individual competition in industry and racial competition in war as instruments of national and international progress. The deep-rooted divergence of species, the strong dominion of heredity, the practical importance of chance individual variations as means of progress, are made to nourish theories of permanent racial and class ascendency based on superiority, and of individual genius and effort as the sole instruments of industrial betterment. Progress is represented as the slow orderly play of physical forces pushing from behind, any attempt to alter or accelerate the pace of which is a baneful disturbance of the order of nature. Any proposed activity of the people through legislation or otherwise is held to involve this disturbance and is denounced as interference with nature.

The neglect of the part which mutual aid or conscious co-operation plays in the true biological conception of the struggle for life is a significant feature of the selective method of this class sociology. Nay, even when the suspension of internecine struggle within the group is recognised as a condition of progress, the lesson deduced is that the suspension implies the fiercer and more effective struggle for life between groups, nations, or races. A whole sociology of imperialism is built on this alleged necessity, ignoring the true central teaching of biology that as man ascends above the rest of animal creation his struggles are directed less and less against his fellowmen, more and more for the control of his material environment.

But the most impudent abuse of biology consists in the assumption that the methods and formulæ of a science concerned with the individual physical phenomena of man can suffice to interpret the social moral phenomena of human achievements, that individual animal evolution constitutes the whole essence of social evolution.

Since the real battle is waged round the fortress of economic privilege, it was only to be expected that the new plastic science of political economy should be moulded and utilised for weapons of defence. And this is indeed the case. That competition secures for the workers in enhanced wages and improved conditions of work the gains of all industrial improvements (in the long run); that the great fortunes secured by entrepreneurs, capitalists, and speculators, are the just and necessary rewards of the social services rendered by their ingenuity, industry, foresight, and organising power; that capital, as the result of thrift, is so mixed up with land values that even rent contains no certain elements of unearned increment; that the workers, as a class, cannot obtain higher wages without increasing their efficiency; that there exists, therefore, no genuine divergence of interests between capital and labour, between employer and employed, landowner and tenant; that all attempts to place increasing burdens of taxation upon capital, or upon the incomes of the rich, will recoil upon the workers by checking business enterprise and the demand for labour; that endeavours to restrict private enterprise in alleged monopolies by municipal or state control or management are alike unjust, and injurious to the common good. These are a few of the weapons of defence taken from the arsenal of conservative economics, and directed against movements of reform.

What speciousness these doctrines contain is dependent on two false assumptions, the first, that free competition, as a general practice, actually exists; the second, that the value of anything depends upon the individual conduct of its owner.

The theories about the benefits of competition, individual efficiency, and rights of property, thus selected out of biology and economics, are supplemented by diverse doctrines drawn from other and more elevated studies. Psychology and ethics are summoned to support a theory of social reform, which concerns itself entirely with the education of the individual character, deprecating the dependence upon legislative aids or any artificial sapping of the self-reliance and self-sufficiency of the individual worker, who has always capacity, if he uses his opportunities aright, to obtain for himself the share of the general wealth which is due to him, and represents his earnings.   The sole sufficient key to all social problems, according to this school, lies in the assertion of the powers of individual character.

The root fallacy here, of course, lies in the false assumptions that any individual living in a social-economic society is capable of self-support, and that he is endowed with a power of will and intellect competent for the effort which he is supposed to be capable of putting forth.   It is bad psychology, for it ignores the reactions of environment upon the springs of individual character, bad ethics, because it ignores the factors of society in forming individual conduct.

Nor do the defenders of the " existing order " disdain such assistance as they can draw from philosophy and religion.   For the less cultured man the crude methods of the orthodox churches still suffice; contented with his place in this world let him occupy his thoughts with bright hopes of another; absorbed in the saving of his particular soul he will not worry himself about the safety of the commonwealth, but will leave politics and economics to his betters.   For the more cultured a finer brand of quietism and mysticism is furnished, sometimes infused with splendid ritual or subtle esoteric appeals, sometimes a colder and more austere philosophy couched, partly in the authoritative conservatism of Hegelian dogmas, partly in the later determinism distilled out of evolutionary science.   These last are the strictly academic contribution to the defences of vested interests, and are particularly calculated to sterilise the liberal sympathies of young intellectuals, so as to deprive the progressive forces of that able generalship which is essential to success.   We can observe how the same selective and deterrent influences are brought to bear upon literature, art and the drama, in a boycott of really critical ideas and fundamental social issues, and a saturation of the public mind with commonplace sensationalism, sloppy sentimentalism, and bizarre frivolity.   The patronage of the finer and the coarser arts of recreation is expressly directed to foster a combative patriotism, and its attendant forms of animalism, a snobbish reverence for rank, fashion and the valuations of the master class, and a contempt for earnestness, sobriety, and reflection : a debased ideal of chivalry is set up with reckless charity in the place of justice, impulse for reason and passing expediency for principle.

There is indeed no close pattern in the texture of this teaching. It is not deliberately woven as a scheme of defence by " vested interests," but is thrown together by the class instinct of self-preservation. In its higher intellectual form it approaches the dignity of a Sociology, in its lower it is a mere appeal to the passions of the animal self. But it is always and everywhere animated by a common purpose, viz., to check the organisation of a popular movement for the overthrow of privileges, and the achievement of " reason " in national and international order.

This is no idly speculative analysis. Nothing is easier than to illustrate in detail how modern theories of Oligarchy, Protection, Militarism, Imperialism, Property and Charity, chief buttresses of the present order, are derived from the sources I have named. As the popular movement for economic justice becomes more conscious, and is carried more into intellectual and moral channels, the more urgent will it become for the vested interests to secure these defences. More and more will the instruments of public education, press, platform, pulpit and lecture room, be paid to impose upon the public mind the sedatives, diversions, and distractions which are found serviceable, and the louder and more indignant will be the genuine disclaimers against the imputation of corruption. But though these grave professors, right reverend fathers, right honourable statesmen, and sagacious editors, may not know it, the finances which support their institutions are derived from rents, monopoly profits, and other forms of unearned income, and they will fight with such intellectual and spiritual weapons as they can wield for defence of the social-economic order which sustains them.

They will be required to deter and to confuse a clear understanding of the economic and spiritual structure of society, and of the rationalisation of progress dependent on this understanding. As an essential of this defence, they must pretend and believe that their teaching is disinterested and unbiassed, and that their financial dependence does not tarnish their intellectual and spiritual liberty.

Can these defences of the ascendant classes be made effective so as to break or to postpone indefinitely the attack of an organised people? I think not. There is a certain growing irony in the situation. For while the ascendant classes are with one hand building these elaborate moral defences, with the other they are supplying their assailants with the sinews of war. For the very conditions of modern profitable exploitation favour the physical and intellectual solidarity of the people: modern capitalism makes directly for moral democracy. The new methods of industry demand individual intelligence and close complex co-operation among large bodies of workers: the mere machine tender and single-process man is not increasing but diminishing in proportion to the workers whose work involves elements of responsibility and skill. The large-city life imposed by modern industry is at length beginning to bear fruit in a clearer civic consciousness and capacity of co-operation for civic ends. Modern industrialism cannot proceed without increasing co-operation and solidarity of the masses as workers and as citizens: these processes of formal integration cannot fail to generate and feed a fuller and more intelligent popular consciousness. It is this consciousness, enlightened and moralised, that forms the soul of the progressive movement. Upon its growth depends the development of plain popular ideas and sentiments, of a reason and a justice, which will neither be coerced, corrupted nor bemused, by the defences set up by the spiritual mercenaries of the vested interests.

If the struggle were merely one of wits, a sophistical swordplay, it might well seem that the longer purse here, as elsewhere, might buy the better advocates, and so make their defences always adequate. But justice is a great ally. When the struggle is on the plane of brute force, numbers and justice may indeed be overborne, but every elevation of the plane of struggle raises their power. Thus the efficacy of the cause of progress is logically justified, as it is practically demonstrated, by a growing use of spiritual weapons. For the great strength of the cause of the people lies in the substantial justice of its demands for economic equality, and in proportion as the popular intelligence and will are enlightened will they be able to resist the great temptation, to revert to the physical force in which they wrongly imagine themselves superior, and to choose the higher struggle, where reason and justice will befriend them.

Popular progress is not rightly measured in terms of material prosperity, nor does it consist in the destruction of the economic monopolies of the possessing classes, but this levelling of material opportunities is the first esential condition to the free development of the higher life of the people: it is the prime basis of all true liberty, and, once substantially attained, opens a new economy of progress in every field of organised activity.

This methodology of progress, asserting a priority in time for economic reforms, implies no disparagement of intellectual and moral reforms, nor does it revert unconsciously to the narrowly conceived economic interpretation of history rejected at the outset of this analysis. While it is desirable that the main body of our reformatory forces should be at present directed to securing these economic bases of popular advance, this process of direction is itself a spiritual movement, involving a rally and an organised arousal of the latent intellectual and moral energy of the people. While, therefore, in the region of concrete reform work temporal priority must be accorded to economic achievement, or in other words, we must improve the soil before we can hope to grow the fruits of a higher humanity, the actual initiative is drawn from the domain of moral character and intelligence. Moreover, each step in the improvement of the economic environment of a people or a class is only secured so far as it is attended by two results; first, a more or less conscious and, therefore, moral readjustment of the entire economic resources of each group or family, raising the quality as well as the quantity of the "standard of comfort;" secondly, an increased power of assimilating the moral and intellectual opportunities presented in that improved spiritual environment which it is the function of distinctively religious, ethical, and educational reformers to mould, for the satisfaction of the higher human appetites and the erection of a higher standard of life.

CHAPTER III

THE SOCIAL PHILOSOPHY OF CHARITY ORGANISATION

It must have occurred to many to ask what the writer of the 13th chapter of the First Epistle to the Corinthians would have thought of charity that was "organised." And yet the need for some organisation is generally admitted. The narrowing process by which the term "charity" has passed from its early place as the expression of the broadest and most elevated principle of spiritual life to describe the perfunctory relief of certain material needs has a significance at once too subtle and too large for treatment here. It is not, however, difficult to mark the definite change by which, even in its narrow connotation of almsgiving, virtue has passed out of it and left it a prey to those abuses which modern rational philanthropy seeks to remedy. So long as gifts or doles are the direct expression of true human sympathy with individual needs—a personal aid which is a natural accompaniment of neighbourly feeling, such help as may be bestowed without condescension in the giver or shame in the receiver—no injury attends the kindly service. The large flow of reciprocal charity which still passes among many sections of the poor, amounting sometimes indeed to an incipient communism of goods, retains the true spirit of the virtue intact. Whole nations in a primitive condition of life, where there exists an approximate uniformity of economic character, still practise a free hospitality and bounty which breeds no wrong. Even where wider divergence of rank and material power exists, as in certain feudal societies, aid could pass harmless from rich to poor when it was regarded as belonging to a social system based on reciprocity of personal services.

But under the pressure of forces which break up these old orders, charity, like other personal services, is commuted for payments of money. This is the origin of evil. The rise and the segregation of a moneyed class, whose moral status seeks to reconcile the sentiment of pity for vaguely known distress with a sensitive shrinking from closer personal contact with concrete cases of suffering, devitalises charity. The outward acts are entirely severed from the inward grace, and charity stagnates and grows corrupt. All the specific defects of ill-ordered charity arise from this separation of the form from the spirit—misdirection, waste, overlapping, professional parasitism of every order and degree.

In setting itself to discover and to stamp out pernicious forms of almsgiving, to order, direct, and economise the charitable energy which comes from the moneyed classes in gifts or endowments to unknown recipients, the Charity Organisation Society performs a service of great and easily recognised value.

Most of the work seems to be performed with zeal and with discretion. Accusations of hard-heartedness from blind sentimentalists are not unnaturally treated by the society as complimentary testimony to the saneness and rationality of its methods. In spite of the unpopularity which must inevitably attach to those who are often compelled to set reason against generous impulse, the society is making in many places a deep impression upon social work. An ever-widening recognition of the evils of " indiscriminate " charity and of the need of a thorough sifting for the discovery of " helpable " cases and right modes of help, attests the educative influence which the Charity Organisation

o

Society is exercising on the public mind. Even the clergy hear and tremble.

The chief work they have essayed is, by establishing a class of expert middlemen, to provide a substitute for the broken personal nexus between donor and recipient. In the course of such work, and the study it involves, it is only natural that certain rules of general application to classes of cases should emerge. For some time the active workers on branches of charity organisation have acknowledged certain *media axiomata* as binding on them in the treatment of their cases. But of late it has become apparent that some of the most active organisers, especially in the Metropolis, are indulging more ambitious claims. From the narrow empirical rules they ascend to principles, or perhaps it would be more true to say, they interpret their rules in the light of super-imposed and externally derived principles. Those familiar with the tone and method of their recent criticism of the new social movements are now aware that this group of influential leaders in charity organisa-tion work lay claim to an exclusive possession of the right principles of social reform in relation to all pro-blems of the poor. What exactly were these principles it was not, until lately, easy to ascertain, though their broader tenor was unmistakable. But we have now a book* which, from the conjunction of its authorship and its avowed object, may be taken as an authoritative revelation of this charity organisation philosophy. Covering, more or less, the whole field of social study, from the minutiæ of Poor Law administration to the vague vastness of " the general will," it brings theory and practice into contact in a most instructive way. We are now able for the first time to test the logic and the " scientific " character of charity organisation.

The value of such inquiry widely transcends any interest which may attach to the conduct or the *personnel*

---

* " Aspects of the Social Problem," by various writers, Dr. Bosanquet, Mr. C. S. Loch, Mrs. McCallum, Miss Dendy.

of the Charity Organisation Society. For the statement of principles which these writers make will be discerned as the clear and conscious expression of the repugnance and distrust strongly but mistily conceived by the great majority of the " propertied " classes, when their attention is directed to the claims which the poorer classes are making for a larger social support in their efforts to attain decent material conditions of life. The book may therefore be regarded as an authoritative statement of the opposition of the propertied classes to schemes of old age pensions, feeding of school children at the public expense, public provision of work for the unemployed, and other proposals of public aid for the poor and needy.

Such schemes are one and all condemned with the same condemnation that is meted out to indiscriminate charity and wasteful doles. They sap the sense of responsibility in the individual, weaken his incentive to effective work, and break up the solidarity and unity of family life. With the practical assumptions which underlie this criticism—*i.e.*, that every willing worker can get work sufficiently regular and well-paid to enable him to provide for himself and his family all that is necessary for a decent life, to set by enough to keep him in old age, and to secure him against all the contingent misfortunes and burdens of a working life—we shall deal later on. It is more convenient to approach the position of this social philosophy by turning to that theory of the " dole " which has arisen most naturally from charity organisation work, and by seeking to understand this theory in relation to the wider principle of property which is laid down as the basis of the social philosophy of this school of thinkers.

It is now commonly recognised that a dole is injurious in its direct effect upon the recipient, and in its indirect effect upon others. It acts as a " demand for idleness " and thus weakens character. But why is a dole injurious to the recipient and to society? Why does it degrade character? The real answer is a simple one. It is an irrational mode of transfer of property. Let Mr. Bosanquet explain.

" The point of private property is that things should not come miraculously and be unaffected by your dealings with them, but that you should be in contact with something which in the external world is the definite material representation of yourself." It is true this passage occurs in an essay defending the institution of private property, but it casts so clear a light upon the theory of doles that I quote it here. A dole is condemnable because it comes " miraculously " to the recipient and not as a natural result of personal effort; it is not a " definite material representation " of himself. These charitable " windfalls " violate the rational order of life, lead weakly human nature to detach the idea of enjoyment from related effort, to expect an effect without a cause. Thus false notions are engendered which break the back of honest regular effort.

Nothing can be more convincing than this condemnation of the dole, derived from the theory of private property. But why stop at doles? Are there no other forms of private property which should stand in the dock with " doles " to the poor? How about gifts and bequests to the rich? Do they too not come " miraculously " ? Are they " affected by your dealings with them " ? Are they " definite material embodiments " of their owners? Here no question arises as to the just limit of the right of the donor or legator over his property. Mr. Bosanquet in his theory of private property has chosen to take his stand by " origin "; his test of valid property is the way it comes into the possession of its holder. Why do the charity Organisation Society and their philosophers constantly denounce small gifts to the poor, and hold their peace about large gifts to the rich? We might press the application of this admirable rule of private property a little further and ask whether the economic rent of land

and certain elements in the profits of invested capital, do not come under the same category of the "miraculous," or, whether they are the natural results, the "material representation," of the productive efforts of the receivers. Can anything be more miraculous than that I should wake up to-morrow and find certain shares which to-day are worth £100 are then risen to £105? These gains which grow "while men sleep," are they sound forms of private property according to Mr. Bosanquet? The positive defence of private property rests, according to Mr. Bosanquet, upon the need which every one has for possessing "a permanent nucleus in the material world" wherewith to help to plan out his life as a rational whole. I here suggest that his view of private property passes a twofold condemnation upon economic rents and other unearned elements of income. Firstly, by enabling a man to reap where he has not sown, by divorcing satisfaction from previous effort, they crush the sense of independence in the recipient and derationalise his life. Secondly, since all "unearned" elements of income are truly the earnings of the work of some one else, or of society, such individual or such society, by losing the natural reward of its effort, is disabled from realising itself. The ground landlord who "realises himself" in the rents he draws from his slum property is preventing the docker and the seamstress from realising themselves, and is destroying for them the possibility of rationally organising life. Do the Charity Organisation thinkers apply their solicitude for the maintenance of moral responsibility in these directions? No! their logic makes a dead halt on the other side of this just economic application. They are all fear lest the poor should suffer from the degradation and the ignominy of receiving something they have not earned. Yet they never lift their voice to save the characters of the well-to-do which are constantly assailed by these same demoralising forces. It never seems to occur to them that charity is perhaps a

feeble sort of conscience money, an irregular and inadequate return of fragments of unearned income to
those who have earned it, and who are disabled from
ordering their lives in decency and reasonable care
because it has passed from their legal possession in those
processes of economic bargain where the poor are taken
at a disadvantage.   If there is any truth in this, indiscriminate and sentimental charity has a certain natural
support which can only be destroyed by a full and
logical application of Mr. Bosanquet's theory of private
property.

I have said that Charity Organisation thinkers do not
face this demand that one and the same law be applied
to rich and poor.   Mr. Bosanquet, however, is far too
keen a reasoner not to perceive the awkward pressure
of this argument, and in a single passage of almost
unparalleled audacity endeavours to turn it :

"The Socialist" he admits, "may say," (why he should give a
monopoly of common-sense to the "Socialist" is not clear!) :
"'Is not, at least, inherited or unearned property an equally
pernicious subvention to the rich as out-relief to the poor?' I
point out one distinction, and then give my general answer.   Property is within the owner's control and is a permission to him to
choose his work—of course, an enormous indulgence.   But Poor Law
relief is not in the recipient's control, is a payment for idleness, and
is not sufficient to set the life free to choose work.   A large pension
or gift of property to a man not yet demoralised would probably do
no harm.   Great expenditure which 'sets a man up' does not as a
rule demoralise ; it is the small chronic subventions, which give no
freedom and are actually consequent on the failure of the social will,
that cause demoralisation.   I do not think that it can be denied
that property *may* have a similar effect.   Wherever it distracts from
one social vocation, without forming the basis of another, then it
operates as out-relief pure and simple."

Now, why is one class to enjoy " an enormous indulgence " at the expense of another class?   Why are some
people to have " permission to choose their work " and
not others?   Why are we told that property *may*
distract from work and not that it has a natural tendency to do so?   These are a few of the questions

which the effrontery of this argument evokes.   But let us keep to his main distinction.   Three criteria of bad " subventions¹" are proposed—insufficiency for freedom, payment for idleness, absence of recipient's control. The first need not detain us.   It is not the design of Poor Law relief " to set the life free to choose work;" but if it were, Mr. Bosanquet would be the last to admit that out-relief of twenty shillings a week to all applicants sufficed to place out-relief on a common basis with the " property " which he champions.   As to " payment for idleness," this is a slipshod way of describing poor relief.   Destitution, not idleness, is the direct condition of the receipt of " relief."   Idleness may or may not be the cause of destitution; but the meagre sum paid as out-relief is not a temptation to a state of idleness commensurate with the knowledge of the safe possession of a private competency.   Take a rough-and-ready test, the only one available; the life of an average out-pauper has embodied far more painful effort for the public good than the life of an average gentleman of independent means.   The test of results would not show that out-relief as actually administered was a demand for idleness to nearly the same extent as the possession of unearned property.   Lastly, Mr. Bosanquet thinks that regularity and full control on the part of the recipient favours good use.   But if Poor Law relief were in the recipient's control, if he had a right to demand his five or ten shillings weekly, and to receive it regularly, would this relief approximate towards sound property?   Surely the united voice of the Charity Organisation Society was clamorous in its repudiation of the enormities embodied in Mr. Charles Booth's Pension Scheme, on the very grounds that the pensions are proposed to be given regularly, and are to be at the free call of the recipient, independently of those considerations of individual needs and merits which are the basis of the social control vested in boards of guardians over the payment of out-relief. If Poor Law relief was large enough to " set up a man," was regular in its payments, and at the call of the recipient—that is if all the true conditions of sound " private property " were observed, we should surely have a form of Socialism the most foolish in conception and the most demoralising in its actual results that could possibly be imagined. Yet if Mr. Bosanquet's distinction has any meaning, he would be forced to admit that these reforms would put our poor-relief on a level with the inherited or unearned property he is defending. If not, what does he mean?

One phrase of positive enlightenment his argument contains. Property is bad when it does not form " the basis of a social vocation." This brings us close to the root fallacy of his reasoning. Private property he justifies solely by the use to which it is put. If an owner uses his ground rents or his monopoly-profits as " the basis of a vocation," returning to society by his voluntary effort what he chooses to regard as a *quid pro quo*, he is blameless. So " unearned incomes " are treated as a social " trust," a " charge." To use Mr. Bosanquet's own ingenious words, " if one has enough to live on, that is a charge—something to work with, to organise, to direct."* Mark what has taken place in passing from the application of the theory of property in the case of " doles " to the case of " unearned " incomes. Doles were shown to be pernicious by reason of their origin, *i.e.*, as windfalls; unearned incomes are to be tested not by origin but by use. If they are put to a good use, we are to keep silent about their origin, and about the injury which their payment inflicts upon those whose work they represent and who need them for self-realisation. The ground rents of London are a trust, a " charge " socially bestowed upon the Dukes of Westminster, Bedford, Portland, etc.; society has designed them so as to give these noblemen " something

---

* "Civilisation of Christendom," pp. 334-5.

to work with," an opportunity to serve London and to be a glory and adornment of our social life; if they faithfully execute this "trust," fulfill their high "vocation," they have earned their ground rents,* if not —well for this not very improbable contingency Mr. Bosanquet and his friends make no provision ! What are they prepared to do when the "trust" is plainly violated? Will they provide means for deposing the fraudulent trustee? Of this we have no word. To speak candidly, this talk about a "charge," a "trust," is a wanton abuse of language, applied as it is to describe elements of income which pass to the owners from exercise of sheer economic might. That this power is generally exercised legally there is no question, but that in any true sense it has received the conscious endorsement of society in consideration of services to be rendered, which alone could justify its description as a "charge" or a "trust," is an absurd suggestion. Such language, it is true, is no invention of Charity Organisation philosophers. Its close parallel is found in the sophistry by which some of the officials of the early Church sought to reconcile the teaching of the Gospel with the tenor of economic practice. St. Clement of Alexandria writes :

"Our Lord does not, as some suppose, command the rich man to throw away his possessions, but to cast from his heart the love of gold, with all those cares and preoccupations that stifle the germs of life. . . . . What new thing does the Son of God teach us in this? *Not an exterior act*, such as many have performed, but something higher, more perfect and more divine, the out-rooting of passions from the soul itself and the renunciation of all that is alien to its nature. . . . . Worldly goods should be considered as materials and means to be used for pious purposes, to be turned to good account by those who know how to use them skilfully. " †

How admirably is this old teaching modernised in Mr. Carnegie's "Gospel of Wealth," the notion that the

---

* The following gem of academic phraseology embodies this idea : " Property is mediate payment with responsibility " (p. 333).
† " Christian Socialism." Nitti p. 70.

"millionaire" is a creature divinely ordered and endowed to make piles of money on condition of spending it freely in his lifetime for the public good, though not always, I fear, in modes that would satisfy the scrutiny of the Charity Organisation Society. This langauge indeed emerges in the philanthropic cant of all ages. When we are dealing with the poor, we are to brace their character and to remove everything that enervates and induces to idleness; when we are dealing with the rich, we must encourage them to make a good use of the means which, in their origin, are helping to maintain poverty. We must simply remember "if one has enough to live on, that is a charge." We need not investigate too curiously how "one" comes to "have enough to live on"! "No, we are not economists," say these gentlemen, when they are invited to trace back "unearned incomes" to economic rents and the superior bargaining power of the rich as compared with the poor. The answer is: "You are economists when it suits your purpose; your condemnation of the effects of indiscriminate almsgiving, or the operations of the Poor Law, is based on 'economic' reasoning, but your 'economics' are selective and partial in their application."

By trying to stop the free flow of charity, while refusing to recognise the social economic forces which cause poverty, Charity Organisation thinkers assume that dangerous position which is known as "sitting on the safety valve." The mediæval Church acted more wisely, winking at the practice of the luxury and monopolies which its theory condemned, on condition that the rich beneficiary gave lavish largess in public and private charity.

> "Yet cease not to give
> Without any regard ;
> Though the beggars be wicked,
> Thou shalt have thy reward"

was the deliberate advice of a divine like Crowley writing in the sixteenth century. With just instinct did theologians recognise that the stoppage or even the narrow restriction of charity was likely to endanger the fabric of feudal society by disclosing to the light of day the foundations of social and economic inequality which supported it. The keener sighted of them saw then, as the keen-sighted business man sees now, that millionaire munificence, by giving back in doles a portion of the profits of monopoly, can not only turn the edge of public envy, but obscure the nature of the true social issue by the plausible suggestion that the social problem can find a safe solution in the " moralisation " of the individual employer.

The rejection of " doles " as a treatment of poverty, combined with a refusal to apply their method of criticism to the economic structure of society as a whole, drives the Charity Organisation philosophers to that assertion of the independence and responsibility of the individual family which is their basic conception. Private charity or organised social support by pensions or other modes of subvention will, they think, crush this individal responsibility which is the only source of social progress.   This brings us to the crucial question : Is this individual responsibility an actual fact, and does it yield a force competent to the gradual solution of the social problem?   Responsibility implies ability.   Are poor families able, each and all, to gain for themselves, by the exertion of such powers as they actually possess, a condition of material comfort and moral decency? The Charity Organisation Society's philosophy asserts this ability, and in support of its assertion adduces (1) evidence of fact; (2) a theory of moral autonomy.

Mr. Loch holds that better administration of the Poor Law has shown " that the alleged impossibility of the poor to maintain themselves or provide for their future has, in fact, disappeared," and that " old age pauperism can be gradually eradicated, except in so far as it is the result of sickness, incompetency, or moral defect." Mr. Bosanquet says : " I look on the exceptional case of destitution by pure misfortune in a manner analogous to that in which I regard a legal offender who is free, by some accident, from moral responsibility "—*i.e.*, there are no economic forces which at present by their normal action tend to maintain destitution. Again, the latter writer informs us : " Material conditions are necessary to existence; but they are themselves dependent to an enormous extent on the energy of the mind which they surround."

What it all comes to is this : that the poor can provide for themselves, and need not be poor if they choose to exert themselves.

Now, so far as the assertion of this fact goes, it is supported, partly from Poor Law statistics, and partly from the *ipse dixit* of Charity Organisation investigators, who allege that poverty is always, or nearly always, associated with personal defects.

So far as Poor Law statistics are concerned, they may be at once ruled out on the ground that pauper figures have no fixed or ascertainable relation to poverty. " Pauperism " can be eradicated by changes in the administration of the Poor Law, but such fact could be no evidence of the disappearance or diminution of poverty.

The argument from personal experience is vitiated by two fallacies. First, the ancient fallacy of " any and all." In American schools it is not unusual to encourage the boys by reminding them that by industry and perseverance, any one of them may rise to the position of President of the United States; but to say that all of them could attain the position would be plainly false. Yet the individualist argument by which our Charity Organisation thinkers seek to show that because A. or B. or C. in a degraded class is able, by means of superior character or capacity, to rise out of that class, no one need remain there, contains the same fallacy. It assumes what it is required to prove—viz., that there are no economic or other social forces which limit the number of successful rises. It assumes that every workman can secure regularity of employment and good wages; that the quantity of "savings" which can find safe and profitable investment is unlimited; and that all can equally secure for themselves a comfortable and solid economic position by the wise exertion of their individual powers. Now if there exist any economic forces, in their operation independent of individual control, which at any given time limit the demand for labour in the industrial field and limit the scope of remunerative investment, these forces, by exercising a selective influence, preclude the possibility of universal success in the field of competitive industry. All economists agree in asserting the existence of these forces, though they differ widely in assigning causes for them; all economists affirm the operation of great tidal movements in trade which for long periods limit the demand for labour and thus oblige a certain large quantity of unemployment. The Charity Organisation Society's investigator naturally finds that the individuals thrown out of work in these periods of depression are mostly below the level of their fellows in industrial or in moral character, and attributes to this " individual " fact the explanation of the unemployment; he wrongly concludes that if these unemployed were upon the same industrial and moral level as their comrades who are at work, there would be work for all. He does not reason to this judgment, but, with infantile simplicity, assumes it. This arises from a curious limitation which the Charity Organisation Society places upon the meaning of " fact." Professing to be devoted lovers of " facts," and to be the exclusive possessors of the facts relevant to the study of poverty, they confine themselves wholly to facts in their bearing on individual cases, ignoring those facts which consist in the relation of individual to individual, or, in other words, " social " facts. This " monadist " view of society we presently shall see illustrated in their theory; here we observe how it vitiates their study of facts.

All larger social and economic facts are consistently excluded from this view. Thus they enable themselves to affirm the individual responsibility of the family as a " fact," in face of all the teaching of social science, which proves that in all the ordinary economic issues of life, upon which the stability and solidarity of family life depends—e.g., the price of labour, the regularity of employment, the effectiveness of saving—the independence of the family is ever less and less. Such " facts " do not come within the ken of the Charity Organisation Society.

The second fallacy rests upon another equally unwarranted assumption. Admitting not only that any energetic individual may solve for himself the social problem, but that all, if equally energetic, might do so, is it possible that this moral energy should be generated in the existing environment of poverty? Let us even admit with Mr. Bosanquet that material conditions are largely dependent on " the energy of the mind which they surround," we have not proved the " ability " to provide, which is of the essence of " responsibility." A true realisation of higher wants and the means of attaining them is the driving force in individual effort. The environment, material and moral, of the residuum, constantly thwarts the growth in consciousness of these higher wants, so that the energy, granting it to exist, remains inert. It is futile to urge, " if a man has energy he can help himself " when you know that the conditions of his upbringing and his whole life preclude the birth and growth of that energy.

The Charity Organisation philosophy, crystallised in the single phrase " in social reform, then, character is the condition of conditions," represents a mischievous half-truth, the other half of which rests in the possession of the less thoughtful section of the Social Democrats and forms the basis of the cruder Socialism. Neither individual character nor environment is "the condition of conditions." The true principle which should replace

these half-falsehoods is a recognition of the interdepend-
ence and interaction of individual character and social
character as expressed in social environment.   The
eloquent exponent of the " general will " and the spiritual
solidarity of society, when he comes to practical applications, ignores the need of corporate institutions of social
support, through which " the general will " may find
expression and achieve its ends, and relies for social
progress upon the unsupported initiative of the
individual will considered as a *primum mobile*.   The
application of this social philosophy by Mr. Bosanquet
and his friends makes it perfectly plain that the " character " which is the " condition of conditions " is
individual character.   Whatever some of them may say
in more enlightened moments, this doctrine underlies
their practice and is sheer monadism; it looks upon
society as embodied in the separate action of individual
wills, without allowance for any organic relation among
those wills, constituting spiritual solidarity.   The
principle that individual " character is the condition of
conditions " is much worse than a half-truth in its
application.   For it is used to block the work of practical
reformers upon political and economic planes, by an
insistence that the moral elevation of the masses must
precede in point of time all successful reforms of
environment.   Plenty of people are only too willing to
listen to insidious advice which takes the form : Why
disturb valuable vested interests; why trouble about
ground values; why stir a general spirit of discontent in
the masses; why suggest " heroic " remedies for unemployment, when all that is needed just now is a quiet,
careful, organised endeavour to induce habits of sobriety
and cleanliness in the homes of the poor, to teach them
how to expend their money more advantageously, to
practise saving habits, and gradually, by gentle persistent
endeavour, to build up individual character?   To most
who have not studied the industrial structure of society
it sounds reasonable to suggest that such moral reforms

should come first. In reality it is a falsehood. In the education of a class, as of an individual child, the historic priority of attention must be to the *corpus sanum*, the material physical environment, in order that the conditions of the *mens sana* may exist. Though moral reform may be prior in "the nature of things," economic reform is prior in time. Each reform of economic and social conditions can only be effectual, it is true, if it act as a means of elevating character, and as a stimulus of individual effort, and a general view of the elevation of an individual or a class standard of life will therefore present itself as a constant interaction of improved conditions and improved character. When prime conditions of material comfort and security are once attained, the conscious activity of the individual will and energy will play a larger part, and will often operate as direct cause of economic betterment. But in dealing with the inert nature of the residuum, direct social support aiming at the improvement of material circumstances will play a larger part, and while each step in economic improvement must be accompanied by a moral rise, the external step will precede in time. This does not, as might appear, prejudge the issue whether the social forces in their ultimate analysis are to be described as moral or economic, does not assume the Marxian interpretation of progress, but simply affirms the fact that so far as the historic order of improvement of the condition of the " residuum " is concerned, the earliest impulses to progress reach them in the form of changes of material environment. The fatal consequences of ignoring this truth are seen in Miss Dendy's treatment of the occupations of " the residuum" which assigns the low nature and irregularity of these occupations as the result of the character of the members of that class, without the faintest recognition of the larger truth that the low skill, irregularity, and inability to undertake hard, solid, and effective work is a direct consequence of the education of environment. The interaction of the two must of course be admitted; but Miss Dendy ignores what is in the case of these people the chief interagent. She simply assumes the individual moral standpoint and rules out all larger economic factors. There are doubtless those who, like Robert Owen, have over-estimated the influence of economic environment; but the general tendency of thought in the educated and philanthropic public, drawn to the study of social reform by moral considerations, and untrained in economic science, makes for the falsehood of the opposite extreme. How much can be achieved in the way of social progress by the aid of forces primarily economic, admits of no general statement, but is a matter for careful detailed experiment. But the history of modern Lancashire is a crucial instance of the power exercised by distinctively economic forces to stimulate industrial and moral character and to lift the standard of life of a working class. Better late than never, our religious and temperance missionaries are coming to recognise the intimate dependence of drunkenness, gambling, and other personal vices upon the economic conditions of industrial life. Take the signal example of prostitution. Does any experienced person really believe that moral influences directed to the inculcation of personal chastity will have any considerable effect, so long as the economic conditions which favour and induce prostitution remain untouched? Here is the case of a trade dependent both in volume and in character upon supply and demand. So long as the ill-paid, precarious and degrading conditions which attach to the wage-work and home-life of many women present prostitution as a superficially attractive alternative, or a necessary supplement, to wage-work or wifedom, supply will be maintained. So long as large numbers of men own money not earned by hard regular work, and not needed for the purchase of legitimate satisfactions, and leisure in excess of the wholesome demands of a natural life, while others are deterred by the economic constitution of society from the establishment

P

of normal family relations, the demand for prostitution will continue. This analysis does not deny the operation of definitely personal vicious forces, not closely connected with the economic factors; but it affirms the latter as larger determinants. The refusal of the " purity " party to face definitely and fearlessly the economic supports of impurity has rightly brought upon them the imputation of shallowness, or even insincerity, for shallowness always implies imperfect sincerity.

Refusing to deal with social reform in this wider scientific spirit, and to apply what they foolishly dub " heroic " remedies (as if a man or a measure were worse for being heroic), the Charity Organisation thinker is driven to base his positive measures of reform upon the voluntary action of well-meaning men and women of the educated classes. The crux of the individual moral method of reform we found to consist in the generation of the necessary moral energy in the crushed or degraded member of society. Even if this energy was universally diffused, we showed it would not, could not under existing economic conditions, be generally effective. But, assuming its complete efficacy, how is it possible to quicken in the inert and often perverted character the quality of true self-respect, the sense of decency, the higher tastes and aspirations by which the individual energy finds expression in its reachings towards a better life? It is suggested that true charity may be the generative force, that the contact of the moral superior may yield the necessary stimulus, that each stronger man or woman might help to lift on to his moral legs a weaker brother or sister. This is the practical proposal upon which Mr. Loch discourses with eloquent faith. He wishes " to create a charitable friendship between the family and visitor,"* by which the latter may become a sort of confidential adviser and a source of moral stimulation to the former.

---

* "Charity Organisation" (Sonnenschein), p. 82.

The conception, in itself, is a noble one, in some rare cases capable of yielding the finest results, but associated with the principles and methods of the Charity Organisation Society generally sterile. If all persons of good strong character and kindly disposition could establish and maintain close friendly relations with two or three degraded or weakly families, it seems as if a mighty force for good might be established. But look at the facts. How many superior persons can be got to do this work in the spirit and the methods of the Charity Organisation Society? To generate the requisite initiative moral force in the superior person is nearly as difficult (or quite as impossible) as to utilise it for the elevation of the moral character of the " residuum." There are reasons why this must be so. Your superior person is often kindly disposed and compassionate. But the views of " property " which form the economic condition and the basis of his superior position and education impel him to emotional and " unorganised " modes of charity. He is often willing to pay subscriptions, sometimes to sit on committees, occasionally to do actual " work among the poor." But his charitable work must yield direct results to his sense of pity. This temperament is capable of getting into kindly personal relations with poor people, but not upon " scientific " lines.

Not merely is it impossible to generate this spirit of scientific charity in a sufficient number of superior persons, but when it is generated it is commonly ineffective.

The theory of the Charity Organisation Society is that they are able to perform a twofold work : (1) To find all relevant facts; (2) To stimulate and raise the individual moral character. In reality they can do neither. The kind of person satisfied with the narrow illogical position of the Charity Organisation Society has educated in himself a view of human nature which is a fatal barrier to the attainment of his ends. We have already seen that though the champions of Charity Organisation profess to include in their range of study "a full acquaintance with the wider social conditions and tendencies within the limits of which we work," in reality they exclude all the larger operations of economic forces, confining themselves to the study of individual cases. But do they get at the vital facts in their " cases "?   I doubt it. The highly cultivated lady or gentleman of the Charity Organisation Society, with keen suspicions and some detective skill, whose mind is busied with knotty points of Poor Law, or delicate problems in the science of character, is just the person whom vital human facts escape. His claim to be the only skilled investigator is a ludicrously foolish one. The detective qualities required for certain valuable portions of his work are just fatal to the attainment of the full facts. They can only disclose certain hard, detached, objective facts, the definite disqualifications, which play the largest part in Charity Organisation reports. The subjective human facts and their organic relation in character escape record or appreciation because the temperament and purpose of the visitor are material to their discovery. The " case " does not truly reveal itself because it feels it is regarded as a " case." The mere husks of fact, suitable for tabulation (a process which full human facts never admit) are what find their way to the pigeon-holes of the Charity Organisation Society's office. The Charity Organisation Society's official may classify a case, marking it out by a number of black dots, but he cannot and does not understand a character. This is the large fact which he misses. He cannot help missing the most material facts. The essentially " inhuman " and illogical view of poverty and property which marks the theory of the Charity Organisation thinker vitiates in a thousand little unseen ways the quality of quick, instinctive, uncalculating sympathy which is somehow necessary to extract facts from the poor. The very voice and mode of speech of some of those who boast their close contact with " facts " must be insuperable barriers in this work.

Before such outward signs of class distinction many essential facts close themselves like clams. The same opinions and moral propensities which shut from their eyes large orders of social and individual facts also disable them as stimulative or educative influences. There is a strong and well recognised antagonism between the detective and the educator even on the plane of intellectual education. The man who can best find out what you do not know is seldom the man who can stimulate an interest in acquiring knowledge, or can best aid the satisfaction of that interest. I do not mean that the educator is to ignore the defects of his pupils, to be utterly devoid of the detective faculty. But wherever it becomes a strong feature of his method (and it is very apt to grow, for it is fed by constant self-flattery) it eats away the formative stimulative influence which is the teacher's true source of power. Much more strongly does this hold of education which is not primarily intellectual but moral. Here the protrusion of the critical faculty is fatal.

Very few persons who are members of a richer and better educated class can really influence their poorer neighbours for good. Even a fairly close and prolonged experience in adult years can seldom give direct, as distinguished from imaginative, sympathy with the ideas and estimates of a poor family; the little differences of manners and even dress form an aloofness which chills the atmosphere of free familiarity in which alone the deeper individual facts emerge, and which is the only medium of transference of best moral influence from one person to another. A single breath of " suspicion," the unconscious emission of a class point of view, the betrayal of some little difference in feeling, and all hope of influence is lost. A moral genius may sometimes descend from the classes and, by linking himself closely to the life of the people, operate powerfully for good upon the minds of individuals. Catholic priests, or others animated by an absorbing religious motive, have done this. But their success has been chiefly attributable to some of those very qualities which the Charity Organisation Society repudiate and denounce. They have been enthusiasts, even fanatics, filled with that faith which for its efficient working requires an element of blindness to the faults and foibles of others; their charity has been temperamental rather than " organised " or scientific; their remedies have been " heroic." They have lived among the people on a level with them, and have not occasionally come down from a superior position to dispense " moral doles " to their inferiors.

A sense of superiority is nearly always discovered and resented. I know that many Charity Organisation Society visitors disown this sense of superiority. Doubtless they do their best to conceal it. But the uneducated classes are preternaturally keen in perceiving it, and it has numberless opportunities for oozing out. Moreover, it cannot and ought not to be concealed —for it is there. These persons do feel they are morally superior; if not, what is the power which they affect to use? They are not drunkards; they are not thriftless; they are not given to petty pilfering, or to violent assault upon the person, or to other common vices or defects of the poorer classes. Now, if this sense of moral superiority were justified, its existence would be, to some extent, admitted by the poor, and it might act as a moral lever. But, though they have not reasoned the matter out, the poor feel and know that they are not fairly matched in opportunity with their " friendly visitors "; they feel " it is all very well " for these well-dressed, nice-spoken ladies and gentlemen to come down and teach them how to be sober, thrifty, and industrious; they may not feel resentment, but they discount the advice and they discount the moral superiority. In a blind, instinctive way they recognise that the superiority is based on better opportunity—in other words, upon economic monopoly. There is a sense in which he who would save the souls of others must lose his own. This saving power is vigorously expressed in a little poem by Edward Carpenter, which, for its plain-spoken truth, might well be pondered by the Charity Organisation Society.

WHO ARE YOU ?

Who are you that go about to save those that are lost ?
 Are you saved yourself ?
Do you know that who would save his own life must lose it ?
 Are you then one of the "lost" ?
Be sure, very sure, that each one of those can teach
you as much as, probably more than, you can teach them.
Have you then sat humbly at their feet, and waited on their
lips that they should be the first to speak—
And been reverent before these children—
whom you so little understand ?
Have you dropped into the bottomless pit from between
yourself and them all hallucination of superiority,
all flatulence of knowledge, every shred of abhorrence
 and loathing ?
Is it equal, is it free as the wind between you ?
Could you be happy receiving favours from one of the most
 despised of these ?
 Could you be yourself one of the lost ?
 Arise, then, and become a saviour.

Those engineers who seek to lift the moral nature of the masses by means of a force which they think will emanate from their correct conduct and elevated tastes are apt to be hoist with their own petard. Be sure your "illogic" will find you out. These persons are not wrong in saying that poverty and the social problem have a moral cause, and that the force which shall solve the problem may be regarded as a moral force; but they are wrong in the place where they seek the moral cause. It will be found ultimately to reside not in the corrupt nature of the poor, worker or idler, but in the moral cowardice and selfishness of the superior person, which prevent him from searching and learning the economic supports of his superiority, and which drive him to subtle theorising upon "the condition of conditions" in order to avoid the discovery that his "superiority" is conditioned by facts which at the same time condition the " inferiority " of the very persons whom he hopes to assist. The work of gradually placing " property " upon a just and rational basis, offering that equality of opportunity which shall rightly adjust effort to satisfaction, is a moral task of supreme importance. Let those who shirk such labour on the plea that it consists of mere external or mechanical reforms, and who prefer what they consider the more perfect way of educating the individual nature of the sunken masses, ask themselves the plain question, why they fail to produce any appreciable result. They will then find they cannot exert a moral educative force which they do not actually possess, and that they do not possess it because their supposed superiority is not a moral, but ultimately an immoral superiority resting upon a monopoly of material, intellectual, and spiritual opportunities.

Only upon the supposition that environment affords equal opportunities for all can we possess a test of personal fitness. Then only should we be justified, after due allowance for accidental causes, in attributing the evil plight of the poor or the unemployed to personal defects of character; then only would the scientific treatment consist, wholly or chiefly, in the moral training of the individual. As matters actually stand, the philosophy which finds the only momentum of social reform in the moral energy of the individual members of the masses is just that smart sophistry which the secret self-interest of the comfortable classes has always been weaving in order to avoid impertinent and inconvenient searching into the foundations of social inequality. This, of course, involves no vulgar imputation of hypocrisy. Most of the men and women who hold these views are genuinely convinced of their accuracy. But they have permitted the subtle, unconscious bias of class interests and class points of view to limit their survey of the facts of the social question, to warp their intelligence in the interpretation of the facts, and to establish false theories of the operations of moral and economic forces, so as to yield an intellectual basis of obstruction to all proposals of practical reform in the structure of political and industrial institutions. Their fault is not that they are too hardhearted, but that they are not sufficiently hardheaded : it is not a lack of feeling, but a lack of logic. They are simply not the scientific people that they claim to be, for they have not learned to think straight against the pressure of class interests and class prejudices. Let them apply the reasoning by which they condemn indiscriminate charity to all other modes of transfer of property. Let them accurately study the nature of economic bargains in the light afforded by the writings of economists. They will then discover how much truth underlies their assumption of the individual responsibility of the poor, and will perceive the urgent need of thoughtful reforms of industrial and political institutions, with the object of securing that property may not come " miraculously " to any individuals or classes of the community, and that all equally may have an opportunity of rational self-realisation in forms of property which are the " definite material representation " of their own energy. The spurious antithesis of " moral " and " economic " in methods of reform they will reject as a mere piece of rhetorical bluff, recognising that every well-ordered reform of economic structure is an expression of the moral force of the community, the " general will " finding embodiment in some stable and serviceable form of social support.

CHAPTER IV

MILLIONAIRE ENDOWMENTS

It is now beginning to be recognised that national efficiency requires (among other things) a very large expenditure of money upon the building and equipment of colleges and other apparatus of higher education. It is not possible that the great capital and current expenditure involved in this work can be supported by a system of voluntary fees. In Great Britain, as indeed elsewhere, a large part of the cost of higher education has always been defrayed out of charitable endowments, with the effect of depressing the commercial value of the commodity far below its " natural " rate. So long as higher education remained a virtual monopoly of the possessing classes, the full significance of this dependence did not appear : it was not felt to be unreasonable that an aristocracy, resting on inherited wealth and the profitable control of political machinery, should absorb the use of the quasi-public property devoted to purposes of an intellectual culture which seemed out of keeping with the life of the trading and working classes. This feeling was not deeply disturbed by the part played by culture in the education of the learned professions, so long as those professions were in some sense an appendage of aristocracy, and were in their own structure close corporations, enjoying privileges in official salaries and other emoluments based in no wise upon equivalence of service or the higgling of the market. To classes living so largely upon unearned incomes and privileges, it could seem no matter of surprise, still less of ignominy that they should get their education out of charity. But, now that higher education is deemed no longer the decoration of a leisured class, or merely a tool for certain select grades of intellectual workers, but an essential of sound citizenship in a civilised state, it is no longer possible to acquiesce in this easy virtue of a policy which takes whatever it can get, without caring to inquire into the implicit terms of this acceptance.

It is well to confront without flinching the first salient fact of the situation, the utter lack of funds adequate to meet the demands of higher education, the urgency of which we already recognise; for it is this urgency that constitutes the danger. In an age when our national revenue is continually strained to support what is regarded as a necessary increase of expenditure on armaments, the public purse cannot bear the cost of higher education : where millions are available for force, thousands must suffice for culture. So, from a disbelief in the possibility of self-help, the public is beginning to turn to private charity; rich men are invited to make up the deficiency of our public resources.

The idea is by no means confined to higher education : a whole crop of public wants is growing up, which the City or the State appears to be too poor to satisfy. It is desirable that our growing cities should have parks. What more natural than that some large ground landlord should present the land? Hospitals, public baths, libraries, technical schools are needed. Why not find some rich brewer, banker, manufacturer, or speculator, and let him " acquire merit " ? The ancient practice of the " pious founder " is thus being developed into a definite social doctrine which accords to the millionaire a special function as a saviour of society. The United States, the classic soil of the mushroom millionaire, exhibits the largest and most numerous examples of the fruits of this " gospel of wealth," especially in its application to higher education. It has been estimated that the annual flow of large donations to educational work during recent years amounts to more than one hundred million dollars. Few names eminent in banking and railroad circles, as trust-makers or successful dealers in real estate, remain unrecorded in some great building devoted to the encouragement of higher learning. The huge pile of college buildings which stands to-day upon the grounds of the Chicago Exposition, absorbing a portion of the profits of the famous Oil Trust, is only the most conspicuous example of a numerous species of collegiate foundations scattered over the States, the product of the charity of millionaires. Not only the new colleges which in scores and even hundreds are springing up in the West, the Middle-West, and the belated South, but even the older and more solidly formed universities of New England and the Eastern States are continually seeking, and obtaining, new large bequests and donations from the princes of industry or finance. To not a few of them funds have flowed so quickly that they have difficulty in concealing their embarrassment of riches; and expensive half-used laboratories and other superfluous apparatus of learning attest their unassimilated wealth. Closer examination will doubtless show that over-feeding in certain depart-ments is attended by starvation in others, that the special interests or whims of donors are represented by abnormal growths, and that, in particular, too much money goes into bricks and mortar and the outward visible signs of educational activity, too little into the inward graces of the intellectual life. Everywhere we find the " campus " with its huge departmental build-ings, its law and engineering schools, museum, libraries, laboratories, gymnasium, theatre, the enormous staff of highly specialised, unevenly equipped, and ill-paid professors grinding out interminable courses of lectures and turning out sheaves of printed matter for the University press. An ever-swelling output of rapidly produced intellectual commodities, good, bad, and indifferent, is hurriedly swallowed by earnest hordes of

industrious but often ill-grounded students, young men
and women fresh from farm or forcing city High
School, to be whirled through an intellectual factory
which shall stock, shape, and stimulate their minds,
depositing them as rudimentary teachers, lawyers,
engineers, or clergymen, when they have passed through
the several productive processes.

A strained activity of academic machinery, a wasteful
competition in volume of intellectual output, and a
marked subordination of the slower, finer, less demon-
strable processes of disinterested culture to the quicker,
cruder, more showy forms of utilitarian achievement,
are plain effects of a higher education which reflects the
valuations of the *nouveaux riches* who supply the funds.
It is doubtless true that these defects of intellectual
valuation, imposing short-range, quantitative, utilitarian
tests, are not confined to millionaire influences, but are
natural fruits of the swift growth in mechanical industry
of which America is the foremost exponent. But this
makes it only the more exigent that the practical control
of the educative forces designed to correct these defects
of valuation shall not rest in the hands of those very
men who, by their pecuniary achievements, are attested
to be the fittest representatives of the false standards of
their age and nation. The great fortunes in America out
of which these endowments and donations come to the
support of colleges are in a few rare instances owned by
men or women who have inherited them, and who may
claim to belong to an educated leisured class; in the
great majority of cases they have come to their present
owners as the result of an early and constant absorption
in business processes, in which assiduity, economy, alert-
ness, and skill have been inextricably interwoven with
luck, fraud, force, and every sort of predatory practice.
It is no part of my purpose here to analyse in detail the
necessary origins of great fortunes; but there are scarcely
any great American fortunes into which corruptly-gotten
charters or tariff-aid, illegal railroad practices, land

speculation, over-capitalisation, Wall Street gambling, do not enter largely as ingredients. There is so much plasticity, so much apparent incongruity in human nature, that rare individuals emerge from such a struggle retaining generous impulses, elevated aspirations, and a desire to help their fellows by a contribution of large sums of money to causes of social service. But the conditions under which such wealth has been acquired are such as must normally disqualify its owners for a wise and socially serviceable administration of a public " trust." If to the rare instances where the acquisitive aptitude is conjoined with some higher tastes and far-sighted discrimination of values, we add the far more numerous cases where pride of patronage, pressure of public opinion, indulgence of a fad, loose sentimentalism, are the dominant motives, we shall come nearer to a recognition of the peril of a higher education directed by millionaires.

I am aware that these general alarms will not weigh much with most English educationists, who are too deeply concerned with the troubles of poverty to heed those which come from plethora. Like the Irishman beholding a man lying along the roadside in a state of complete alcoholic stupefaction, they will be inclined to wish for " half his malady." So urgent is the need for money in the equipment of our higher educational system, that educationists seem generally willing to shut their eyes and open their mouths in order to receive whatever they can induce millionaires to give them. It is, in their judgment, sheer captiousness or ignoble cynicism to look such gift-horses in the mouth. " What matter how the money comes if we have the spending of it? " represents the " common-sense view " which is prevalent.

If we adopt this " common-sense view," refusing to enter into origins or motives, and accepting donations from all sources, we are bound to defend the position that origins and motives can exercise no appreciably injurious influence on uses. Now is it a true or a reasonable proposition that dependence upon the large benefactions of contemporaries has no tendency to injure the efficiency of a university, and in particular to impair its liberty of teaching? On these important questions recent American experience is closely relevant. The educational needs of our population, and the economic interests and business methods which produce great fortunes, are substantially the same in the two countries. The existence in Great Britain of a small number of great families in enjoyment of inherited fortunes from land or trade does not materially impair the analogy, for, though our older seats of learning sometimes court this class with academic decorations, it is the new rich, with their ampler superfluity of income over conventional expenditure, that form the real hope of the educational angler. Now no student of American higher education can fail to perceive that the living hand is there far more oppressive than the dead. A first conspicuous result of this necessity is seen in the *personnel* of the College President. An advertising presence and deportment for public occasions, personal weight and persuasiveness in wealthy quarters, plausibility, tact, adroitness, and, in general, the business equipment of a successful " beggar," form the first and most indispensable requisites. Scholarship, science, or philosophy is a decorative parergon, the serious cultivation of which is inconsistent with the duties of a president. Even the. work of internal administration must be subordinated to the necessity of keeping the claims and needs of the college before the public in such wise as to recommend it to the favour of the rich. A College President regards it as an important function of his office to take a leading part in all sorts of non-academic gatherings, save those closely associated with machine politics, and to deliver public addresses upon all manner of " subjects of the day." On morals, education, economics, literature, civics, and politics, not merely in their graver academic bearings, but as practical issues of current conduct, the

College President is regarded as a standing counsel to the public. On the great public questions of the last few years, the Philippine annexation, the anthracite coal strike and the wider aspects of relations between capital and labour, the policy of curbing Trusts, the Panama Question, and the recrudescence of race-feeling in the South, College Presidents have been incessantly talking on public platforms, and writing in the Press, not at all in the capacity of specialists bringing some particular points of academic learning to bear on new events, but as intellectual authorities at large. All this implies a diversion of energy from that work of close internal administration which is so all-important in the building up of a new edifice of learning. Where ancient traditions prevail, less depends upon the personality of a president; but in a new seat of learning it is a prime condition of successful progress to secure a man whose first aptitude and whose absorbing interest are those of an education-ist, not those of a public character or a skilful mendicant. Every well-informed, thoughtful American can point out a score of ambitious colleges which are suffering in their early growth from their showy, scheming presi-dent, whose character is impressed on their plastic institutions. The college dependent on private dona-tions is driven to cultivate the arts of advertisement: it must show numbers of students rather than quality of work, it must lean to utilitarian studies, or captivate the imagination and the purse of impressionable benefactors by novelty of projects and experiments. Though this spirit of novelty has advantages which I would not decry, it certainly involves much waste and some considerable dangers in the early growth of higher educational establishments.

The vulgar saying that " he who pays the piper calls the tune " is operative here as elsewhere. A college which makes itself dependent for its capital or income upon the munificence of rich donors will submit its teaching to be moulded by the will of these donors; and this will must, in the nature of the case, conflict with the true order of educational growth. The real nature of the growing control of the American millionaire over the higher education of America is very subtle; and its subtlety will be imitated here, if we submit our educational forms to the same pressure. The explicit conditions which may be attached to large bequests or donations form the least of the dangers. Most colleges of any standing would have enough dignity or discretion to reject gifts accompanied by express conditions which visibly and grossly infringed liberty of research or of teaching, or imposed any palpably injurious test. Though an uneven or lop-sided development of education is often due to conditioned donations, this has some tendency to right itself by directing subsequent munificence to the neglected parts; and in no case can it be regarded as a permanently serious damage.

Nor does the real dimension of the danger appear in any personal attempt of the living founder, or other large benefactor, to interfere with the teaching of the college, though some instances of such interference have recently disgraced the annals of higher education in America. The dismissal of Professor Bemis from his professorship of Political Economy at Chicago University for taking part, as a citizen, in a movement for municipalisation of industry opposed to the interests of Mr. Rockefeller, the founder of the University, and the dismissal of Professor Ross from the professorship of Sociology in the Leland Stanford University for expressing certain economic and political opinions which aroused the resentment of Mrs. Stanford, are the most familiar instances of an extreme abuse of patronage which wrought the gravest injury upon the reputation of two important universities, and aroused a feeling of insecurity among scores of other colleges similarly fed out of the profits of monopolies or privileged interests. In well-informed academic circles in America I have heard many instances of less open and direct interference with liberty of

Q

teaching, indicating that munificent donors were not indifferent to the uses to which their donations were put. Why should they be? What more natural than that Mr. Rockefeller, or his confederates in the Oil Trust, should object to a plain handling of the Trust issue with local illustrations, or should object to their money supporting a teacher who was engaged in helping to break their control over the gas monopoly in Chicago? Why is it to be expected that the widow of a Californian million-aire, who made his rapid pile out of cheap Chinese labour and land speculation, should value perfect liberty of speech so highly as to endure what seemed to her false and pestilent pronouncements on the Land and Immi-gration Questions?

But these may well be taken as abnormal instances of a sort of interference, to which it may seem extravagant to suggest that any English seat of learning would consent to be subjected. Self-respecting academic bodies in this country, it will be urged, may be trusted to resent the least approach to meddling on the part of actual or would-be patrons. Self-respecting colleges in America use similar language in seeking to reconcile economic dependence with academic liberty. Rich men with generous impulses, touched by admiration of their work, place large sums of money at their disposal, which they utilise as a public trust in the sacred cause of education! Where conditions are attached, the limita-tion commonly arises upon the suggestion of the college, which announces some special need for an exten-sion of material plant or teaching staff. This, it is stoutly maintained, involves no loss of liberty. Such is the theory of the function of the millionaire-donor genuinely held by many American educationists; and, though it ignores the arts of stimulation which commonly precede the " spontaneous " bounty, it contains a large element of truth. There is little direct interference by donors, and very little sense of loss of liberty. The graver peril is a more insidious one. It is not the past or present, but the future patron, whose influence curbs liberty—the unknown prospective donor whose good-will must be conciliated, or, what comes to the same thing, his ill-will averted. For, in order to provide for educational growth, a constant succession of donations is desired. Now it is idle to pretend that this necessity will not impose upon college officials a sort of discretion not exclusively determined by educational considerations. The new rich, like others, have their special interests and susceptibilities in politics, in trade, and sometimes in religion; in special States or cities these interests may be rigorously defined, and certain plain differences of social and even of ethical outlook will mark what, for convenience, may be called the millionaire class in America or in England. Now, so long as the older educational traditions kept colleges absorbed upon dead languages, the mathematics, and those sciences which did not nearly affect living human interests, no difficulty would arise, except an occasional flare-up in the department of theology. But the new trend of higher education is towards an increasing stress upon studies replete with modern human issues and charged with explosive subject-matter. A modern university sets an ever-growing importance upon modern history, economics, and other social sciences, while its philosophy, psychology, and even its biology seethe with political and economic implications.

It is, of course, possible, on paper, to mark out a mode of academic handling which shall maximise the light and minimise the heat of this inflammatory matter. But there can be no way of securing a live effective treatment of many of the subjects which is not liable to offend the feelings of the donor class. This will apply with peculiar force to the departments of economics and sociology. It would be childish to pretend that a scientific analysis of the subjects of rents and monopolies, which exposed the economic and moral soil out of which great mushroom fortunes grow, will recommend a university to the munificence of the possessors of such fortunes. The soreness which appears everywhere in academic centres of America when this question is broached, is itself a strong testimony to the reality of the danger. It is not so much a matter of heresy-hunting or forcible suppression, as of selection. The tendency is to find " safe " men, who will find " safe " materials, for " sound " handling. Teachers, programmes, text-books are all subjected to careful sifting. The process is of course somewhat precarious. In several " kept " universities, men of very advanced views are members of the teaching staff; indeed their presence is commonly adduced as an answer to the charge of millionaire control. But the fact is, that no man known to be of advanced views would be appointed to such a post; and considerable discretion must be exerted in the avoidance of the detailed subject-matter which carries the explosives. Again, advanced doctrine may be tolerated, if it is kept well in the background of pure theory; but, where it is embodied in concrete instances drawn from current experience, the pecuniary prospects of the college are instinctively felt to be endangered.

Now it is evidently not the function of a teacher to assume the rôle of a social agitator in his class room; and the difficulty which must arise in severing the personality and duties of a teacher from those of a citizen may reasonably be held to impose special moderation upon a professor of economics or politics, who takes an active part in public affairs in his capacity of citizen. But the attempt to argue that these restraints, imposed purely in the interests of education, preclude a thorough treatment of the actual phenomena of industry and politics, enforced by live instances drawn from the " here and now," is a virtual repudiation in the department of the social sciences of what are elsewhere recognised to be the soundest scientific methods of instruction. Again, to require of men, whose knowledge and training peculiarly qualify them to give light and leading to their fellow-citizens, that they shall abstain from active participation in public movements where interests are divided and strong feelings are evoked, is a policy of moral and intellectual mutilation, as degrading to those who are curtailed in their citizenship, as it is injurious to the public.

It will not be easy for academic authorities in this country, wedded to antique standards of educational values and admitting the new studies with slow reluctance, to realise the size of the issue. Oxford and Cambridge, with their existing curricula of studies, might receive little injury from the munificence of millionaires; such gifts might even help to liberalise and modernise their teaching—within certain limits.* But our new colleges in the industrial towns must found their culture upon a more modern standard of values, in which the sciences and the literatures charged with current human interests play a larger part, and where, moreover, the claims of professional training will reinforce the modern movement. Culture and utility will conspire to give to such studies as political economy, psychology, law, modern history, and modern literature, places of great prominence in the higher education of efficient citizens.

The intellectual traditions and vested interests in this country are so conservative, that it will be no easy matter for the new studies to make good a claim which to our academic authorities will appear preposterously arrogant. The difficulty of this conflict will impose sufficient

---

* These limits are, however, transgressed by the conditions attached to the recent endowment of teaching in Colonial History by Mr. Beit at Oxford.   The subject, as defined by the donor and accepted by the University, is one which gives great prominence to the History of the South African Colonies, in whose recent story Mr. Beit and his business associates have played so prominent a part.   Does any thoughtful person believe that, if scientific historians, appointed under this trust, apply their science to a faithful analysis of the actual influences exerted upon politics in South Africa by the financial combination of which De Beers, Wernher, Beit, and Co., and the Chartered Company are chief constituents, the trust will be renewed at the expiration of its term of probation ?   If he does, a careful study of the "educational propaganda" conducted through the Press, the political party, and the pulpit, by Mr. Beit and his friends, during recent years, may help to enlighten him.

timidity upon the new aspirants in the formulation of their studies and the methods of their pursuit. Unless there is financial independence, it is easy to perceive that this timidity will prove most detrimental to efficiency of teaching and to the progress of the sciences. If the rulers of these new colleges are conscious of dependence on the voluntary favours of the rich for the needed accessions to their income, a secret, usually unconscious, but persistent spirit of repression will pervade the college, determining the choice of teachers, ordering the curriculum, and making for intellectual quietism which will be misnamed " thoroughness." Those studies will suffer most where freedom and some measure of originality are most needed; the wings of thought, kept clipped, will not pass beyond the careful barriers of orthodoxy. Let me put the case quite plainly. The bolder thinkers in the forefront of the modern sciences which touch the conduct of man and of society are undermining, by newly organised knowledge, many of the supports of the existing social system—religious, moral, political, and economic; and their analysis is being made the basis of strong attacks upon the fortresses of privilege. These forces seem to many to converge in a movement against those organisations of capital and business enterprise which are producing millionaires. The rich are everywhere becoming more conscious of the perils of a movement which represents itself to their eyes as an attack upon the institution of property. This danger they associate with others threatening the ecclesiastical, political, and social institutions with which they have formed an instinctive alliance for mutual defence. Is it likely that this class will finance colleges which are free to promote " revolutionary " doctrines under the name of science, philosophy, or literature? Nay! Is it not reasonable that they will use their financial powers to purchase the sort of intellectual support they need, endow colleges which shall teach a safe economics and a sound sociology, and expel the organic conception of society from ethics and philosophy?

Those who have studied the history of the development of the classical political economy in this country well know how such a class defence can be secretly constructed, by persistent selection and rejection among the ideas and formulæ of a plastic science. In such a manipulation of intellectual forces there is little consciousness attending the process, either among the manipulators or the manipulated. There may be keen-witted business men who know that it is good business to endow a School of Commerce, as it is to build a church; there may be college professors who recognise that their views are being formed or modified by consideration for the welfare of the college. But it is quite unnecessary to assume dishonesty or conscious cunning; the instinct of self-protection works more surely. If the class from which rich donations come has any private interest opposed to that of the public, these donations will serve to buy off close scrutiny into that interest, and, if necessary, will select thinkers who shall formulate a specious defence of its privileges, and teachers who shall propagate its views. Although the free development and teaching of Political Economy would suffer most in such colleges, other subjects would be exposed to similar corruption and retardation, in proportion to their capability of harbouring dangerous doctrine. Endowments of colleges proceeding from vested interests will, in effect, be devoted to the defence of those interests; and the cause of education will suffer accordingly.

The deceitfulness of riches is such, that it will induce colleges to a contemptuous denial of this inevitable chain of moral and economic causation. Unless the popular intelligence can be made alive to the urgency of the danger, our new system of higher education will be a mortal enemy to the cause of democracy. If we once have established in our centres of population colleges which are founded by millionaires and expect to be fed by millionaires, an era of castrated culture is the inevitable sequel.   The doctrine of individual self-help has been dinned into our ears *ad nauseam*: it is an essentially false doctrine, because no individual is capable of self-help in the full sense that is implied. But a city, a nation, is capable of self-help.   If then an individual is degraded by charity, if his self-reliance and energy are sapped by unearned and unmerited gifts, how much more is a city or a nation injured if she permits individual charity to do for her what she ought to do and can do for herself?   Our national, our civic life is surely demoralised if it is robbed of the wholesome effort required to provide out of our own resources for the public needs of education.   If we do not, as a nation, so value education as to take the course which nature and morals alike mark out for its attainment, it is far better, hard though it may sound, to wait for our colleges. We cannot really get our intellectual efficiency by the grace of millionaires.

Chapter V

SOUTH AFRICA: A LESSON OF EMPIRE

Those who ten years ago insisted with so much assurance upon the inevitability of war in South Africa, failed to recognise that the sequel of the war was equally inevitable. That the most redoubtable Boer Generals, who eight years ago were in the field against our troops, should be in London imposing on the British Government the terms of a national Constitution which will make them and their allies in the Cape the rulers of a virtually independent South Africa is, indeed, one of the brightest humours of modern history. The irony gets a broader touch of humour when Generals Smuts and Hertzog are gravely summoned to advise in the defence of the Empire. The general view of the British public towards this outcome is one of mingled amazement and goodwill. This popular sentiment is in part penitence for a half-recognised misdeed, in part pride in our magnanimity and in part a curious feeling that union has justified the war. In fact, there are not wanting persons who believe not merely that there would have been no union without the war, but that the sole motive of the war was to bring about the union. But those who fasten their eyes on the abiding factors in the history of South Africa know that, war or no war, the achievement of political union between the free self-governing States lay in the early future as a settled fact. Even before the spread of railways, and the new direction thus given to the course of trade, the issue was assured. For though the premature endeavour of

British statesmen to force the pace by pressure from without in 1878, and again by conspiring with financial politicians on the spot in 1895, paralysed for a time the internal forces working for union, these latter had too much vitality to suffer more than a brief check. Even had there been no war, the needs of union were ripening so fast that it is quite likely that consummation might have been achieved as early, though the Dutch supremacy which it embodies and assures would have been less conspicuous and the form of the union would probably have been less closely knit. The absence of strong national barriers, save in the case of Natal, the similarity of racial, industrial, political, and social conditions throughout the country, the free interchange for purposes of business and of settlement between the white inhabitants of the several States, the community of interest in customs, transport, education, sanitation, finance, and above all else, in native policy, were forces whose acceleration and direction were constant and uniform. The devastation of the war, with its fearful aftermath of poverty and universal distress may, indeed, have precipitated action in its final stage. Adversity makes strange bedfellows and perhaps rendered easier that co-operation of Boers with Randlords, Bondmen with Progressives, which has been so interesting a feature in the making of the Constitution. One thing is certain. It welded into a passionate spirit of unity and fixed resolve that somewhat torpid and precarious sympathy between the Dutch of the Colony and of the two erstwhile Republics, which hitherto had failed to keep them to any lasting co-operation. So defective, indeed, was this sympathy before the war that within a single decade the members of a race alleged to be possessed by the single passion to drive the British into the sea were several times upon the very verge of an armed struggle among themselves over some question of trade or of right of way. The war has not made the Union, but it has made Dutch mastery within the Union. To some it seems that the present control of the Dutch in three of the four provinces and so in the Union is the mere turn of the scale in the changing fortunes of popular election. But I feel sure that the keen-witted and loyal statesmen, who ten years ago defeated our armies and to-day rule our South African colonies, gauge the situation more truly. Our national sentimentalism befogs our vision. It delights us to imagine that at the close of a bloody and prolonged struggle, in which we wore down resistance by sheer dint of numbers, Briton and Boer should grasp hands of friendship, mutual respect warming into affection, every past unpleasantness at once forgotten, and all determined to live together happily for ever afterwards. A nice propriety of loyal speech in some of the Boer leaders may, indeed, be adduced in support of this romantic view of history. But it is foolish for those who wish to understand and estimate the future of the country where such bitter deeds were done to accept at their face value these polite assurances of oblivion. Loyalty under a flag which shall allow them perfect liberty to use their superior solidarity and persistency in shaping the destiny of the country they regard as peculiarly theirs, it is, indeed, reasonable to expect, but forgetfulness of the violence of the conquest, of the thousands of children whose death by disease and starvation in the concentration camps blackens almost every family record in the two new colonies, such amnesty is not bought by the new glory of entering an Empire upon which the sun never sets, with its alien heritage of history.

I do not dwell upon this necessary imperfection of Imperial sympathy to suggest that it is likely to affect the practical relations between the South African Union and Great Britain. When the Peace of Vereiniging was made, the future of South Africa was marked out quite irrespective of the shifts of party power either in that country or in this. If Lord Milner had looked before he leaped ten years ago, he would have recognised that

the surest way to render certain for the future that
" dominion of Africanderdom " which he hated, was to
convert the two Republics by force into two self-governing British Colonies. For, even if the Government
which had made the war had képt the reins of office
afterwards, with Lord Milner as their authoritative
adviser, the utmost they could have achieved would have
been a postponement of complete self-government for
a few years, accompanied with jerrymandering of constituencies designed to favour British voters; a policy
which might have goaded the Boers to political reprisals
when they entered on the full colonial status which the
first entry of a Liberal Government in England must
have secured to them, but which could have had no
abiding influence upon the further course of events.

But though it is probable that the greater stability
and the more prolific character of the Dutch will make
them the chief formative stock in the amalgam of the
new South African nation, while the persistence of the
Taal and of the Dutch-Roman law will maintain
strongly distinctive features in this section of our
Empire, the trend of national development will not
differ materially from that of Canada or Australia, so
far as its relations towards Great Britain and her sister
nations in the Empire are concerned. How are these
relations shaping? Among those who accept as final
the sharp distinction which has hitherto been drawn
between those white colonies ripe or ripening for self-
government and the unfree remainder of our Empire,
it is natural that the achievement of South African
Union should bring this question into new prominence.
For to Mr. Chamberlain, as twenty years before to Lord
Carnarvon, this union, however desirable upon its own
account, had its chief significance as a step towards a
larger federation, or other reconstitution of the self-
governing sections of the British Empire. Group
federation was to be followed by Imperial Federation.
The former process is now nearly complete in the

Canadian Dominion, the Australian Commonwealth, and the South African Union. Whether New Zealand elects still to stand alone, or, as is not unlikely, is drawn into an Australasian union by the supreme need of a strong pacific policy, is a question of no present urgency. Other fragments still remain for inevitable absorption, Newfoundland in Canada, Rhodesia in the South African Union. But does this grouping of adjoining colonies into nations evidently favour the ideal of a close linked British Empire of which Imperialists have dreamed?

Does the smaller centralising process imply the larger one? The general trend of colonial history during the last three-quarters of a century supports no such implication. As each colony has grown in population, wealth, and enterprise it has persistently asserted larger rights of independent government which the Mother Country has, sometimes willingly, sometimes reluctantly, conceded: each colony values among its most prized traditions the successful resistance to some acts of interference on the part of the Imperial Government which it has deemed injurious to its vital interests or offensive to its sense of dignity, some endeavour to restrict its territorial growth, to force upon it undesirable immigrants, to coerce its commercial liberty. But in general the colonial lesson contained in the American Revolution has sufficed to teach us acquiescence in the continuous assertion of larger independence. The actual bonds, alike political and commercial, between the several colonies and the Mother Country have been growing every decade weaker, in spite of the greater physical accessibility which the steamer and the telegraph have brought, and in spite of the great machinery of modern investment which every colony has used so freely to draw capital from Great Britain for her own development. Nor is it without significance that the oldest and the nearest colonies, and those which federated first among themselves, have gone furthest in the practical assertion of an independence which now leaves Imperial control and obligations well-nigh divested of all corresponding rights even in issues of foreign policy.

When the power to place protective tariffs on our goods and to make their own commercial treaties with foreign countries was once conceded, it needed no undue insistence upon the economic interpretation of history to see that a continual evolution both of commercial and of political self-sufficiency must follow. As each colony fell into federation with its neighbours, this spirit and this practice of autonomy naturally grew, and the four nations now forming part of our overseas Empire are firmer in their confident self-sufficiency than ever were the constituent colonies. Those British Imperialists who, with the events of the last few years before their eyes, still imagine a closer Imperial federation in any shape or form practicable, are merely the dupes of Kiplingesque sentimentalism.

It is true that these colonies sent gallant troops (at our expense) to our assistance in the Boer War, and that for purposes of Imperial defence the British Flag may remain a real asset, though, as the recent Conference will clearly show, the same spirit of separatism exhibited in politics and in commerce demands that even in defence, National shall always take precedence of Imperial interests. Though in each colony aspiring politicians have been found to fan Imperialist sentiment to a glow and to utilise the heat for electoral purposes or for personal glory, these bursts of effervescent feeling, however genuine while they last, cannot be taken as serious factors in the shaping of their national policy. The pride in the British connection may bring Canadian, Australian and South African statesmen to toy with suggestions of political or commercial federation on decorative occasions such as Imperial Conferences: it may even evoke some sentimental dole of preference in a colonial tariff, or some eleemosynary contribution towards a British fleet, but it will not lead the people of these countries on this ground to abate one jot or one tittle of their fixed determination to go their own way, to develop their own natural resources for their own sole advantage, and to be guided in all important acts of policy by purely National, as distinct from Imperial, objects. The very notion that Canada, Australia, New Zealand, or South Africa will even consider the advisability of entering a close political union, through the formation of some Imperial Council, which, whether vested with legislative powers or not, could only act by restricting liberties hitherto enjoyed by each colonial unit, is acknowledged to be chimerical by most of those who in the 'nineties were enamoured of the project.

Mr. Chamberlain soon saw that the front-door of political federation was shut, bolted and barred. He thereupon sought the tradesman's entrance, claiming to knit the colonies and the Mother Country into an indissoluble union by means of a set of preferences which he hoped might eventually give free trade within the Empire. We now perceive that the appeal to community of trading interests is as futile as was the earlier appeal, and for the same reason. Each of our offspring nations is determined to consult its own interests, and it finds that these interests are opposed to any commercial union. This for two reasons: first, because such commercial union to be valid must imply some subordination of its own immediate interests to the co-operative trading ends of the Empire, and to such restraint it will not submit; secondly, because experience, as registered in trade statistics, shows that its commercial interests lie more in the development of profitable trade relations with foreign countries than in British or intra-Imperial trade. The recent commercial history of Canada and Australia proves that each nation has made up its mind to utilise its tariff system, first for its own industrial development, secondly, for its own financial needs. If British preference is retained at all, it can afford no substantial gain and no considerable bond, for British import trade must neither compete with colonial industries nor hamper the colony in negotiating special trade agreements with foreign countries. A detailed examination of Canadian preference proves how flimsy is this bond of union.

It remains for the future to show whether Imperial defence can draw the Empire nearer together, or whether it also will yield to the disintegrating forces. One thing, however, is certain. If the Colonial Office is used again as it was used by Mr. Chamberlain to procure offers of colonial aid, if British Governments, Unionist or Liberal, angle for colonial gift-ships by scare-cables with crooked phrases, all that is generous and genuine in the colonial concern for the old Motherland will perish. No one can have consorted freely with colonial visitors last summer without noting the tone of surprised contempt for the " jumpy " nerves evinced during the months of the German panic. The impudent perversion of the Imperial Press Conference to the same single purpose provoked significant protests from leading colonial journalists whose indignation was aroused at the materialistic interpretation given by British statesmen to Imperial unity. Just as participation in the Boer War opened the eyes of Canadian and Australian volunteers to the military weakness of England, so this eager pleading for Imperial defence rouses reflections upon the character of the Empire, the risks it involves for the self-governing nations, and the unequal influence which they will exercise in determining Imperial policy. It might well appear a profitable and glorious task to co-operate in the protection of a " free, tolerant, unaggressive Empire." But it is not equally glorious or profitable for a free-born Canadian or New Zealander to enter a confederation under which a necessarily dominant partner can claim his blood and money to help hold down India, to quell some struggle for liberty in Egypt, or to procure some further step in tropical aggrandisement at the bidding of some mining or rubber syndicate. In other words, it is our huge, " unfree, intolerant, aggressive " Empire which may well give pause to our self-governing colonies when invited to enter a close unity of Imperial defence. For this Empire is no real concern of theirs, they have nothing in common with its modes of auto-cratic government, they are unwilling even to admit its " British subjects " on to their shores. Why then should they feign enthusiasm for an Imperial defence mainly directed to maintain and enlarge this unfree Empire by quarrels to which they are no willing parties, in which no true interests of theirs will be involved, but in which they may be called upon to squander their resources and even risk their independence.

Though the full logic of the situation may not yet be manifest, we may be sure that it is a sound prophetic instinct which makes colonial statesmen so reluctant to commit their countries to any of those schemes of close central control which our home-made Imperialists have been so anxious to bind upon them. Nothing is more significant than the determined way in which the. Colonies, Canada leading, are urging the conditions of their participation in Imperial defence, viz., the priority of Colonial to Imperial defence with all its necessary limitations in Imperial strategy, and the retention of the *personnel* of the command in the hands of the Colonial Government.

Of the real meaning of this movement there can be no doubt. As in political self-government and in com-merce, each colonial group has long established a vir-tually complete autonomy, so now it is proposed to take over the duty and the right of its armed defence from the Mother Country. As soon as the so-called "Imperial Defence " is consummated, there will be no Imperial troops or ships in the " free " colonies, but only national troops and national ships. Whatever language is used to describe this new movement of Imperial defence

R

it is virtually one more step towards complete national independence on the part of the colonies. For not only will the consciousness of the assumption of this task of self-defence feed with new vigour the spirit of nationality, it will entail the further power of full control over foreign relations. This has already been virtually admitted in the case of Canada, now entitled to a determinant voice in all treaties or other engagements in which her interests are specially involved. The extension of this right to the other colonial nations may be taken as a matter of course. Home rule in national defence thus established reduces the Imperial connection to its thinnest terms.

To speculators upon the larger problems of history it will be a particularly interesting and delicate consideration whether our colonial nations will best consult their safety and their liberty in the future by remaining formal members of the Empire, sharing both the risks and the resources of this association, or by taking their destinies entirely into their own hands, forming their own alliances, and meeting out of their own resources the rarer risks which might attend such severance.

But the formation of the South African Union emphasises in another way the instability of the British Empire. " I believe this Government," said Abraham Lincoln, " cannot endure permanently half slave, half free." Equally true is it that no abiding unity can be found for an Empire half autocratic and half self-governing. One force of dissolution we have already recognised in the divorce alike of sympathy and interest between the self-governing colonies and the rest of the overseas dominions of the Crown. But the corruption of self-government itself in the case of the new nation is a perhaps more subtle sign of weakness and decay. The Constitution of the South African Union is, indeed, in some respects a more satisfactory instrument of government than either that of the Canadian Dominion or of the Australian Commonwealth. In this country it has been subjected to very little criticism. Both parties appear to regard the sanction of the Imperial Parliament as an act destitute of real responsibility. It is, indeed, understood that the Colonial Office procured some minor modifications in the South African proposals. But all effective criticism or amendment was denied to the House of Commons by a bold and very simple form of bluff. The South African delegates, who came here to impose this Act of Union, were well aware that the denial of any real representation to civilised natives and coloured people over the greater part of the Union, the imperilling of the coloured franchise in the Cape, and, in particular, the formal adoption of a colour-line for membership of the Union Assembly, would be unwelcome to the majority of the members of the most Liberal Parliament which has ever sat in Westminster. Aware that any free exercise of Imperial legislative power would amend their Act so as to secure the standard of equality formulated by Mr. Rhodes, " equal rights for all civilised men south of the Zambesi," they agreed upon the terse formula that any such amendment would " wreck the Union "! The device was well calculated to secure its end. For though it is utterly unreasonable to suppose that the South African States, each with such carefully bargained ends to gain by union, would, in fact, withdraw their sanction because the Imperial Government chose to exercise its undoubted right to secure for the majority of British subjects in South Africa the right to qualify for civilisation, the firm assertion of this peril proved enough to overbear the opposition of all save a negligible minority. It was inevitable that this should be so.

The fast confederacy of Dutch and British politicians was certain to bear down principles of Liberalism already compromised and enfeebled by acquiescence in the modes of government applied in India and Egypt to the subjects of our unfree Empire.

So it has come about that a Government has been established in South Africa, in form resembling that of Canada, Australia, and New Zealand, in substance very different. To describe as a self-governing nation the white oligarchy that has, with our connivance, fenced itself against admission of the ablest and most progressive members of races living in their midst and by general admission capable of a civilisation at least as high as that of the ordinary white wage-earner, is an outrage to political terminology. Deliberately to set out upon a new career as a civilised nation with a definition of civilisation which takes as the criterion race and colour, not individual character and attainments, is nothing else than to sow a crop of dark and dangerous problems for the future. Such a government, such a civilisation, must fall between two stools. There is, indeed, no parallel without or within the Empire for a self-government in which five-sixths of the governed are excluded from all rights of citizenship. In other colonies where the population is mainly composed of "lower races" bureaucracy is never more than tempered by representation, and that representation is mostly free from colour-lines: such government can at least secure order, if at the cost of progress. It is conceivable (though our Empire affords no present instance) that sound order and political security might be obtained by a white oligarchy which kept in economic servitude the lower races of inhabitants, barred them from skilled industries, from any large participation in modern city life, and from religious and intellectual instruction of any kind. This was virtually the old Boer policy, though adopted as readily by British settlers on the land; it was absolutely successful. But it is not conformable to-day either to the conditions or the sentiments of the more progressive white citizens of South Africa, even in Natal. There is no intention to refuse all technical and intellectual education to Zulus, Fingos, and other natives capable of profiting by it: much of

the hard work which Europeans will continue to require
and will refuse to do themselves involves and evokes
knowledge, intelligence, and a sense of personal responsibility.   Not even the most carefully sophisticated
Christianity furnished by " kept " white missionaries,
can prevent the democratic doctrines of the New Testa-
ment from doing this revolutionary work.

To take away the political liberties enjoyed for a third
of a century in Cape Colony would prove too dangerous : to leave them will be to set a continuously
growing ferment at work throughout the length and
breadth of the Union.   For there are very deep and
very real native grievances.   In the Transvaal and
Orange River Colony the elementary freedom of movement from one place to another is denied, the right of
buying and holding land is denied : whenever in South
Africa a dispute arises between a white and a coloured
man it is tried in a white man's court, by white man's
justice.   Indeed it is needless to labour such an issue :
political rights are everywhere the indispensable condition of civil rights, and without them can be no security
of life, liberty and property for an " inferior " race or
class.

I am well aware that public opinion is very unenlightened among the bulk of the white population of
South Africa.   Many of the political leaders confess
themselves favourable to a carefully restricted native
franchise, but insist that " the people will not have it."
But I cannot help feeling that if these statesmen had
taken a little more time to forecast the troubles which
are certain to arise from an essentially inconsistent
native policy, such as I have here described, they would
have thrown the full weight of their personal authority,
never likely to be greater than now, against the popular
prejudice, and have welcomed the aid of our Liberal
Government to support a Constitution free from this
stain of colour.   There can be no enduring peace, no
steady progress and prosperity in a South Africa where

the vast bulk of the work of industry is done by men who are denied all opportunity to participate, proportionately to their proved capacity, in the government of the country which is morally theirs, in the sense that they are genuinely interested in it, and have put their personal effort into its development.

At the best such a South African Union as is now established will be a close replica not of Canada, but of the Southern States of the American Commonwealth, where the races subsist side by side in the same land in no organic spiritual contact with one another, each race suffering the moral, intellectual and industrial penalty of this disunion. As the recent spread of education and of skilled industry among the negroes of these Southern States has only served to develop and aggravate the situation, so it will be in South Africa. There, as in the Southern States, the black population grows at least as fast as the white, it cannot be expelled or put into reserves because it is required for white men's wants, it cannot be permanently kept in ignorance, and knowledge means not only power, but the demand for rights and a rising discontent at their denial.

The higher mental calibre and capacity of many of the Bantu peoples and the presence of considerable numbers of intelligent Asiatics will be likely to ripen in South Africa even more rapidly than in the Southern States this sense of wrong and this demand for justice. This claim is misunderstood when it is resolved into a race question. Though the form of the exclusion gives it that aspect, it is not at root a race question, but a question of personality. The Zulu, the Indian, who is denied a voice in his country, does not say, " Give me a vote because a Zulu, or an Indian, is as good as a white man." He says, " Give me a vote because by any reasonable test of manhood you lay down—work, knowledge, personal character, even property—I am as fit a man to serve the State as others whom you admit." Unless and until the sentiments of the white peoples

in South Africa can be adjusted to the acceptance of this
humane and just view of a State, one which can only
operate by raising the average standard of citizenship,
its destiny will move upon an unstable axis, and it will
remain a source, not of strength, but of weakness to
the group of self-governing nationalities to which it
falsely claims to belong.

Chapter VI

THE MORALITY OF NATIONS

It has never been clearly admitted that Nations are moral beings in the same sense as individuals, having rights for which they are entitled to receive respect and obligations to respect the rights of others, thus forming units in a moral system, a Society of Nations. The general trend of the conduct of States and Governments towards one another has been one of moral isolation, each concerned exclusively with the supposed good of its own nation and only using treaties or alliances with other nations as instruments to secure its own gain. Even in recent times when civilised nations have established for their several convenience a permanent machinery of diplomatic relations, and have become inured to various sorts of temporary or permanent co-operation, no clearly-established basis of moral obligation supports this co-operation. So far as statesmen have ever brought the problem into the region of conscious consideration, they have usually maintained the non-morality of international relations, confining the duty of a ruler or government to the area of its own people.

Though vague sentiments couched under such terms as " Christendom," " The Cause of Civilisation," the " progress of humanity " have operated to some slight extent to cosmopolitanise individuals or little groups within the nations, they have had no perceptible influence in securing a moral basis of international relations.

Though the political principles of Hobbes and of Macchiavelli, in imposing the narrow self-interest of each State as its supreme law, have sometimes been contravened by great political theorists, they have dominated practical statecraft through the centuries. While occasional spasms of generosity or sympathy for struggling or oppressed nations have momentarily modified the pure play of national selfishness, they cannot be taken to imply any definite recognition of duty or of rights. In the concrete art of statecraft the policy which stood out naked and unashamed in Bismarckism has always prevailed among politicians; nor has the mind of the educated public or of the populace adopted or conceived any other standard. Patriotism is sometimes couched in the single phrase, " My country, right or wrong." This, however, misrepresents such patriotism, which is contented with the shorter phrase, " My country right," not even contemplating any possibility of wrongness.

Curiously enough a modern *rationale* is afforded to this non-moral view of international relations by some of our otherwise most enlightened modern political philosophers. There is a phrase, to which Professor Giddings has given a good deal of vogue, " consciousness of kind," used to imply the limitation of areas for the play of sympathy. Only within such areas as afford a common fund of experience and a free material and spiritual contact, can we say that a group of persons has this " consciousness of kind." Now this common consciousness is the essential basis for feelings of right and obligation; where there is no adequate community of experience and feelings, there can be no real moral communion, no human society. Peoples living in neighbouring valleys were once so isolated in their actual life as to make them strangers or " barbarians " to one another; meeting hardly ever save in strife, they recognised no clear rights or duties towards one another. Civilisation has broken down many barriers, and enlarged the areas of common experience. With this enlargement has grown an enlargement of moral areas. But, urges Professor Giddings, the nation is still so rigorous a limit as to preclude any considerable " consciousness of kind " outside the national area. For individuals or little groups there may be more community of experience, interest, and feeling outside the national area than inside; but the general and collective life of one nation is so separate from that of another as to furnish no sufficient basis of sympathy on which to build any recognition of right and obligation. Professor D. G. Ritchie and Mr. Bosanquet put what appears to me to be substantially the same point when they urge that " the general will " cannot be deemed to have any real meaning outside the nation, for there is no adequate community of needs and interests through which it can function.

The real issue involved is, I think, better tested by consideration of rights than of duties, for there is a tendency among many thinkers, quite illogical, to acknowledge a wider and looser range for the play of duty than of right. It is, for instance, argued by Professor Ritchie, that though we as human beings have duties towards animals, they cannot be said to have corresponding rights, or indeed any sort of rights. What the nature of a duty is for which no one has a right to claim fulfilment, I cannot myself conceive. But this issue is one I only raise in passing, because in regarding groups of human beings it appears essential to insist that any moral relations which subsist between them must imply some system of rights and obligations.

As, in the case of animals, the tightness of this principle is shirked by substituting " kindness " or " humanity," or some protective feeling for justice, so it is with the claim which probably all modern political thinkers would admit, that a strong nation has some obligation to help a weaker nation, and that the mission of civilisation even on the national plane has a meaning and a validity. But, they would be disposed to insist, no right exists on the part of a weak nation to *claim* such assistance. Now I maintain that we can never get a sound basis either for individual or national ethics until this pestilent falsehood of distinguishing justice and generosity has been got rid of. Ruskin pricked it in one of his most penetrating phrases when he spoke of justice as including such kindnesses as we *owe* one another. If we have any sense, as a nation, that we owe it to ourselves to help another nation struggling to be free, that it is a proper and noble thing to do, that is in effect an acknowledgment of a " right " in that other nation to *claim* our aid, an admission that the two nations are members of a human society.

What is our present position as a nation towards such a nation as the Russian? Individuals, perhaps a majority of the individuals of our nation, have some genuine sympathy with the Russian people in their struggle for self-government : there is even what must be called a national sentiment in this country favourable to that cause. But we are told that our State and our Government, the only instruments by which this general wish of the people could exercise any direct influence over the Russian struggle, have neither an obligation nor a right to interfere, even to the extent of withholding voluntary manifestations of good will towards a government which is one of criminal oppression. It is true that this policy of non-intervention is not absolute, but the exception proves the rule, for where a nation affords moral or material support to another, such conduct is always presumed to be directed to secure some balance of power or some other interest of the intervening power. Such an instance is afforded by the international guarantee of the integrity of Belgium. That there have been cases where a Liberal statesman, inspired by a personal enthusiasm for liberty, has directed the policy of his State in disinterested support of struggling nationalities is familiar to us from the recent careers of Palmerston and Gladstone. But such conduct is usually regarded as quixotic, and even those who advocate and practise it would admit that it belonged to gallantry and generosity rather than to the realm of positive obligation. Nor would they be prepared to incur heavy risk or cost in such charitable enterprise. Even when the Turk was most "unspeakable," the proposal to expel him "bag and baggage" hardly passed outside the region of rhetoric, and had it taken shape in definite policy would have been adopted as an interested measure of European police rather than as an obligation to the peoples under Turkish misrule.

But perhaps the most interesting test of the rudimentary character of international ethics is furnished by the attitude towards treaty obligations. The entering upon such agreements implies some recognition on the part of governments that their States are moral beings capable of respecting rights which they have sanctioned, and of fulfilling obligations. A network of such agreements may be deemed to constitute an incipient Society of States, not bound indeed by any general consideration of their common good, but recognising a duty to carry out certain defined undertakings. This relation perhaps serves best to mark the comparison between the actual state of individual and national morals. An individual is not confined in his obligations to benefit his fellows to the terms of any contract which he has entered with them, or even to the more numerous and larger obligations which the law of the country imposes on him; he admits, in theory at any rate, a general duty to do good to his fellow-citizen and fellow-man, and that there is some right vesting in the latter to demand such services. This duty, he will even allow, transcends the limits of nationality, though losing some force when passing from neighbours to strangers. But for States and Nations such obligations seem to be confined within definite contracts; ethical considerations based on humanity, are hardly held applicable to States.

Nor is that the only difference between individual and national morality. The history of treaties shows that the moral attitude of States towards their most solemn and explicit undertakings differs from that of individuals. Every civilised modern State is willing to break or repudiate or neglect the performance of treaty contracts under the pressure of strong national interest, without expressing the sense of shame, or evoking in other nations a moral indignation, at all corresponding in kind or intensity with that which is evoked by a similar act of individual perfidy. If a treaty obligation is of old date, or some change of circumstances makes adhesion to it highly inconvenient, or if some slight undetected or permitted breach can be construed into a precedent, or simply if the national advantage of breaking it be large enough, an international agreement is broken. Even where no absolute breach takes place, the failure to fulfil a quite definite promise, as in the case of the British evacuation of Egypt, is treated on a widely different moral footing from any individual failure to carry out a pledge. This instance is, I think, peculiarly serviceable in showing the loose ethics of internationalism. When the case of our unfulfilled promise to evacuate Egypt is adduced, two demurrers are put in. First, it is denied that any actual public pledge was given, though the plain declaration of intention made by our Government was understood by everyone as an undertaking at the time when it was made. But the answer usually deemed relevant and adequate is that we are remaining there for the good of the Egyptians themselves. Interpreted in terms of individual ethics, this would imply that one party to a contract insists that he has a right to vary the terms of the contract on the ground that in his judgment such variation is advantageous to the other party. But though this irrelevant argument is usually adduced and accepted, the fact that it is so accepted is a crucial instance of the demoralising effect of forcible Imperialism. For it is not the real reason why England broke her word. The real reason for not quitting Egypt is that we deem it advantageous to continue to hold the country, not advantageous to Egypt, though incidentally we hold that also, but to ourselves. The hypocrisy of pretending that we are actuated primarily by the good of Egypt is simply the tribute that national selfishness pays to international morality.

My point is that the actual history of treaty obligations indicates that a nation, as a moral personality, is on a lower level of development than an individual. Here we come to the central difficulty. A nation, in its political aspect as a State, using as an instrument a Government, is not fully realised as a moral being, a personality at all. Much as the ethics of business life has indisputably suffered certain injuries by the substitution for the individual employer of a company, without a soul to be saved, or a body to be kicked, a sort of " person " which even the law finds it hard to bring to book, so with all other sorts of human aggregates or collectivities.

It is in part the abstractness of a State which seems to diminish its moral responsibility, in part it is the lack of continuity in the composition of the Governments which wield its power. Where, as in this nation, Governments are run on lines of party politics, the notion that one party Government should be able to give pledges to foreign Governments which its successors are bound to fulfil seems inconsistent with the operation of the party system. It is for this reason that the secrecy which shrouds the conduct of our Foreign Office is so dangerous to the cause of political democracy. The power of a Cabinet to form a Japanese treaty or to enter a Brussels Sugar Convention, without disclosing the nature of these grave national undertakings to Parliament and the nation, and obtaining their assent, is fraught with double peril. If every succeeding Government felt bound to adhere to such undertakings, however damaging they deemed them to be, grave injury would be inflicted on the liberties of representative Government. If, on the other hand, a Government should seek to evade the chains forged by its predecessor, the stability of the personality of the State is greatly impaired.

But if the attitude of States towards the performance of treaty obligations indicates a feeble conception of moral personality, what shall we say of international morality as indicated by the relations between stronger and weaker, advanced and backward States. Stronger nations have everywhere and always been liable to invade, subdue, and impose their power upon weaker nations. They have almost always acted so, because they have deemed it advantageous to their own national interests to do so. But the fact that they have generally, in modern times at any rate, pretended and persuaded themselves that their forcible encroachment is either an act of reprisal or a preventive attack, indicates some sense of a " right " to independence on the part of the weaker nation, or at any rate some sense that other nations may regard the forcible act as an infringement of a right.

There is of course a school which utterly repudiates such rights, a *real politik* which virtually regards weaker nations as legitimate prey of stronger ones, and considers that the sole moral duty of a statesman is to promote the strength and well-being of his own State, disregarding utterly the interests and so-called " rights " of others. Under such a creed imperial aggression requires no justification, and admits of none. But this *politik* is not truly *real*: it does not conform to actual State feelings and practices, which everywhere, as we have seen, admit some sense, however feeble, of right and obligation even beyond the limits of express contracts.

The real issue of international morality which lurks in modern Imperialism consists in the secondary motives which qualify the purely selfish greed for power and territory, trade, and riches, that is the main propeller. May not one nation ever conquer and rule another for its own good and for the wider good of the civilised world? Though few would have the hardihood to

claim that our seizure of India or Egypt, or other parts
of our Empire, was mainly prompted by disinterested
considerations for the good of these peoples, it is contended that, blended with our commercial and political
motives, was some genuine desire to extend the benefits
of Christianity and the Western arts of civilisation, and
to increase the area of orderly government in the interest
of the backward peoples and of humanity at large.   If
England, France, or Germany can confer such benefits
on backward peoples and on humanity, have they not a
right, a duty, a " mission " to do so?   And is this right
or duty cancelled because in realising it they also seek a
private reward for themselves?   The defender of the
doctrine of natural rights of nationalities may here,
perhaps, put in a prior plea, urging that if even England
or France is capable of improving the condition of
another people, and is disinterested in her desire to do
so, this other people, by reason of its inalienable right
of independence, is entitled to cry " hands off," and to
claim the " moral " support of all other nations in her
resistance.   A people in actual possession of a country,
it may be argued, has an inherent right to its use and
abuse, to let its rich resources run to waste and to maintain the most degrading arts of life, so long as it does
not injuriously interfere with its neighbours.   Now, as
we have seen, a right which implies no duty in another,
which pre-supposes no sort of social sanction, is mean-
ingless: the term " absolute," when applied to natural
rights, is as empty as when applied in any other way.   If
this rigorous view of rights of independence means
anything, it means that the true interests of civilisation
are served by allowing every nation to work out its own
salvation or damnation by itself, and that the claim of
any nation to force its assistance on another is so certain
to be abused that it ought never to be entertained.   In
other words, the doctrine of the " sacred rights of
nationality " implies that there is at any rate an incipient
society of nations which sets its sanction on this right.

With this interpretation of the "rights of nationality," I have strong sympathy. But can it carry us so far that we reject as injurious and immoral all forcible interference by one nation with another? Is it not relevant to the ethics of the case to consider whether in point of fact such interference may not be beneficial to the interests of the society of nations and the particular nations subjected to such force. In the case of so-called civilised peoples it would easily be admitted that no such benefit was likely to accrue, and that we should be entitled to denounce as unwarrantable any interference by a stronger with a weaker, a larger with a smaller people living on the same general level of civilisation and capable of following their own line of progress. The worst moral iniquity in our plea for conquering the Boer Republics consisted in the false and fatuous pretence that British government was essential to promote civilisation in those countries.

But what are we to say of the mission of civilisation which consists in the forcible subjection and government of definitely lower peoples and the seizure of their lands? Setting aside the barbarous treatment of the American Indians as irrelevant to the essence of the issue, can we assert that the greater colonisation of North America was unjustifiable, because a few hundred thousand savages incapable of utilising the resources of the country were its wandering occupants. Or taking as a more recent instance, the partition of a large part of Africa among European powers by spheres of influence and protectorates, what is to be our ethical interpretation of this act? It is admitted that in such partitions and annexations the encroaching powers are each animated primarily by selfish considerations. But if they put in the plea that humanity, as represented by the civilised peoples of the world, has given a tacit sanction to this encroachment on the ground of the incidental benefits which will accrue both to humanity and to the subjected people by this extension of

Imperialism, must we reject this plea as merely hypocritical and fundamentally vicious?   It is a moral
problem of much delicacy.   The Imperialistic
encroaching State virtually says, or ought truthfully to
say : "Although my chief direct motive in forcibly
annexing this backward country is my own gain and
aggrandisement, I claim that, since the methods of
attaining these objects must bring benefits to the world
at large and to the subject people in particular, these
benefits shall be considered to compensate any damage
which *primâ facie* may be considered to have been inflicted by infringing the rights of the invaded peoples."
    More fully developed, this doctrine seems to run
thus : Certain civilised white nations agree that the
common interests of humanity, as interpreted by them,
imply that integrity of national domains is among
themselves a "right" which must not be infringed,
either for purposes of national gain or with a view to
conferring benefits by better government, but only for
the purpose of repelling an actual or anticipated
invasion of their "rights"; whereas, in the case of
uncivilised peoples, they have a "right," in virtue of
their higher standard of civilisation, either collectively
or separately, to over-ride the "rights" of such peoples,
wherever there is reasonable ground for maintaining
that benefits will be conferred on the world and on the
invaded people by this course of conduct, and they are
entitled to judge whether there is such reasonable
ground.   Finally, they contend that this superior right
shall not be annulled by the fact of any special advantages which may accrue to the encroaching nation, or
even by the fact that the attainment of this advantage
may be the chief or the sole conscious directing motive.
    The slippery nature of this ethical justification of
Imperialism is undeniable.   The admission that the
chief motive is one's own gain must be held certain to
prevent one from discriminating between encroachments which will in fact be beneficial to the subject

people, and those which will not; the conscious pursuit of one's own gain as the first consideration must certainly impair one's ability to secure, adequately or at all, the incidental advantages which were to accrue to the subject people. Finally, the government by force, not by consent, of another people, and the chronic temptation hypocritically to feign that the dominating motive in our rule is their good, not our own gain, may react so powerfully and so insidiously upon the mind of an Imperialist nation that it loses the capacity not merely to recognise the advantage of leaving lower peoples to follow their own paths of progress or regression, but to perceive the fatal injuries which domineering practices abroad inflict upon the efficiency of national self-government at home. Even if Imperialism can in some instances make good its claims to benefit certain lower races, and to maintain good order in otherwise disordered regions, such gain may be purchased dearly by the damage done to democracy at home. But the radical moral defect of Imperialism is due to lack of any true sanction from a society of nations to the interference of an Imperialist nation with the life of a lower people. If there existed a fairly developed form of international society, in which all peoples, great and small, higher and lower, were in some sense represented, and such a society delegated England or France in the interests of civilisation to take under her tutelage some backward or degraded people which lay on their borders, maintaining order, developing the natural resources of the country, and helping to teach the arts of civilisation, this would afford some moral basis for Imperialism. Actual Imperialism differs widely from this condition. Each Imperialist nation claims to act primarily for its own, not for the general good; it does not even pretend to have received a sanction of civilised society for its action, and its own *ipse dixit* is its only guarantee of fitness to carry out a civilising mission.

These are the wide divergencies between the actual

ethics of individuals and those of nations. But that does not imply any essential difference in the ideal of conduct in the two. It only implies a feebler development of moral personality in the Nation, and a feebler structure of international society. But in both these growth is going on, faster than before and at an accelerating pace. Both the utility of nationality and the recognition of that utility are gaining ground, and with such recogni-- tion the rights and obligations appertaining to the moral personality of Nations become more real facts and forces in history. Practical internationalism of various forms is teaching us more clearly that co-operation, not antagonism, is the distinctive character of national activity, that nations are primarily neighbours, not strangers. This definite sense of neighbours in friendly co-operation for mutual services is the growing nucleus of that national personality which is creating the Society of Nations. When that Society is as firmly developed as that of the individuals within a national Society, and is provided with a growth of laws, customs, and sentiments of corresponding complexity and of tested experience, the morality of nations will be found to correspond on a larger scale to the morality of individuals.

This national morality implies three plain obliga-tions : (1) a recognition that it belongs to the common good of nations to leave each nation liberty to govern itself in all matters where such liberty does not directly and clearly contravene the common good; (2) a repudia-tion of the practices of parasitic Imperialism, or forcible interference with the life of another nation so as to secure a gain in excess of net services rendered; (3) the positive practice of mutual aid between nations upon equal terms, extending to the conduct of nations the sound organic principle of moral conduct " from each according to its powers, to each according to its needs." In such manner, as the individual realises himself in a democratic nation, so the nation best realises itself in a democratic society of nations.

CHAPTER VII

THE TASK OF RECONSTRUCTION

It is not without significance that the term rationalism should have acquired a destructive rather than a constructive meaning. Why this should be so is not at first sight obvious. Man's use of reason as a guide of life would seem to give an equal value to the selection of the true and the rejection of the false, and rather to lay the stress upon the former process as containing the stronger appeal to human interest. It is no doubt intelligible and inevitable that the defenders of things and ideas as they are, finding their strongest support in the emotional forces of usage and authority, should strive to represent reformers as mere destroyers and their intellectual engines as fitted only for this work. But as regards the later decades of the nineteenth century there was considerable justification for this attitude. The spirit of the age in the cultured circles of Europe was coldly sceptical and tending towards an ever-narrower specialisation. In both these respects it differed widely from the rationalism of the early portion of the century, which was still filled with the enthusiasm of revolution and with dreams of an age of reason which, out of the breakdown of the old order, should establish at once in politics and industry, in religion, education, art and literature, as well as in the practices of private conduct, a new moral and intellectual order. Such a dream of rational humanity did not only fire the imagination of the younger poets of two generations, Wordsworth, Coleridge, Shelley, even Tennyson: it possessed the minds of the most representative thinkers from Paine and Godwin to Owen, Bentham and J. S. Mill. Poetic prophets, co-operative socialists, utilitarian theorists and philosophic radicals, whether their primary impulse was drawn from romantic art, philosophic reflection, or from some passion of practical reform, all aimed consciously and avowedly at a general transformation of life. This vision of some new harmony of life and the glow of confidence in its achievement which inspired the Socialism of Owen and its weaker revival under Kingsley and Maurice, which even flickered in the earlier writings of Carlyle and Ruskin, had its counterpart in many other movements of the times. Wordsworth, with the romantic naturalism for which he stood, the new literary force of the novel in the hands of idealists like Dickens, Disraeli, the young Bulwer, the magnificent audacity of the Pre-Raphaelite Brotherhood, the infinite vistas of human power opened up freshly by the new physical and organic sciences—there was no mere narrow intellectualism, no economy of "Ca' canny," in any of these movements. These leaders of thought and action believed that the time was come for a new general plan of life, thought out afresh and freely carried out, in which a clear assessment of the past and the established order should be made so as to secure "a new moral universe" based on a free application of the mind of man to the control of his destiny upon this earth. There were wide divergences in the assessments of the new economy, according to the materialistic or spiritual standards of human welfare adopted : nor could it be claimed that all were equally or mainly rationalistic in the tests applied. But each of these movements had what may be regarded as its philosophic import and basis, it did endeavour to see life steadily and to see it whole : moreover, it designed to apply reason for constructive changes, and these changes were conceived, not departmentally, but in their bearing upon the general life.

Now no sober student of our intellectual and moral life during the later nineteenth century can help recognising that this tide of intellectual and practical progress was checked and broken. Not that less intellectual and practical energy was generated and applied : improved education placed a great increase of raw force for progress at the disposal of the nation, and it was applied along innumerable channels of detailed work. But the larger purpose had passed out of it. Instead of flowing freely to the fertilisation of the whole kingdom of humanity, it was drawn off into numerous little channels to turn little private mill-wheels or to irrigate separate enclosures. The whole idea of the economy of progress had shifted. Large synthetic schemes of thought and action were renounced as wildly, wastefully speculative : evolution was the new watchword, and its substitution for revolution meant the assertion, as a primary doctrine of general application, that progress must be slow. This doctrine was derived from scientific records in fields of inquiry where the ordered consciousness of man played no part; but once " discovered " it was applied with easy confidence to human history. Related to this doctrine of progress was another, viz., that progress can only be secured by rigorous division of labour. Thus retarded and divided, the powers of reason were no longer available for co-operation in the great work of human reconstruction. Rationalism almost inevitably became identified with destructive criticism. For such was the work that came easiest to hand under the new conditions. This is not at first sight the obvious result of the application of evolutionary formulæ to the world process. It might rather have been expected that the linking of the natural sciences by the application of the law of the conservation of energy, the new conception of continuity secured by the acceptance of the Darwinian hypothesis of the origin of species, and especially the bridging of the chasm which hitherto had separated man from Nature, with the finer application of causality to the innermost life of man, would have bent the systematic thought of all intellectual workers towards the making of a new all-embracing synthesis. As Comte, on the very threshold of the new scientific epoch, so Spencer, a generation later, felt himself impelled along this plain road of intellectual duty. The failure of each to win the acceptance or co-operation of more than a scanty handful of followers in his life-time was not due to any flaws there may have been in the synthetic system which he presented. It was due to certain forces which worked towards the postponement of any synthesis. What these forces were it is not now difficult to recognise. First one would place the important demands of material utility, the great bribes of fame and gain by which men of trained scientific intellect were harnessed to the trades and the professions. The heroic struggle of Herbert Spencer to enlarge evolution into a cosmic philosophy when what his practical countrymen required was aniline dyes, chemical manures and cheap electric lighting, dramatised the issue. Though the main stress of this utilitarian specialisation was com-mercial, drawn from the rapid discovery of innumerable profitable applications of the physical sciences, other more disinterested motives co-operated with this economic drive. Biology, the keystone of the new intellectual system, fell too early and too completely under the sway of particularist research directed to the solution of hygienic problems. The case of sociology was still more significant. It may be said to have been taken from its very cradle into the factory, forced before its frame was set to hard tasks of solving anthropological conundrums and devising remedies for social diseases. The same is true of psychology, put before it could well stand to grind grist in the educational mill, or to furnish sensational hypotheses for alienists and criminologists. No doubt a genuine though mistaken economy of scientific energy made in the same direction. It required a race of intellectual giants to handle the great conceptions of such men as Comte and Darwin, and to do the work of re-orientation they involved. No such crop of giants rose. Small worthy men, shrinking from so large an adventure, pleaded plausibly the economy of spade-work, how bands of humble patient students, set to work with test-tube, microscope, and note-book in every patch of ground, would best advance the cause of learning. This doctrine of "thorough," under the guise of modest industry, was in large degree a cloak for intellectual cowardice. The trend was everywhere towards division of labour, breaking "the one" into "the many." Now division of labour is only a true economy when a sound principle of co-operation underlies and dominates division, maintaining the supremacy of the unity and harmony of the whole process. Modern science has preserved no such economy. There is no strong centralising force to keep the special sciences in their proper orbits in the intellectual heavens : within each science numbers of little un-coordinated kingdoms and principalities arise : local self-government is carried everywhere into a licentious extreme. There exists no proper intellectual authority, correlating the work of the innumerable groups of scientific hodmen, sifting their results and forming them into the material for a higher grade of research, so step by step working by the inductive method towards great scientific laws which may finally be incorporated in a new intellectual system. There is no warrant for believing that the notion that "a simple system of natural liberty" and "enlightened self-interest" is any better economy in the intellectual than in the industrial world. Intellectual individualism is quite as injurious as industrial individualism. Neither indeed is anarchy. In each case there does survive and operate some principle of harmony. But in each case alike it operates feebly and wastefully. As in our industrial system failure of central control is responsible for the survival of the twin monsters of luxury and poverty in nations possessing natural resources and technical arts fully adequate to secure comfort and opportunity for all, so in our intellectual system a similar defect retards even more disastrously the production and distribution of the highest forms of wealth. It is not that intellectual labour is over-divided, but that there is no proper correlation of its specialisms, no proper harvesting and assimilation of its fruits. This can only be attributed to an abandonment of central intellectual control.

I have discussed this tendency to sacrifice unity to multiplicity in science at some length, because the nature of this false economy is there more visible than elsewhere to the naked eye. But the same tendency to prefer small specialised to large general activities of mind is seen in literature and the fine arts. And the forces at work are evidently the same. It is the tyranny of the market, the demand for immediate crude utility in conventional enjoyment, co-operating with a timidity which seeks shelter in some little bypath of expression whose peculiarity may figure as originality, without incurring the risks which attend audacity, that explain the failure of great creative work in the later years of the last century.

But there still remains something lacking in this explanation of the failure of intellectual synthesis, and the prevalence of destructive rationalism. It is hardly possible to follow the early controversies to which the startling doctrines of Darwinism and Marxism gave rise in the middle century without recognising a curious phenomenon, which, though discernible in every civilised country, is studied to best advantage in England. As soon as the shattering impact of these new thoughts upon the established beliefs and institutions had been felt, the conservative instincts began to assert themselves, not in a formal repression or boycott, but in a steady silent refusal to face the intellectual consequences. The familiar advice tendered by the aged divine to the young student who inquired how he should deal with the arguments of sceptics, "Look them boldly in the face and pass on " is hardly needed in this country. Our literature is full of proverbs expressive of, or rather concealing, this proclivity. It is not our habit, we boast, to cross a stream until we come to it. We might add that, if the stream is deep and strong, we do not come to it. There are three adjectives commonly recognised by foreigners as peculiarly representative of English valuations, the terms " respectable," " comfortable," and " shocking." They denote the inward fortress of conservatism, primarily in conduct, but secondarily in thought. The English temperament stands for " comfort " and stubbornly resists anything that disturbs this aspect of " the good." Its method of defending " comfort " is by endowing it with " respectability " and by regarding all disturbing influences as " shocking." Our standard of " comfort " is solidly material, consisting *au fond* of " creature comforts." Though in its higher strata it appears as intellectual or even spiritual, so that we speak of the comforts of religion or philosophy, it will be recognised that anything which makes us feel really " uncomfortable," any sentiment or opinion that is " shocking," inflicts on us a physical disturbance. As a fundamentally respectable, moral, and religious people, we are very sensitive to all large disturbing thoughts which thus present themselves as shocking. Though our real feeling towards them, as I say, is mainly physical, compact of inertia and apprehension, we represent it to ourselves as moral. This bit of national psychology is necessary that we may understand how it could come to pass that our thinking men were successfully prevented for two generations from setting their minds to the large task of intellectual and spiritual reconstruction which the destructive criticism of nineteenth-century science involved. Feeling " in our bones," as nurses say, that the inflowing realism of modern science and of a literature and art which was drinking eagerly the realistic spirit, would wash us away from all our old conventional moorings, we set ourselves, doggedly, to stem the tide, and by diverting its force into the thousand little practically serviceable channels which I have described, to render it innocuous. We really succeeded for nearly half a century in keeping the " educated " public of England from facing the deep searching questions lying at the foundations of our institutions, our religion, morals, art, and literature, which the new evolutionary conception of the cosmos involved. Intellectual men and women were sometimes half conscious of the process; they felt that somehow they were not so " free " as they professed to be, that subtle influences, in which they came to acquiesce, prevented them from thinking out root questions. The few bolder ones who were not deterred from thinking out, found that impenetrable barriers stopped publication. It was not, as is sometimes thought, mere mischance that kept the revolutionary discoveries of Mendel buried for a generation. It was the tacit conspiracy against disturbing thoughts. Every broadminded scientist can point to similar repression in his own province. It was not so much a rigid orthodoxy, still less an active hunting down of heresy, as a persistent avoidance of certain lines of thought, where what may be called the modern spirit was likely to be encountered. Just in proportion as a subject was likely to contain this spirit was it " doctored " for witchcraft. Not science alone, but every branch of learning has suffered this sterilising process. The true story of the modernising movement in our seats of higher education would be most instructive if it could be given in adequate detail. We should see how the newer branches of natural science were stoutly refused entrance, until their claim to culture was endorsed by proved utility and their fiery spirit tamed by slowly acquired orthodoxy. Religion and philosophy were secured against the new

ferment, partly by authority, partly by a slow inocula-
tion. But the most instructive cases are naturally to
be found in what were termed the moral sciences. For
here the erosive power of the new ideas could not be
excluded. The efforts of the older ethics to apply
evolution to its utilitarian or its idealistic standards
proved singularly futile, while the accepted politics
quickly crumbled into ruin with no serious attempt at
ordered substitution. Political economy, as the study
naturally most exposed to explosive thought, sought
protection by dropping all organic unity and breaking
into a variety of detailed historical and statistical
researches. It has often been made a matter of amazing
comment that our universities have ignored the great
literature which their own language offers for the
nourishment of English youth, or still worse have
murdered it in order to dissect. For this systematic
" doping " of all studies to which the new disturbing
thought might obtain access, there is no other explanation than that this is the instinctive self-defence of vested
interests and established causes. This formal resistance
of the educational and intellectual world was supported
by the equally instinctive cunning of " society " in
refusing to discuss or even to recognise the graver
questions of the age. The effrontery of this attitude
was only equalled by its consistency.

Let me state the issue in its most general form.
Our life and all it signifies for good and evil, happiness
or misery, to ourselves and others, rests upon a number
of feelings, thoughts, and actions which, hardened into
customs and institutions, constitute " the foundations
of society." Such are the family, property, the State,
the industrial system, the Church. Now the old fixed
faiths on which these foundations were laid were
undermined by the new thought. The engines of
criticism were battering each of them. Not only the
theories but the practice was assailed. The old clear-
cut convictions of the permanency of a single type of

monogamous family, of the sanctity of individual property, of the limits of government, of the private control of industry, of the conception of a God and of personal immortality, to name some crucial instances, have all been seriously and even fiercely assailed by free thought. Yet until quite recently the ostrich attitude has everywhere prevailed. The modern intellectual forces could be kept under but could not be kept out, everywhere they were seen at work, corroding the old cast-iron dogmas, eating away the old theology, the old politics, the old social conventions. In vain did we shun as " uncomfortable " and " shocking " the early inroads of realism into fiction, poetry, and the drama. Tolstoy, Zola, Ibsen, Shaw, Brieux, we held back for a generation. But they are now visibly upon us. Meanwhile in the churches and the orthodox political parties, the work of erosion had been steadily advancing. The great blasting processes of interrogation have proceeded far. The seeds of scepticism, sown in the last generation, are bearing timely fruit and a new vigorous generation is beginning to demand that the constructive work shirked by their fathers shall be taken in hand. There are signs of a great intellectual and spiritual revival. At the very moment when blind critics are deploring the decline of genius and the barrenness of the age, an abundance of fresh inspiration is beginning to breathe through new forms of realism in poetry, the drama, prose, fiction, and art. The censorship, not Mr. Redford's but Mr. Podsnap's, is being brushed aside. The very problems which, springing directly from scientific history, biology, and economics, had hitherto been most successfully evaded, have forced their way into a drama and a fiction which are actually becoming popular. Heredity, alike in its physical and moral bearings, the origins of poverty and luxury, the struggles of sex, of capital and labour, the corruptions of politics and religion, not merely furnish the material of art and the drama, but they are treated in modes of demonstration which, challenging the fundamental assumptions of the older art, give it a novel intellectual and emotional authority. Not less significant is the demand, issuing from the more liberal sections of the Christian Churches and from their outcast sects, for a new spiritual synthesis in which the constructive as well as the destructive criticism shall find expression. Twenty years ago it would have been impossible for such a publication as the *Hibbert Journal* to have obtained the influence it wields to-day. The whole modernist movement in Catholic and Protestant countries is a striking confession of the failure of the silent protest to keep the new wine out of the old bottles. In every church the new bottling industry is going on with more or less success.

It is unnecessary here to illustrate from the field of practical politics a similar decay of faith and a similar demand for new principles and a new policy. It is the same penetrating force of realism, exposing the falsehood of the ancient party watchwords and cleavages, and craving intelligible and mentally satisfactory principles. Here Socialism has been the great educator, breaking down at last in this country the boycott of disreputability, and forcing politicians to fight it with some champion more substantial than the ghosts of Whiggism and Toryism. In a word, just as the theologians are beginning to seek a re-statement of religion that is " real," comprehensive, vital, so it is with the more enlightened politicians. The age of shirking, vapouring, and opportunism is passing. A larger and larger number of modern men and women are possessed by the duty and the desire to put the very questions which their parents thought shocking, and to insist upon plain intelligible answers. What is more, they want all these questions answered at once. In other words, there is an instinct to reverse the dissociative current, which everywhere made for separatism, and to lay the main intellectual and spiritual stress on harmony and unity. It is significant that this unifying process has been so counter to our national habits in the past that, when we seek to express it, we are obliged to have recourse to some foreign term such as *Welt-anschauung*, the barbaric look of which seems to give artificiality to the process. Yet it is some such orderly assemblage of ideas that thousands of men and women are beginning consciously to seek after. For lack of intellectual guidance or effective co-operation, many of them became the dupes of some narrow doctrine which appealing powerfully to some single craving of their nature, sets up as a religion and a philosophy. So Spiritualism, Christian science, Socialism, Quietism, even Anarchism and Agnosticism, in spite of their negative character, furnish to many a binding principle and a central enthusiasm which otherwise are lacking. They are the spiritual makeshifts of an age of disillusionment. Those who adopt them testify to their provisional character by their inconstancy. It is a time of short intellectual leases, not of permanent abodes. This restlessness is due not so much as is often held, to a nomad state of soul, as to an experimental discovery of defects in these improvised syntheses.

We have had, it is true, even in the age of scepticism, little schools of intellectuals who have soared into some loftiness of thought where they have claimed to find the one and absolute. But the logical athletics of their ascent preclude most, and leave the climbers in an atmosphere so high and dim that unity seems only got by blotting out diversity, not by harmonising it. Whatever may be said about the logic of the pragmatists, their protest against the " unreality " of the idealistic synthesis remains valid. What is needed is not so much a system of thought, whether monism or pluralism, not so much a single faith, religious, ethical, intellectual, æsthetic, practical, as a single spirit in the conduct of life. Now it is the supreme claim of science that she has given form to the spirit of truth-seeking, embodying it in that realism which to-day is struggling for positive expression in every art of man. At first sight realism may appear an extremely inadequate word to express that striving of head and heart which is replacing the dissipation and distraction of the earlier rationalism. And indeed there is no term that is adequate: if there were, instead of the striving we should have the thing. But if we are to gather together the various efforts of enlightenment, reconcilement, and reconstruction, presented in religion, politics, art, science, literature, we shall admit that there are two dominant features. The first is the persistent strenuous desire to reach, present and represent facts, not excluding fictions, illusions, superstitions, but disentangling this sort of facts from the others. The second is a firm conviction that every sort of salvation or success lies in a clear-eyed following of fact.

We shall be told that the realism which consists in a mere following of fact will not give us any ordered scheme of life. Realism, like other isms, has suffered much from its friends. Neither naïve realism nor sophisticated naturalism will do what is wanted, for their " Nature " and " reality " are doubly defective : they lean too heavily on the material side of things, and they give Nature too much independence. Modern thought, correcting this cruder realism, sees the whole of Nature as a psycho-physical process, interprets human history as a spiritual-animalism, and recognises clearly that so far as the selection, valuation, and utilisation of " realities " go, Man is the maker of the Universe. Philosophers may busy themselves with the design of the pattern according to which man makes his universe, or with some ultimate hypothesis which shall regard the whole of human history as an episode in the self-realisation of the Absolute. It is unlikely that this sort of metaphysical unity will ever occupy the minds of men, will furnish them with any substitute for religion, will animate their art and literature, or will incite them to

T

daring deeds for their own good and that of others. What men are seeking for is a wholeness without strained unity, a freedom of thought, of feeling, of conduct, which shall enable each man to confront an object of nature, an idea, an event, a situation, not as appealing for acceptance or reprobation to some specifically moral, intellectual, or æsthetic faculty of him, but as a reality to be seen clear-eyed and to be taken for what it is worth. This " worth " or " value " must be given on a human consideration which transcends the distinctively moral, intellectual, æsthetic.   In fact the virtue of the realist outlook upon life will consist primarily in closing up this false division of the human standard, which especially in England, has done more than anything to keep us uncivilised.   The time of the Renaissance did not find us ripe for humanism, nor was a humanism so deeply impregnated with obsolete or obsolescent culture, truly realistic.   So we have lived in separate strata of barbarism and philistinism with a growing but un-assimilated tincture of cold intellectualism. But unless I read wrongly the signs of our time, there is a genuine awakening not in one but in many quarters.   In the religious world the new term " comparative " religion is indicative of much, and the anxious *rapprochement* to science is in effect, though not in intention, a capitulation to the spirit of realism.   In politics the same spirit is seen in the weakening hold of the "romantic" view of aristocracy and democracy, the critical re-statement of the revolutionary formulæ, the bolder expression of " real politics " in the organised craft and force of Bismarckism and political machines, but more particularly in the clear emergence of industrial and financial interests as the directing and dominating factors of national and international relations.   In literature and art eager, even furious, endeavours are afoot to break down the barriers which have forbidden the keen presentation of the most disturbing thoughts and topics of our age.   Wagner, Millet, Whistler,

Nietzsche, Tolstoy, Whitman, Ibsen, have not laboured in vain. It is true that in our compromising English way we have at first received them, reluctantly, as freaks. We did not even recognise there was a new and common spirit in their work. Now, too late, our guardians of public order struggle to shut the conservatory windows. The invigorating air has already quickened a new perception of the purposes of literature and art; we are no longer content to grow exotics under glass, we want the free growth of the natural flora of our country. Not less potent, though different in its working, is the new spirit in science. There it acts chiefly as a correction of the narrower realism of detailed research, by the healing process of ever wider and more fruitful speculation. For the sort of facts which speculative science sees, its creative or interpretative hypotheses, fall under the fuller realism and indeed serve admirably to distinguish it from the cruder realism whose only facts were hard and dead.

What is most needed now is a fuller consciousness among those who in different fields of thought and work are moved by this spirit, a recognition of their unity of purpose and a fruitful co-operation. This is more possible and more desirable, because it is not sought to secure adhesion to any common formulæ or any creed, but only to a common temper and a common outlook. But we have so much faith in facts as to believe that this temper and this outlook will work towards a community of thought and feeling, not indeed fusing or subjugating personality but representing fairly and truthfully in a " practical philosophy " of life what is common to mankind, while leaving liberty for the uniqueness and waywardness of the individual. There will doubtless be some to whom this realism will seem either a false generalisation or a movement which being inevitable in its direction and its pace cannot profit by seeking self-consciousness. But those who accept the view that experiments in collective self-consciousness, as a means of accelerating and directing the " urge of the world " towards human enlightenment and well-being, are likely to yield great results, will recognise that a rendering of realism in many fields of thought and art is the most profitable task of our age.

INDEX

.

www.ingramcontent.com/pod-product-compliance
Lightning Source LLC
Chambersburg PA
CBHW020526270326
41927CB00006B/460